Michael Oakeshott on the Human Condition

Michael Oakeshott
on the
Human Condition

══ Essays by Timothy Fuller ══

WITH AN INTRODUCTION
BY TIMOTHY FULLER

Liberty Fund

Preface, Introduction, and index © 2024 by Liberty Fund, Inc.
Articles reprinted by permission.
All rights reserved. Published 2024.

Cover and jacket art: Portrait by Paul Gopal-Chowdhury, *Michael Joseph Oakeshott, Senior Fellow*, oil on canvas. Used by permission of the Master and Fellows of Gonville and Caius College, Cambridge. © Paul Gopal-Chowdhury, Artist.

Printed in the United States of America

24   25   26   27   28   C   5   4   3   2   1
24   25   26   27   28   P   5   4   3   2   1

Library of Congress Cataloging-in-Publication Data
Names: Fuller, Timothy, 1940– author.
Title: Michael Oakeshott on the human condition / essays by
    Timothy Fuller; with an introduction by Timothy Fuller.
Description: Carmel, Indiana : Liberty Fund, [2024] | Essays
    prepared, 1976 to 2020, some previously published, some
    published for the first time. | Includes bibliographical
    references and index.
Identifiers: LCCN 2023033712 | ISBN 9780865979314 (hardcover) |
    ISBN 9780865979321 (paperback) | ISBN 9781614872962 (epub) |
    ISBN 9781614876731 (kindle edition) | ISBN 9781614879435 (pdf)
Subjects: LCSH: Oakeshott, Michael, 1901–1990. | Humanity. |
    Philosophical anthropology.
Classification: LCC B1649.O344 F85 2024 | DDC 128/.4—dc23/
    eng/20231218
LC record available at https://lccn.loc.gov/2023033712

Liberty Fund, Inc.
11301 North Meridian Street
Carmel, Indiana 46032
libertyfund.org

Contents

Preface

LIBERTY FUND'S PUBLICATION of my essays on Michael Oakeshott is a source of great satisfaction for me, the culmination of my forty-one-year association with Liberty Fund. My introduction to Liberty Fund was a ten-day summer conference on political economy at Blacksburg, Virginia, directed by James Buchanan and Gordon Tullock. I was a student of political philosophy who, having up to then paid little attention to economics, found myself at a conference made up almost entirely of notable economists, including Douglass North (along with Buchanan eventually to be a Nobel Laureate in Economics), Geoffrey Brennan, Karen Vaughn, Charles Plott, Dwight Lee, and others. My interest thus kindled I began to read in the tradition of political economy, especially Adam Smith, and eventually I started teaching, and still teach, a course called "Foundations of Political Economy." Oakeshott did not write much about economics but in one remarkable essay, "The Political Economy of Freedom," he discusses the work of Frank Knight (Buchanan's teacher) and of Henry Simon, commenting on fundamental elements of the classical liberal tradition.

I contributed to the expansion of Liberty Fund's attention to the study of the classics of political philosophy, encouraging political philosophy colleagues to participate. Michael Oakeshott's thought became prominent in Liberty Fund's exploration of the idea of a society of free and responsible individuals. I have edited and introduced a number of Liberty Fund editions of Oakeshott's works. Liberty Fund has played a vital role in making Oakeshott's work accessible to a wide audience.

My essays in this volume range from 1976 to 2020, some previously published, some published here for the first time. When I set out finally to bring these essays together—something I had been urged to do by many for some time—it was clear to me that Liberty Fund was the right place for them. Happily, they agreed. I count my association with Liberty Fund to be among the most important elements of my intellectual and professional life.

In preparing this volume I want to acknowledge and thank Jessica Gryzywa for her first-rate technical assistance in preparing this work, Emilio Pacheco for his support and encouragement, Laura Goetz for overseeing the initial preparation of this book at Liberty Fund, and Jana Stefanciosa whose high editorial standards contributed numerous improvements to the text. Whatever flaws may remain are entirely mine.

I dedicate this work in memory of my wife, Kalah, and to my daughters Margaret and Amy, for whom Michael Oakeshott had great affection. They exemplify what it means to be free and responsible.

Introduction:
Encounters with Michael Oakeshott

MY FIRST ENCOUNTER with Michael Oakeshott was on a Saturday afternoon in the library of Kenyon College in the fall of 1959 when, with the place mostly all to myself, I found on a shelf the Blackwell's Political Texts edition of Hobbes's *Leviathan*, edited by a certain Michael Oakeshott. I was just then deciding to change my major field of study. I had started as a premed student, then considered Classics and English. I was taking my first course in political philosophy, a subject which immediately attracted me. Finding Oakeshott's *Leviathan* confirmed my intuition. I was about to write an essay on Hobbes for the course. I sat down at a secluded library table to look through what this author, hitherto unknown to me, had to say. From the first sentence, "Thomas Hobbes, the second son of an otherwise undistinguished vicar," I was captivated. I read through the entire essay as the afternoon wore on. I was taken by what I later learned was a famous and controversial interpretation among Hobbes scholars. As I finished it, I looked up and thought to myself that I must someday write an essay like this, that to desire anything less was not to be serious about what I now knew I intended to do.

The following Monday I burst in on my political theory professor asking if he had ever heard of Oakeshott. Providentially, one might say, he also was an Englishman who had read modern history at Trinity College, Cambridge, before coming to America to do graduate work at Harvard and to teach. Not only had he known Oakeshott but he had worked with him on the *Cambridge Journal* in the 1940s. He was the first of those I was to encounter who described what it was like in the 1930s and '40s to hear the legendary Oakeshott lecture on the history of political thought (others I met later include Brian Tierney and Peter Laslett). My teacher was patient with my enthusiasm to take up political thought and teach it. It is, of course, what I did and do, and I have never regretted it for a moment. I owe my direction, in significant part, to the Oakeshott I was to meet face to face only much later.

He was legendary among Cambridge students, not alone for his lectures but also for somewhat dandyish ways and for his love of horse racing. He was said to have abandoned his scheduled lectures on certain occasions when the races at Newmarket were on. The latter interest found expression in the book he wrote with his friend, Guy Griffith, *A Guide to the Classics or How to Pick a Derby Winner*. The book was published in 1936 by the distinguished house of Faber and Faber, whose esteemed editor was T. S. Eliot. At least a few people, looking hastily at the title, must have bought it thinking it was an essay by two scholars on the classics. Eliot mentions the book in passing in his 1944 address to the Virgil Society, "What Is a Classic?" Careful readers used its prescription for betting with occasional success and, so I am told, one such sent Oakeshott, in appreciation, a case of Chateau Margaux.

Oakeshott lurked in the back of my mind for a few years until, while I was in graduate school, *Rationalism in Politics* appeared in 1962. This was the book that launched him in America and remains today his most widely read book. At this point, my interest was rekindled and, when I came to writing my doctoral thesis on John Stuart Mill, I deployed numerous ideas of Oakeshott's in examining and criticizing Mill's basic political doctrines. In part, also, I was responding to the very controversial view of Mill that Maurice Cowling, at that time a follower of Oakeshott, had recently published in his *Mill and Liberalism* to the effect that Mill was a "moral totalitarian." This accusation is not one Oakeshott himself would have pronounced. In 1979, through Shirley Letwin, I finally met and began a rewarding friendship with Cowling who, by then, had overturned a number of his earlier Oakeshottian views and who, characteristically as I came to know, rebuffed my praise of his early work. When I started teaching at Colorado College in 1965, reading Oakeshott became a regular part of my courses on modern political thought.

My first meeting with Oakeshott came in 1974, the centennial year of Colorado College (he was to return once more, in June 1982, to receive an honorary degree). I had proposed, and the college had put me in charge of, organizing a year-long lecture series on the present and future state of liberal learning. I wrote to Oakeshott, inviting him to spend a week at the college and to present the first lecture. He accepted, and offered, in Tutt Library at Colorado College on September 17, 1974, to an audience of nearly four hundred, "A Place of Learning." This now well-known essay was printed in the *Colorado College Studies* in January 1975, later reprinted numerous times in various places, ultimately to appear as the lead essay in *The Voice of Liberal Learning* (1989). The latter was the first of my editions of Oakeshott's essays on various subjects.

Oakeshott electrified the audience with extraordinarily powerful, and beautifully conceived, formulations issuing from the mouth of a slight, unassuming man who might go unnoticed unless and until he spoke with you. Oakeshott was, of course, highly critical of the contemporary social sciences, but he made his points with a grace that led one of my colleagues in sociology to remark that he had never been so charmingly demolished.

At the same time, his evocation of what liberal learning really is was so heartfelt, and expressed with such an effortless invocation of the great resources of the Western tradition, that he instantiated and made real to all present what, in lesser hands, would have seemed romantic. Apart from his lecture, he spent much of his week in residence talking with students and faculty, and I began to glimpse his greatness as a teacher. In later years, when I witnessed Oakeshott performing in the general seminar of the History of Political Thought at the London School of Economics and Political Science (LSE), I enjoyed another version of the same experience.

His visit to Colorado was the beginning of our friendship, which lasted until his death in December 1990. I took him around Colorado to admire the skill of cowboys on horseback punching cows, to see the aspen groves turning to orange and gold, and to clamber about the hills of the Cripple Creek goldfields. I asked him why he had agreed to come to Colorado since, although my letter had made it clear that I knew something about him, he surely had never heard of me. This was not quite true because, as I later found out, we had several mutual acquaintances who had vouched for me.

He told me that two things influenced his decision to come: First, he had an uncle who had migrated to California at the turn of the century to grow tomatoes; this had excited in him an interest in the American West and he read widely on the topic from childhood. He had a lot of western literature at his disposal. Although he had been to the East Coast of the United States, this was his first chance to see the West of his boyhood imagination. It seemed to him exactly like what he had read about. Second, he was charmed by the thought of an encampment of liberal learning nestled at the foot of Pikes Peak which, as he imagined it, had been founded by pioneers crossing the great plains in covered wagons bearing Shakespeare and the Bible. This was not quite accurate but not altogether wrong either. He endeared himself to us all when he began his now famous lecture by saying: "I have crossed half the world to find myself in familiar surroundings: a place of learning." We felt and he felt genuine kinship between ancient Cambridge and pioneering Colorado College. This quintessential Englishman had a romantic attraction to the "frontier experience."

We corresponded, and then in 1977 I began my annual pilgrimages to England to spend time with him. My wife and I arrived in London in August of that year and Oakeshott took us for a drink to the bar of the Ritz Hotel (introducing me to one of his favorite drinks, Campari and soda) before going along to lunch with Shirley and Bill Letwin at 3 Kent Terrace. This was to result in another extraordinary friendship and my entry into the most rewarding society of friends and companions I have known. Meeting Shirley Letwin for the first time could be a test of one's poise. If you got through the test satisfactorily, you could bank on a permanent commitment that taught me what fierce and devoted friendship really means. I did not yet know that, of course. Michael had alerted her about me and had shown her a seminar paper I had written about his thought. He had written to me to say of that paper that I "understood him better than he understood himself." She started by telling me it was among the best things she had seen on Michael, but then went on to pummel me with questions about all the American political theorists whom she seemed to despise, many of whom were friends of mine. I managed to maintain myself until Michael, in his marvelously graceful way, turned the engagement to a more conversational topic. I owe to Michael the chance of such high, Aristotelian friendship with Bill and Shirley Letwin.

In 1979, I arrived at LSE to spend time as an academic visitor in the Government Department. Oakeshott had long since formally retired but he retained his room in Lincoln's Chambers and, as he only came to the School officially on Tuesdays for the History of Political Thought seminar, I was given the other desk in his room that had been before me that of his former colleague, Professor Pickles. On Tuesdays when he was to give his papers on the study of history, which were later published in *On History and Other Essays* (1983, 1999), he would spend the day at his desk rewriting the papers. He did this every time he presented them, refining them over a number of years before they finally were published. In the meantime, photocopies of various versions of them circulated among his devoted student followers. Unless he was to see a student, I remained in the office working back-to-back with him. He smoked continuously until it was time to leave our cloudy space for the seminar meeting at 4 p.m. We often went out to eat together after the seminar, his two favorite places being *Luigi's* on Tavistock Street and *Mon Plaisir* on Monmouth Street. The latter especially remains a favorite of mine. It was during this time that I came to know well Bill and Shirley Letwin, Ken Minogue, Elie Kedourie, Wolfgang Von Leyden, Maurice Cranston, Robert Orr, John Morrall and John Charvet, and also Maurice Cowling at Cambridge. I still think of this as a golden era at the LSE, a time when many of my best students came there to study in the History of Political Thought program.

Oakeshott could enchant students even when, as was often true, they understood him only in part. He was, at eighty, more attuned to the young than teachers half his age. He never forgot what it was to be young, and he could forgive students for much because he loved what he saw as the glorious, transitory inconsequence of youth. Like Socrates, he was young when old. He never imposed his ideas except so far as their natural force would take them. He would listen patiently to virtually any question students posed and would answer them by making them better questions than they started out to be. Study in the university, he famously said, is the gift of an interval: a liberation from the unavoidable drills of school and a momentary release before the limiting responsibilities of adulthood set in. He thought work should balance play, enjoyment ambition, and conversation debate. He urged that we should be conservative with respect to the rules of the civil life in order to be radical in everything else. He was a Bohemian in the right way. He told students arriving at the university to think of themselves as strolling minstrels stopping off to perform before they were moved on by the local constabulary, and he encouraged them to think this far superior to occupying a niche in the social organization. He counseled students to be, as it were, irresponsible for a time so that liberal learning could enter in. And yet no one could doubt that what he was urging, and what he exemplified, was the profound seriousness of the life of the mind.

In the 1980s, Oakeshott decided to give up his flat at 16 New Row in Covent Garden to live year round in his Dorset cottage in the tiny village of Acton on the edge of the Purbeck marble quarries. His cottage was the combination of two quarryman's cottages which he had bought years before, knocking out the central partition to make one larger cottage. I first visited the cottage in the summer of 1977. In the decade of the 80s I visited him often there. There was no central heat, and only late in his life was there a telephone and a TV for his wife. He had minimal regard for any features of modern life. The computer did not exist for him. He thought most modern inventions had done the human race little good. He wrote everything by hand. From his cottage one looked out on the country of Hardy. One felt oneself transported back before World War I, even to the nineteenth century, to a world where one might meet Jude the Obscure coming down the path. This is exactly how Oakeshott wanted to feel. Life was, to him, sweeter then.

Oakeshott kept most of his books at the cottage, including many rare volumes that he was able to collect in the good old days when old books were relatively cheap and mostly bought by people who would read them rather than treat them as collectibles, antiques, or investments. The cottage had, at one end of the main room, a large fireplace that gave off much heat—at least at that end of the room. I would often huddle at the fireplace while Oakeshott would roam the farther reaches of the room complaining that it was rather hot. He was an excellent cook and gardener, and he owned a blue 1958 MG-B which, as I experienced, he drove at excessive speeds through the hedgerows.

The cottage was a place of conversation that often lasted until late into the night. It was genuine conversation. It could be witty and frivolous, up to a point. It could be sophisticated and often philosophical. It could be literary or theological. It could be, but infrequently, about current politics for which Oakeshott had little taste even though he was well informed. If you posed a serious question to him, he would often sit entranced for a time, until you began to think he hadn't heard you and you started to speak to fill in the void or to repeat yourself when, all of a sudden, a considered, precise, and elegant response would come forth, and you realized that, in such moments, elapsed time had no significance for him.

In his learned brilliance, Oakeshott made shrewd judgments about people and arguments, but he was, in a way, the least judgmental of all people. He was an intellectual aristocrat, but his sense of the universal predicament of being human (what he called the ordeal of consciousness) was authentically democratic. He was a true individualist. He spent no time worrying whether others had more or less than himself, he treated every encounter with another person as a unique circumstance, a potentially poetic experience. However, if an encounter was not fruitful, he went his way happily, awaiting another opportunity to present itself. He had the capacity, like Montaigne and Pascal, to sit alone in a room, to think and to write. He was certainly a companion to himself and, perhaps for that reason, he was a marvelous companion to others. When he found himself talking with someone of modest talent and little thought, he would look up at a corner of a room, jangling the coins in his pocket, and respond, "Oh, you think that! Do you? Do you?" His "do yous" were famous. And at the Oakeshott memorial meeting at LSE in 1991, John Casey, a fellow of Oakeshott's Cambridge college, suggested that if God had spoken to Oakeshott rather than Moses, saying "I AM that I AM," Oakeshott might have replied, "Are you? Are you?"

Oakeshott was a great teacher but he thought of himself as a learner, occasionally disclosing to others what he thought he had learned, inviting them to say what they might think of it.

The original impetus to his becoming a teacher was the impact of his teachers at St. George's School. He always thought of himself, first, as a learner, but those of us who saw him at work lecturing, or in seminars, knew that here was an extraordinary teacher. Even in his seventies when he limited himself to attending the General Seminar in the History of Political Thought at LSE, and occasionally reading papers on the idea of history, he identified with students in a special way. He had an immense appreciation of what it means to be young, he never forgot what it is to be young: "Everybody's young days," he said, "are a dream, a delightful insanity, a sweet solipsism. Nothing in them has a fixed shape, nothing a fixed price; everything is a possibility, and we live happily on credit. There are no obligations to be observed; there are no accounts to be kept. Nothing is specified in advance; everything is what can be made of it. The world is a mirror in which we seek the reflection of our own desires.... Urgency is our criterion of importance; and we do not easily understand that what is humdrum need not be despicable. We are impatient of restraint; and we readily believe, like Shelley, that to have contracted a habit is to have failed."[1]

He was also a writer in the deepest sense. He wrote, so far as I can tell, every day of his life from his undergraduate days until well into his eighties. He kept notebooks in which he copied out quotations, analyzed what he was reading, tried various opening gambits

---

1. Michael Oakeshott, "On Being Conservative" (1956), in *Rationalism in Politics* (1991), 436. "On Being Conservative" was originally a lecture given at the University of Swansea in 1956.

for essays, and so on. As we now know, he wrote numerous essays and lectures that he did not publish.

In his will he appointed Shirley Letwin his literary executor to do with his papers as she thought best. She and I went to the cottage in Dorset in May 1991 to remove the papers to the new Letwin house in London at 15 Arlington Road where they were kept before coming to the LSE library. She and I worked together on the joint venture to publish some of these with the Yale University Press. Since most of this archive, with the exception of some private correspondence, is now accessible to all interested parties, I need say no more about it. I read all of it, but so can anyone else now. In the meantime, more recent scholars have continued to publish much of his archive. Rather, I want to remember him in terms of some of the most memorable things he had to say on the topics dearest to his heart.

Oakeshott was eloquent on old age and mortality: "For most there is what Conrad called the 'shadow line' which, when we pass it, discloses a solid world of things, each with its fixed shape, each with its own point of balance, each with its price; a world of fact, not poetic image, in which what we have spent on one thing we cannot spend on another; a world inhabited by others besides ourselves who cannot be reduced to mere reflections of our own emotions."[2]

He spoke of love and friendship as only one who has felt and considered both could do: "Friends and lovers are not concerned with what can be made out of each other, but only with the enjoyment of one another. A friend . . . is somebody who evokes interest, delight, unreasoning loyalty, and who (almost) engages contemplative imagination. . . . Neither merit nor necessity has any part in the generation of love; its progenitors are chance and choice—chance, because what cannot be identified in advance cannot be sought; and in choice the inescapable practical component of desire makes itself felt."[3]

"In conversation," he famously remarked, "thoughts of different species take wing and play round one another, responding to each

2. Oakeshott, "On Being Conservative," 436–37.
3. Michael Oakeshott, "The Voice of Poetry in the Conversation of Mankind" (1959), in *Rationalism in Politics*, 537. "The Voice of Poetry in the Conversation of Mankind" first appeared as *The Voice of Poetry in the Conversation of Mankind* (London: Bowes and Bowes, 1959).

other's movements and provoking one another to fresh exertions. . . . There is no symposiarch or arbiter; not even a doorkeeper to examine credentials. . . . Voices which speak in conversation do not compose a hierarchy . . . it is an unrehearsed intellectual adventure . . . with conversation as with gambling, its significance lies neither in winning nor in losing, but in wagering. . . . It is the ability to participate in this conversation, and not the ability to reason cogently, to make discoveries about the world, or to contrive a better world, which distinguishes the human being from the animal and the civilized man from the barbarian." Conversation is also the sign of liberal learning for "Education, properly speaking, is an initiation into the skill and partnership of this conversation."[4]

Universities are places of learning ideally set aside to achieve conversationality: "A university will have ceased to exist when its learning has degenerated into what is now called research, when its teaching has become mere instruction and occupies the whole of an undergraduate's time, and when those who come to be taught come, not in search of their intellectual fortune but with a vitality so unroused or so exhausted that they wish only to be provided with a serviceable moral and intellectual outfit; when they come with no understanding of the manners of conversation but desire only a qualification for earning a living or a certificate to let them in on the exploitation of the world."[5]

Of course politics, the "necessary evil," is always with us: "The pursuit of perfection as the crow flies is an activity both impious and unavoidable in human life. It involves the penalties of impiety (the anger of the gods and social isolation), and its reward is not that of achievement but that of having made the attempt. It is an activity, therefore, suitable for individuals, but not for societies."[6]

"In political activity, then, men sail a boundless and bottomless sea; there is neither harbour for shelter nor floor for anchorage, neither starting-place nor appointed destination. The enterprise is to

4. Oakeshott, "The Voice of Poetry," 489–90.
5. Michael Oakeshott, "The Idea of a University" (1950), in *The Voice of Liberal Learning* (2001), 117.
6. Michael Oakeshott, "The Tower of Babel" (1948), in *Rationalism in Politics*, 465.

keep afloat on an even keel; the sea is both friend and enemy; and the seamanship consists in using the resources of a traditional manner of behaviour in order to make a friend of every hostile occasion."[7]

His views on politics resulted from considering politics philosophically: "Thinking is at first associated with an extraneous desire for action, and it is some time, perhaps, before we discern that philosophy is without any direct bearing upon the practical conduct of life, and that it has never offered its true followers anything which could be mistaken for a gospel. Of course, some so-called philosophers afford pretext enough for this particular misunderstanding. Nearly always a philosopher hides a secret ambition, foreign to philosophy, and often it is that of a preacher. But we must learn not to follow the philosophers upon these holiday excursions."[8]

"Philosophical reflection is recognized here as the adventure of one who seeks to understand in other terms what he already understands. . . . It is, in short, a well considered intellectual adventure recollected in tranquility."[9]

It is hard to say, in reflecting on the distinct activities of philosophy and poetry, which he came to value more. "Poetry has nothing to teach us about how to live or what we ought to approve. Practical activity is an endless battle for noble or for squalid but always for illusory ends, a struggle from which the practical self cannot escape and in which victory is impossible because desire can never be satisfied. . . . Poetic activity has no part in this struggle and it has no power to control, to modify, or to terminate it. If it imitates the voice of practice its utterance is counterfeit. To listen to the voice of poetry is to enjoy, not a victory, but a momentary release, a brief enchantment. . . . Poetry is a sort of truancy, a dream within the dream of life, a wild flower planted among our wheat."[10]

---

7. Michael Oakeshott, "Political Education" (1951), in *Rationalism in Politics*, 60. "Political Education" was Oakeshott's inaugural lecture at the London School of Economics in 1951, and it was then published as a pamphlet by Bowes & Bowes in 1951.
8. Michael Oakeshott, *Experience and Its Modes*, 1.
9. Michael Oakeshott, *On Human Conduct*, vii.
10. Oakeshott, "The Voice of Poetry," 540–41.

Throughout, Oakeshott felt the pressure of the eternal on our temporality, and he reflected on the resulting tension—the tension characterizing the civilization in which he was a loving voice—over the whole of his life: "Religious faith is the evocation of a sentiment (the love, the glory, or the honour of God, for example, or even a humble caritas), to be added to all others as the motive of all motives in terms of which the fugitive adventures of human conduct, without being released from their mortal and their moral conditions, are graced with an intimation of immortality: the sharpness of death and the deadliness of doing overcome, and the transitory sweetness of a mortal affection, the tumult of a grief and the passing beauty of a May morning recognized neither as merely evanescent adventures nor as emblems of better things to come, but as *aventures*, themselves encounters with eternity."[11]

The essays collected here constitute my reflections over a period of forty-five years on Oakeshott's understanding of the human condition, beginning with the "achievement" essay of 1976 leading most recently to the essay on what we can learn from him in 2020. Most gratifying is the fact that numerous of my students, who studied political philosophy with me, have gone on to highly successful careers, often going well beyond me in their accomplishments. Some of them had the good fortune to meet and study with Oakeshott at the LSE. Later students have discovered his work and the spirit of inquiry it inspires. They have become courageous defenders of the life of the mind who, with Oakeshott, neither despise nor overrate politics. They see that the practical life is an essential, unavoidable feature of the human condition, that it reveals much of what is true of the human condition. Yet at the same time politics does not exhaust the possibilities in human experience. As he did, they look for and are receptive to the poetic moments in the midst of life's ordinariness. They are in the world while resisting worldliness. For him and for them my gratitude knows no bounds.

11. Oakeshott, *On Human Conduct*, 85.

Michael Oakeshott on the Human Condition

The Achievement
of Michael Oakeshott

T O UNDERSTAND OAKESHOTT one has to see him making a series of formulations of his thought understood as acts of self-disclosure. Their consistency with each other is the revelation of a character, despite the transposing of images of one sort into another over a lifetime. He has been disclosing what he has learned, and here the emphasis will be on what he has learned as related to the political life.[1]

I

According to Oakeshott, human beings are what they learn to be. What they learn depends on the state of the world into which they are born and initiated. It is not a mere world however. The human world is entirely a world of experience dividing itself into various

Previously unpublished essay reprinted by permission from Timothy Fuller. This 1976 essay was Fuller's first effort to interpret Oakeshott's thought. He sent it to Oakeshott, who gave him a positive response. This confirmed a friendship lasting until Oakeshott's death in 1990.
1. A bibliography complete up to 1968 is to be found in *Politics and Experience, Essays Presented to Michael Oakeshott*, ed. by Preston King and B. C. Parekh (Cambridge University Press, 1968). A bibliography of Oakeshott's writings since 1968, and of recent criticism of his work, is provided by Josiah Lee Auspitz: "Bibliographical Note," *Political Theory*, vol. 4, no. 3, August 1976, 295–300.

modes of experience as a whole whose characteristic feature is the achievement of an increasingly organized arrangement of postulates or assumptions which shape an image of experience. At some point in the evolution of this image, it achieves a sufficiently distinctive form so as to qualify itself for consideration as the key to initiation into the world as a whole. It can be taught to those who have not yet learned it, and thus impart the possibility of a guide in the endless engagement to understand ourselves, which is the human condition. The emergent distinctive images of experience struggle toward completion. Each mode of experience seeks completion in an explanation of experience as a whole, recasting in terms of its own assumptions, as they are clarified, whatever is an incipient incoherency. In itself each mode of experience poses a challenge to the alternative modes since the expression of its completeness proclaims its self-satisfaction, and its adequacy to subsume, suppress, or ignore other modes. However convincing this argument may appear from the perspective of the proponents of a mode of experience, for the philosopher such a proclamation of self-satisfaction must be treated with skepticism. The rest of this formulation is to be understood as an exploration of what the "philosopher" has learned to be, and a disclosure of what is to be seen from the perspective he has learned.

The philosopher has no interest whatever in arbitrating the merits of the various claims of completion or self-satisfaction of the modes of experience. As each mode seeks completion or satisfaction by limiting experience—preventing experience from spilling over the boundaries its own assumptions permit—the philosopher contrarily seeks experience unmodified in its fulness. He cannot accomplish this by establishing a hierarchy of modes because each mode, when fully explored, reveals an exclusivity, each implies a claim to the understanding of experience as a whole.

One cannot encounter a mode of experience recognizable as such unless what is encountered has assumptions sufficiently clear to permit its systematic exposition. Moreover, the systematic exposition of the assumptions which give a mode its coherence, cannot avoid presenting the mode in its exclusivity—indeed, it is the discovery of this decisive exclusivity that is the emblem of the mode's qualification to be considered a mode of experience at all. Failing this we are confronted not with a mode but with an uncertain occurrence, a derivative of a mode not yet brought into view, or an incipiency which may or may not eventually establish itself for consideration as a mode. These occurrences cannot be explained clearly because what is not yet distinctive cannot be systematically expounded, it is not yet a *world* of thought or ideas as opposed to a jumble, not yet a challenge that the philosopher must accept in order to insure himself that he has not overlooked the treasure he seeks. Nor can the philosopher reconcile the modes: Compromise is a sign of makeshift, the invention of a spurious mode to explain the modes and thus a turning-away from the quest for the whole of experience unmodified. A makeshift is a confusion, a chaos of mixed modes, a hopeless argument in a hazy context. This conciliation has the substance of a shadow.

The philosopher does try to clarify the interior logic of each of the modes of experience he encounters. He articulates what the interior logic of a mode of experience must be if it is to believe itself coherent. This construction of the philosopher adds nothing to the capacity to act of those who see the world in the perspective of a certain mode. Nor can the exposition be understood to be an "ideal" which sets a "standard" for the mode's adherents to emulate. The explanation shows instead why everything must be just as it is.

II

Oakeshott's original discussion of "practice" may be summarized as follows: The attempt to explain the whole of experience from the perspective of the practical is sufficiently developed to be expounded by the philosopher in terms of assumptions which can be shown to be unavoidably necessary, whether acknowledged as such or not, for those who make the attempt. To have clarified the matter this way shows also what assumptions must be attractive to the person initiated into explanation of the world as a world of practice, that is, what kind of person the practical person learns to be. If the philosopher can show that the whole of experience, understood from the viewpoint of the assumptions of practicality, is distorted, that is, that all experience cannot be satisfactorily explained in terms of the assumptions of practicality except by remaining uncritical of its own assumptions, and there exist alternative explanatory assumptions of sufficient clarity to be brought forward by the philosopher, then the explanation of the world, as if it were entirely a world of practice, is an abstraction. An abstraction is an obstacle to the quest for experience as a whole unmodified and the philosopher must reject it.[2]

For "practice" to constitute a "mode" of knowing or interpreting the world it must be able to produce an image of experience that is a "world of ideas." If it is not a "world of ideas" then it is not a systematic way of knowing. Perhaps, then, it is the basis of worlds of ideas—the source from which "theories" about experience arise, that is, it is a "world of action" as opposed to a "world of ideas." But, for Oakeshott, this is impossible because there are no "worlds" of any kind that are not "worlds of ideas." There is no experience without thought and judgment, and there is nothing knowable to us which we do not experience, and thus nothing that is not thought which we can know. The "world of action" thus must be a "world of ideas" being spoken of as a "world of action" and not a mere "world of action."

"'What happens' in practical life is not the material of thought, it belongs itself to the world of thought; 'action' is not the product of thought, it is itself a form of thought. An 'eternal' or 'objective' world of doings and happenings which is not a world of ideas, is a mere fiction. Events and actions, if they are to fall inside the world of experience, must conform to the character of that world; and to remain outside is an acknowledgment of nonentity. . . . Further, it is impossible to accept the view that practical life, because it is concerned with volitions, is therefore not a world of thought. For such a view is meaningless unless we are to believe that the will is a faculty independent of the intellect, and that volition is experience, yet not judgment; . . . Volition is itself thought and not the mere result of thought."[3]

---

2. This summary is primarily based on Michael Oakeshott's *Experience and Its Modes* (Cambridge University Press, 1983; reprinted, 1966). Hereafter cited as *EM*.
3. Oakeshott, *EM*, 251–52.

But even if it is granted that practical life is experience as a kind of thought, does it constitute a *world* of experience, that is, a distinctive imagining of coherency as opposed to a "tissue of mere conjunctions"? Those who believe that the practical life is composed of feelings, intuitions, or immediate responses are likely to see only a tissue of mere conjunctions. But, for Oakeshott, there are no immediate responses, because an immediate response implies no thought, no experience, and where there is not experience there can be no response. "To suppose a wholly irrational element in practical experience is to suppose a mode of experience which not merely falls short of, but which explicitly contradicts, the character of experience. And whatever defects this 'irrational' world of intuitions may suffer from, they are defects which belong to a world of experience capable of becoming a world of knowledge."[4]

But do we not encounter the practical life of mere opinions? What is good for one is bad for another; what is right for you is wrong for me—are these not irreducible differences?[5] Here surely is a world of endless incoherence. On the contrary, says Oakeshott: "If anything were a matter of *mere* opinion. It belongs to the character of a mere opinion that it can never be contradicted: in the region of mere opinions, what one asserts the other never denies. Yet not only does practical experience assert the possibility of a difference of opinion, but it is obliged to assert it. A 'mere opinion,' in this sense, must fall outside possible experience. Everywhere there is the possibility of contradictory opinions, and where these are possible we have left behind a collection of mere opinions and have, at least, entered a world of opinions. . . . Everywhere in opinion there is implicit assertion, reference to reality."[6] Therefore, however unsatisfactorily arranged the practical world may seem to be when we come upon it, its unsatisfactoriness lies not in its failure to imply a coherent visualization of itself but in its unfulfilled realization of that coherency.

We turn, then, to the exposition of the idiomatic imagining of coherency in practical life: "Practical life comprises the attempts we

4. Oakeshott, *EM*, 253.
5. Oakeshott, *EM*, 254.
6. Oakeshott, *EM*, 254–55.

make to alter existence or to maintain it unaltered in the face of threatened change. It is both the production and the prevention of change, and in either case it is not merely a program for action but action itself. Our practical world is the totality of such actions, together with all they imply. Practice comprises everything which belongs to the conduct of life as such."[7]

This means that we cannot restrict the notion of the practical life to the vulgar conception of it derived from "the restricted tastes and defective genius of the majority of mankind. He who determines to do away with his life is no less conducting his life than the man who spends it in satisfying his ambitions: and the man who seeks satisfaction in imagination or devotion to God requires to be no less active than he who looks for it in conquest or an empire. Indeed, we cannot deny the name of practice to the life of one who, following some creed of quietism, passes his unproductive existence in contempt of all that the world holds active and practical, for here also is involved the change or maintenance of existence. Practice is activity, the activity inseparable from the conduct of life and from the necessity of which no living man can relieve himself."[8]

Practice is characterized by conducting ourselves in terms of the "to be" which is "not yet." Even to maintain is to change, to seek an alteration pointing toward the "not yet." The practical world is a world of the "wished-for." It is the world of experience *sub specie voluntatis*. Thus, even though it is a characterization of experience which makes volition *prominent*, it is not a characterization that could stand on the idea of *mere* volition. That is, there can be no volition without a context which gives shape to the issue of change and maintenance, no volition that does not proceed in a world of opinions about change and maintenance, for without such a world of opinions there could be no "wished-for" "not yet."[9]

7. Oakeshott, *EM*, 256.
8. Oakeshott, *EM*, 257.
9. By contrast, in the historical mode one might seek to explain how a world of opinions came to be, but in so doing one could not show how that world came to be by speaking of it as a "to be" which is "not yet." It is a world characterized by "pastness" and the demonstration of why it is the way it is is performed in terms of the details of how it came to be the way it is. This demonstration

Now, if we are dealing with a world that is something more than a jumble of mere opinions, we cannot be dealing with a *mere* "to be" which is "not yet." We must be dealing with a "to be" of which we must unavoidably say that it "ought to be." The "to be" which is "not yet" takes shape through its connection to a notion of fulfillment, completion, or coherency intimated, however dimly, in the wished-for outcome. The intimation of coherency brings forward the "to be" as what "ought to be" since if it did not it would be inexplicable that the current condition was not entirely satisfactory, that is, satisfactory in no lesser or greater degree than any alternative condition. But then it would not appear unsatisfactory or point beyond itself. We must, therefore, be dealing with a world of ideas which implies completion or systematic coherence, and that implication suggests the unavoidability of the characteristics previously attributed to that world of ideas—it is a mode of experience with distinctive features. Its distinctiveness consists in its mutability, its transiency, its constant exhibition of the desirability of what is not yet, its insistence that the only way to see the world as a whole is to see it *sub specie voluntatis*, while nonetheless pursuing the completion that would release volition into a world where the "not yet" loses its seductiveness. To be clear on this point we must also notice that this is a world of ideas, that is, we are seeking its interior meaning as a world, we are not seeking to comprehend it in terms of what is outside it. To do the latter would be to fail to notice it as a world. It cannot be said, therefore, that this world is "caused" by desire and aversion, or by desiring. On the contrary, "desiring" is a way of explaining which is

---

undoubtedly involves thought and judgment but what is prominent is not volition but the characterization of an occurrence as past. On the other hand, concern for the conduct of life also involves consideration of the past; not the past as that which is over and done with but the past as suggestive of what is desirable in the future. To put it another way, it is possible in the historical perspective that the world of experience, understood as past, however unsatisfactory, is not unsatisfactory because of our unfulfilled desires. It is unsatisfactory because the evidence is lacking to complete the story of how it came to be. As soon as it becomes unsatisfactory because it brings to mind a desirability not yet achieved, we have shifted from historical perspective to the practical, and we cease to be concerned with demonstrating how it came to be and seek in it, instead, the inspiration to guide our conduct.

interior to, and emerges in the context of, this world of ideas when understood as a world of ideas. To think of the human situation in terms of "desiring" is to notice a feature within this practical world of ideas. "Desiring, of course, is not the cause of activity in a hitherto inactive self; we do not first 'have a desire' which causes us to move from a condition of rest to one of movement: desiring is merely being active in a particular manner, reaching out one's hand to pick a flower, or feeling in one's pocket for a coin."[10]

Oakeshott here leads us to the combination of particularities constituting the concrete character of practicality, of which "desiring" is a misleading abstraction. "I do not want to be happy," he says, "What I want is to idle in Avignon or hear Caruso sing." In other words there is no desiring without something desired, and nothing much is revealed in merely saying that there is desiring. It occurs to us, then, that this is a world in which what is true today may have been false yesterday, and may again be false tomorrow. This world, like any other, hopes for satisfaction or coherence. How, then, is this coherence to be achieved when what was true yesterday, an intimation of satisfaction, is false today, a misstep? Today's coherency "is merely preliminary to its transformation,"[11] suddenly appearing as the not now acceptable consequence of yesterday's "not yet" which sought "to be." This is a world of endless transformations, and its peculiarity is in the supposition that transformation will lead to the world unmodified, to the whole. Like every other world of ideas that distinguishes itself as a world of ideas, there is implied a method to reach out to that which would be fully and finally satisfactory. But it can be seen already that it convicts itself, by its own method, of abstraction—of coming to an arrest in the quest for the whole. The practical man claims the wisdom to know how to find coherence in transformation, taking it for granted that coherence presupposes transformation. He is uncritical with respect to this assumption. What might otherwise suggest contradiction he has learned to know as a fascinating image of the not-yet transformed, and he finds his world confirmed. For

10. Michael Oakeshott, *Rationalism in Politics* (New York: Basic Books, 1962), 206. Hereafter cited as *R*.
11. Oakeshott, *EM*, 267.

him, the seas are an energy resource, not: "The moving waters at their priestlike task/Of pure ablution round earth's human shores—"[12]

We come, then, to describing the one who inhabits this world of ideas: He is, for Oakeshott, the self-determined self who is an end in himself. This is so because: "Whatever be our principle of reality or individuality, that which is real or individual is, for that reason, an end in itself; and where the principle of reality is taken to be separateness and uniqueness, that which has demonstrated its separateness and uniqueness, has demonstrated also its character as an end in itself."[13] In the practical world action is impossible without such a self. Without separateness and distinction the practical begins to disintegrate. There ceases to be agency for the particular desires and aversions which compose practical reality. However many occasions there may be to lose ourselves in what is other, and to believe that our singularity is an illusion, we always come back to it. To pass beyond what divides the self from what is other is momentary, it cannot be permanent. For Oakeshott, the union of satisfied love is followed by the confession that "we two must be twain/ Although our undivided loves are one."[14]

Philosophic contemplation, as he sees it, is the making of images whose distinctiveness is their appeal even though they do not constitute signs or symbols of something else.[15] And poetic expression is a composition of images pointing not to something else but exhibiting the delight to be found within the arrangement. "Poetry is a sort of truancy, a dream within the dream of life, a wild flower planted among our wheat."[16] "There is no *vita contemplativa*; there are only moments of contemplative activity abstracted and rescued from the flow of curiosity and contrivance."[17] Whereas:

> Practical activity is an endless battle for noble or for squalid but always for illusory ends, a struggle from which the

12. Oakeshott, *R*, 208.
13. Oakeshott, *EM*, 270.
14. Oakeshott, *EM*, 272.
15. Oakeshott, *R*, 220.
16. Oakeshott, *R*, 247.
17. Oakeshott, *R*, 247.

practical self cannot escape and in which victory is impossible because desire can never be satisfied: every attainment is recognized to be imperfect, and every imperfection has value only as an incipient perfection which is itself an illusion. And even "forgiveness" is only an emblematic break in the chain of the fatality of doing; every action, even those that are forgotten, is irreparable. Poetic activity has no part in this struggle and it has no power to control, to modify, or to terminate it. If it imitates the voice of practice its utterance is counterfeit. To listen to the voice of poetry is to enjoy, not a victory, but a momentary release, a brief enchantment.[18]

18. Oakeshott, *R*, 247. Likewise, the philosopher who ascends out of the shadows of the cave and, upon returning from his travels, brushes aside the "cave-understood conditionality of 'the truth, the whole truth, and nothing but the truth' and were to insist that matters should be delayed while the question, What is truth? was explored, or if he were to lecture judge and jury about the postulates of justice, those concerned might be expected to become a trifle restless. Before long the more perceptive of the cave-dwellers would begin to suspect that, after all, he was not an interesting theorist but a fuddled and pretentious 'theoretician' who should be sent on his travels again, or accommodated in a quiet home. And the less patient would be disposed to run him out of town as an impudent mountebank. In short, what the cave-dwellers resent is not the theorist, the philosopher . . . but the 'theoretician,' the *philosophe*, the 'intellectual'; and they resent him, not because they are corrupt or ignorant but because they know just enough to recognize an impostor when they meet one." Michael Oakeshott, *On Human Conduct* (Oxford University Press: Clarendon Press, 1975), 30–31. Hereafter cited as *HC*.

For Oakeshott, "Mortality is the presiding category in practical experience" (*EM*, 273). But if love, poetry, and philosophic contemplation cannot invade and complete the mortal world of practicality, what of religion? Here, too, Oakeshott maintains the practical world as a world with a by now not surprising result. As he sees it, the man of faith enjoys a sentiment "in terms of which the fugitive adventures of human conduct, without being released from their mortal and their moral conditions, are graced with an intimation of immortality: the sharpness of death and the deadliness of doing overcome, and the transitory sweetness of a mortal affection, the tumult of a grief and the passing beauty of a May morning recognized neither as merely evanescent adventures nor as emblems of better things to come, but as *aventures*, themselves encounters with eternity" (*HC*, 85).

For Oakeshott there is no getting rid of the world of practice even when we have agreed that it is an abstraction. Abstraction though it may be, it is a world of ideas. To enter it is to be governed by its terms. We may leave it, we may ascend out of it, we may expound its character, but if we return into it it surrounds and enfolds us with its conditions and requirements. To know what such a world must assume in order to make sense to itself is not to know how to refute it. To explain its premises, is not to utter a magic formula by means of which its leadenness may be turned into gold, or its multiplicity into unity. Properly understood we see it is a world that must be exactly as it is, and there is in this some release from its persuasiveness. All intimations of what transcends the self are explorations of other worlds which, however significant, are not substitutions for the practical world. To have shown the postulates of the practical world is to have convicted it of abstraction without having shown its avoidability. Likewise, the experience of the self as individual has not been shown to be dispensable whatever longing for fulfillment it may suffer.

The individual is the agent of evaluation. All the goings on of his world are considerations in the pursuit of coherency. "Whatever virtues there be, whatever judgments of value, each must submit itself (and does submit itself in the mind of anyone who leads an 'examined life') to the world of value as a whole, and from this it derives both its status and its truth. For here, as everywhere, absoluteness belongs solely to the coherent world as a world and as a whole."[19] The evaluations of individuals, consequently, must emerge from the already imagined image of coherency. To make a judgment of value is not to pull something out of nothing, from nowhere, into our world. Evaluation is the consideration of what is intimated by the incoherency of our world as we construe that incoherency. This tells us something about how we recognize the difference between "rational" and "irrational" conduct. Thus, in the Victorian era, it was discovered, by careful anatomical and mechanical observation, that "rational dress" for girls riding bicycles was, undoubtedly, bloomers.

19. Oakeshott, *EM*, 278.

But how was it that these inventive minds, set free from all lingering prejudices, "paused at bloomers instead of running on to 'shorts'"?[20]

At least part of the answer must be that those inventive minds considered anatomy and mechanics in the context of the considerations of coherency we designate Victorian. The notion that there is a method of rational problem-solving independent of the circumstances in which the problem to be solved takes its shape is here rejected. It is rejected because it does not constitute a "way of behaving" but only a "theory of behavior."[21]

"Mind as we know it is the offspring of knowledge and activity; it is composed entirely of thoughts. You do not first have a mind, which acquires a filling of ideas and then makes distinctions between true and false, right and wrong, reasonable and unreasonable, and then, as a third step, causes activity. Properly speaking the mind has no existence apart from, or in advance of, these and other distinctions. These and other distinctions are not acquisitions; they are constitutive of the mind."[22] Doing something depends on knowing how to do it, and it is only possible to describe, in propositions, the nature of this doing when the knowing how is already exhibited in the doing so that propositions may be distilled from it. The propositions are the retrospective distillation of what we have already learned to do. One evaluates, invents, imagines, constructs, suggests, proposes, responds in the context of what he has learned. There is no other possibility. Evaluation involves learning to understand ourselves, and this seeking to understand ourselves is emergent out of what we have learned to become. Oakeshott often thinks of this as "an adventure": "It has no preordained course to follow: with every thought and action a human being lets go a mooring and puts out to sea on a self-chosen but largely unforseeable course. . . . It has no preordained destination. . . . It is a predicament, not a journey."[23] The conduct of selves in the context of each other involves not finding out the answer to the question of the meaning of

20. Oakeshott, *R*, 82.
21. Oakeshott, *R*, 88.
22. Oakeshott, *R*, 88–90.
23. Michael Oakeshott, "A Place of Learning," 11, hereafter cited as *PL*.

life but rendering their interaction intelligible. Hobbes explored this predicament in depth by tenacious reflection on the dependency of self-regulation on self-knowledge. A human being may be understood to be in contention with himself: On the one hand, he is moved to peace as the premise of the self's continual wish to explore itself. On the other hand, there are the temptations of self-assertion bespeaking the madness of the proud, and the seductions of self-forgetfulness in the "mob" incited by "eloquence." These polarities are understood by Oakeshott to play a major role in the constitution of the political life which he sometimes describes as the *bellum omnium contra omnes* carried on by other means.[24] There is no self-regulation that guarantees safety from the arbitrary, incomplete, unfulfilling, lacking. The flow of desire and temptation is endless. This circumstance cannot be ignored. What is not given to us we must learn to become. It is not altogether unreasonable to find a modicum of nobility in this perpetual process of learning to become human, to portray to ourselves our task and to show to the others what is proper for us, what we have learned to become. It is not inconceivable that one can come to feel that knowing what is appropriate is a greater achievement than overpowering others (or submitting to them), since conquering others has little to do with elucidating the self one wishes to know. A self may learn to accommodate the others in order to save himself. And, in learning to direct himself the self may bring himself to believe that he is immersed in a task of such significance as to make the direction of others superfluous business. This holding together of pride and humility Oakeshott shares with Hobbes whose *Leviathan* he has variously characterized as the greatest masterpiece of political thinking in English, and as a "work of art of superb integrity." Hobbes's was the expression, at its most intrepid, of the morality of individuality, and of the civil society that corresponds to it. "Any abridgment" of his "carefully pondered and exceedingly complicated image of human nature is hazardous."[25]

---

24. Cf. Michael Oakeshott, *Hobbes on Civil Association* (1975) hereafter cited as *HCA*.
25. Oakeshott, *EM*, 252; Oakeshott, *HCA*, 79.

Practice, then, is understood to be the engagement of the self *inter homines* to become what it has learned to become, and to do so by breaking down the discrepancy between what is here and now and what ought to be. "The only means which practice recognizes for this purpose is action, the actual point-by-point qualification of what is here and now by 'what ought to be.'"[26] There can be no reduction of what is here and now to what ought to be, for that would be as much as to say that there is another world in terms of which the here and now could be arranged. But the here and now can only arrange itself according to what it knows how to do. It requires the here and now already to know how to be what ought to be, to know what ought to be, to overcome the so-called "deficiency" or "prejudice" of the here and now. But it is that deficiency or prejudice which constitutes the possibility of what ought to be. What is actually possible to us, therefore, are particular efforts to make whole the paradoxical simultaneity of the here and now and the ought to be. The "ought to be" which is "not yet" is a present experience and can be explicated only in terms of what is present to us. What is not present to us is not in our experience. It is the genius of the world of practice to organize everything around the experience of the discrepancy between what is here and now and what ought to be. Those who assert the possibility of ending this discrepancy, and who revile the failure hither to have done so, mistakenly suppose that this condition is a sign of avoidable incoherency. In fact, they are noticing the distinctive character of the world of practice, the thing that gives it its shape. They mistake the arbitrariness of its organization of experience for a failure to have understood its full potential. We may convict this world of abstraction, but because it is a world of experience, its modality may not be satisfactorily subsumed into another. Thus, it fulfills its potential, so to speak, at every moment. There is no additional postulate to be added to it to make it complete and so, if we wish to go beyond it, we must abandon it altogether for another world of ideas. It is not experience unmodified, but within its premises it is consistent. It

26. Oakeshott, *EM*, 290.

is a barrier to the philosopher's quest for experience unmodified and he must reject it outright. It is not his task to add to it, nor to overthrow it, but to abandon it to its self-congratulatory assertion that it knows what is important. "Its truth is true so far as it goes, but, because it stands in the way of our going further, it must be rejected *in toto*. Practical experience, to gain the whole world, must lose its own soul. Not until we have become wholly indifferent to the truths of this world of practice, not until we have shaken off the abstractions of practical experience, of morality and religion, good and evil, faith and freedom, body and mind, the practical self and its ambitions and desires, shall we find ourselves once more turned in the direction which leads to what can satisfy the character of experience."[27] As a philosopher inevitably remains a man, so he must nevertheless acknowledge his fellow men. He can neither overthrow nor lead the world. "Great achievements are accomplished in the mental fog of practical experience. What is farthest from our needs is that kings should be philosophers. The victims of thought . . . are self-confessed betrayers of life, and must pursue their way without the encouragement of the practical consciousness, which is secure in the knowledge that philosophical thought can make no relevant contribution to the coherence of its world of experience."[28]

III

Oakeshott's thinking formed along these lines early in his career, and he has exhibited remarkable consistency from the appearance of *Experience and Its Modes* in 1933 on. His major essays on Hobbes and the collection in *Rationalism in Politics* elaborate his original thoughts. His response to the way we live now has centered around refusing obsession with practice, opposing the incessant politicization of modern life and scholarship, and revivifying the ear for the poetic. Among the various releases from the world of practice it is

27. Oakeshott, *EM*, 310.
28. Oakeshott, *EM*, 321.

clear that poetry is paramount for Oakeshott. Indeed, it is with respect to poetry that Oakeshott has made the only explicit major alteration in his thinking. In *Experience and Its Modes* he located poetry within the practical world as an activity which provided a fleeting taste of the overcoming of the discrepancy between what is and what ought to be. Poetry was seen there as motivated by the occasional felt need of release from that endless chain of transformations— it was the illusion of escape from the sometimes dreadful consistency of practical life. But in his essay, "The Voice of Poetry in the Conversation of Mankind" he retracted what he came to think of as a foolish view of poetry and attempted to establish poetry as a world of its own wholly other than the worlds of practice, science, and history. He ceased after *Experience and Its Modes* to make serious reference to the task of the philosopher or to the attempt to grasp the whole unmodified. On the contrary, if I am not mistaken, from the publication of the essay "Rationalism in Politics" in 1947 until the publication in 1962 of that and a number of other essays in the collection of the same name, a cautious but distinct transposition of attitude toward the practical world is evident. The marks of this shift are the alteration in the status of poetry, and Oakeshott's proposal that the hallmark of humanity is conversation. The conversation of mankind is ecumenical and conciliatory. The disdain of the distinctive voices of the different modes or worlds of ideas that seeps through *Experience and Its Modes* has disappeared. The voices are no longer convicted of abstraction but are simply described for what they are. The descriptions are largely consistent with what is to be found in *Experience and Its Modes* but the tone has altered. It is in the conversation that humanity is to be found. It is in conversation the different voices must forever seek to understand themselves. It is not too much to say that the poetic evocation of the conversation of mankind has replaced the philosopher's effort to abandon abstraction. Conversation becomes "the appropriate image of human intercourse—appropriate because it recognizes the qualities, the diversities, and the proper relationships of human utterances." Again: "In conversation, 'facts' appear only to be resolved once more into the possibilities from which they were made; 'certainties' are shown to be combustible, not by being brought into con-

tact with other 'certainties' or with doubts, but by being kindled by
the presence of ideas of another order; approximations are revealed
between notions normally remote from one another. Thoughts of
different species take wing and play round one another, responding
to each other's movements and provoking one another to fresh exertions. Nobody asks where they have come from or on what authority they are present; nobody cares what will become of them when
they have played their part. There is no symposiarch or arbiter; not
even a doorkeeper to examine credentials. Every entrant is taken at
its face value and everything is permitted which can get itself accepted into the flow of speculation. And voices which speak in conversation do not compose a hierarchy. Conversation is not an
enterprise designed to yield an extrinsic profit, a contest where a
winner gets a prize, nor is it an activity of exegesis, it is an unrehearsed intellectual adventure. It is with conversation as with gambling, its significance lies neither in winning nor losing, but in
wagering."[29] It is not too much to say that these expressions, poetic in
nature, seek a different attitude toward the world. However indirectly, there is here an attempt to add something to the world of
practice. It is an addition not by way of adding a postulate to the
postulates of the practical world—that remains impossible—but by
way of the poet who, having glimpsed and taken up the poetic intimation in the interstices of practical life, elaborates it and brings it
to our attention. This conversational gambit offers cooperation in
the human venture of self-understanding in the hope of restoring
to balance the interplay of self-knowledge and self-regulation. The
conversational attitude becomes, in Oakeshott's thinking, preser-
vative of tradition, moderation, and sympathy. In alliance with this
new task he has written a series of essays on education, teaching,
and learning, and on the idea of the university, defending as essential the setting aside of places of learning wherein careful initiation
into the conversation might be possible. There we might learn to
think of a culture "as voices, each the expression of a distinct and
conditional understanding of the world and a distinct idiom of
human self-understanding, and of the culture itself as these voices

29. Oakeshott, *R*, 198.

joined, as such voices could only be joined, in a conversation—an endless unrehearsed intellectual adventure in which, in imagination, we enter into a variety of modes of understanding the world and ourselves and are not disconcerted by the differences or dismayed by the inconclusiveness of it all . . . an education in imagination, an initiation into the art of this conversation in which we learn to recognize the voices; to distinguish their different modes of utterance, to acquire the intellectual and moral habits appropriate to this conversational relationship and thus to make our *debut dans la vie humaine*."[30]

He has done as much as any recent political thinker in the Anglo-American world to outline the possibility of a conservative disposition that is conversational without sinking into mere accommodation.[31]

There is little doubt that Oakeshott initiated a conversational gambit with the presentation of his inaugural address at the London School of Economics in 1951, "Political Education."[32] From that moment forward he has been a controversial conversationalist. His attack on the "ideological style" in politics, and his understanding of politics as "the pursuit of intimations," together with his perhaps ironic insistence that he was only representing "a further stage in the intellectual pilgrimage" of the liberal John Stuart Mill, all stated with quiet uncompromisingness, elicited an outcry among many who saw no point to a conversation in which there is no symposiarch, and where utterances suggest poetic as well as programmatic meaning in life. This was taken to be "mere conservatism" or sometimes "aestheticism." Yet it would be a mistake to suppose that

---

30. Oakeshott, *PL*, 28.
31. The basis for this disposition can be constructed out of the essays in *Rationalism in Politics*, the essay, "The Masses in Representative Democracy," reprinted now in William F. Buckley's anthology of *American Conservative Thought in the 20th Century* (Indianapolis, IN: Bobbs-Merrill, 1970), and most importantly in *On Human Conduct* (1975) and his two-part essay "The Vocabulary of the Modern European State" in *Political Studies* 23, nos. 2–3 (June 1975): 319–41, and no. 4 (December 1975): 409–14. A distillation of the ideas in these essays in somewhat simpler form, "Talking Politics," is available in the anniversary issue of the *National Review* 27 (1975): 1345–47, 1423–28.
32. Reprinted with additional comment in Oakeshott's *R*.

Oakeshott is a mere conservative. The primary emphasis is on being conversational not on being conservative. Yet conversation is a great activity, it is the beginning of one's humanity, and, for Oakeshott every great activity is necessarily conservative.

In brief, Oakeshott's conservatism is a disposition to be skeptical about private dreams which seek to become a compulsory public manner of living, and to be reserved toward the impatient who pursue perfection as the crow flies. Such a disposition takes its bearings from the current condition of life, learning to enjoy and to explore the possibilities of what is present, and to find the resources for this venture within ourselves. Its accomplishment is a settled manner of living that resists frenzied anticipation of the future, believing the present an unfortunate barrier against "real life." Nothing can be required that cannot be confirmed in the experience of selves. There is no unifying interpretation of the meaning of life. There is only the possibility that the conduct of the affairs of selves in relation to each other can be rendered intelligible and regular without having to answer questions about the *summum bonum* or *finis ultimus*. Men cannot raise themselves above themselves. A man can see only with his own eyes, and seize only with his own grasp.[33]

There is a theme here: the recognition of friendship and affection as always desirable even though not all of human experience can be contained in them. It is the finding of a way for different kinds of men to take delight in each other, not by eliminating differences

---

33. By training myself from my youth to see my own life mirrored in that of others, I have acquired a studious bent in that subject, and when I am thinking about it, I let few things around me which are useful for that purpose escape my notice: countenances, humors, statements. I study everything: what I must flee, what I must follow. So I reveal to my friends, by their outward manifestations, their inward inclinations. I do not attempt to arrange this infinite variety of actions, so diverse and so disconnected, into certain types and categories, and distribute my lots and divisions distinctly into recognized classes and sections. . . . I, who cannot see beyond what I have learned from experience, without any system, present my ideas in a general way, and tentatively.
—Montaigne, "Of Experience," in *The Complete Works of Montaigne*, trans. Donald M. Frame (Stanford: Stanford University Press, 1958), 824.

but by exploring them; not by calculating the advantages of alliance, but by defending each other's idiosyncrasies; not by rooting out variety in human motives for the sake of an ideal type; not by judging how well each plays his role, but by encouraging each to introduce a character to the stage. In this understanding one renounces mere traditionalism fearful that the future has no possibilities; mere individualism which finds every obligation a burden; and that moralism which seeks accommodation between rival tendencies by means of hollow exhortations to do better and be progressive. If there is a crisis it is a crisis of imagination resulting not from the suppositious shackles of inherited resources but from the attempt to abandon a ground from which to work. The remedy can only be discovered in a more profound appraisal of political life. We must cease to expect of politics what it cannot give, and we must recapture the ability to see the engagement and its frustrations for what they are. We must *attend* to political things, not obsessively dote on them. We cannot give up—but we should not overvalue—the terms of political discourse: social justice, freedom, rights, progress, liberation, exploitation, civilized, barbaric, liberal, conservative, radical, reactionary, imperialist, and the like. These terms have currency; they are both intelligible and yet without specific meaning. Their uncertainty is the hallmark of the political life. To pretend the irrelevancy of these peculiar terms would be foolish. How shall we make our way without ever employing or inventing the very sorts of terms on which the conduct of the political life depends? But, equally, it is foolishness to be seduced by the spurious solidity such words lend to the tales we tell ourselves about our most secret hopes and fears.

It seems obvious that this describes a world made by and for adults. Admission to this world implies graduation from the status of a student. It implies self-enactment tempered by patience, the conviction that every great activity is unavoidably conservative, and that utterances in the indicative mood are corrective to what we intend and claim to have accomplished. In everyday life "language is like a coinage, the more fixed and invariable the value of its components, the more useful it is as a medium of exchange. . . . If I say, 'I am sad,' I am not seeking to add a fresh *nuance* to the word 'sad';

I expect the word to be understood without quibble or difficulty, and I expect as a reply not, 'What do you mean?' but 'What's happened?' or, 'Cheer up.'"[34] To put it this way is, however, to run the risk of contentiousness in conversation. Whatever one may think of this disposition Oakeshott is in no doubt that it has ceased to be predominant in the practical world: "We are acquisitive to the point of greed; ready to drop the bone we have for its reflection magnified in the mirror of the future. Nothing is made to outlast probable improvement in a world where everything is undergoing incessant improvement: the expectation of life of everything except human beings themselves continuously declines. Pieties are fleeting, loyalties evanescent, and the pace of change warns us against too deep attachments. We are willing to try anything once, regardless of the consequences. One activity vies with another in being 'up-to-date': discarded motor-cars and television sets have their counterparts in discarded moral and religious beliefs: the eye is ever on the new model."[35]

The man of conservative disposition, on the other hand, according to many, was "last seen swimming against the tide, disregarded not because what he has to say is necessarily false but because it has become irrelevant; outmanoeuvred, not on account of any intrinsic demerit but merely by the flow of circumstance; a faded, timid, nostalgic character, provoking pity as an outcast and contempt as a reactionary."[36] But the man prepared to die will not be beaten cheaply. There is a clear note of cheerfulness in Oakeshott misunderstood entirely if one cannot entertain the idea that refusing the current preoccupations of our world is something more and other than nihilism. From Oakeshott's point of view such a conclusion would be nonsense. There are some activities "which can be engaged in only in virtue of a disposition to be conservative."[37] Wherever "present enjoyment" takes precedence over extrinsic profit, and there are still many such occasions, the conservative disposition is

34. Oakeshott, *R*, 212.
35. Oakeshott, *R*, 174.
36. Oakeshott, *R*, 175.
37. Oakeshott, *R*, 175.

"exclusively appropriate."[38] The conservative disposition, therefore, does not need to predominate in every human activity. Undoubtedly it should not seek to do so: to seek "to enjoy what is present and available regardless of its failure to satisfy any want and merely because it has struck our fancy and become familiar, is . . . an irrational inclination."[39] Wherever the transactions of life are utilitarian in nature an implied willingness to change is unavoidable. The world of practice in its characteristic modifications of experience demands this. We can resist this tendency of the affairs of life, but the logic of the world of practical affairs is not to be dispensed with: In the world of practical affairs, "every image is the reflection of a desiring self engaged in constructing its world and in continuing to reconstruct it in such a manner as to afford its pleasure. The world here consists of what is good to eat and what is poisonous, what is friendly and what is hostile, what is amenable to control and what resists it."[40]

In short, it is not a matter of rejecting private dreams, which would amount to rejecting human beings, but of learning to handle them appropriately. For Oakeshott, it was Hobbes more than anyone who sought to map the contours of the world understood as a composition of private dreams. The first thought might be to fill one's world with images of pleasure.[41] But we must think further because we are selves in the midst of other selves, and we must suppose that our first thought is not beyond their imagination. Moreover, we are never content to have an image of pleasure if we think it a mere image and not a reality, if it is not confirmed, for example, by the unavoidable others. The image of a world without interfering others is a case in point. This image seeks fulfillment only to discover the unavoidability of what it seeks to ignore or eliminate. Consequently, whatever images of pleasure we conjure up it is not enough that they appear—we must assess and approve them. This implies something of a moral skill which, says Hobbes, a man has if "when weighing the

38. Oakeshott, *R*, 176.
39. Oakeshott, *R*, 176.
40. Oakeshott, *R*, 207.
41. Oakeshott, *R*, 206.

actions of other men with his own, they seem too heavy, to put them in the other part of the balance, and his own in their place, that his own passions and self-love may add nothing to the weight."[42]

It would be a mistake to suppose that this view of things, because it requires a balancing of the self against the other selves, excludes pride, passion, or delight. On the contrary, neither Hobbes nor Oakeshott have much to say on behalf of the purposeless, the dull, or the cringing. Oakeshott's point is that engagements of delight, pride, and unfettered connoisseurship are predominant mainly outside the realm of practicality and are able to be what they are because the logic of their engagements is different. What is needed, therefore, is not a universal conservative disposition, or, indeed, a universal disposition of any kind, but an agreement not to turn private dreams into public policies nor to apply utilitarian standards, generated from practical life, to all human engagement. Required also is a rule of law and a willingness to be law-abiding. Associating ourselves requires specificity, so that we may attend to our political arrangements instead of living for them. And we need a government of a certain style: "Into the heat of our engagements, into the passionate clash of beliefs, into our enthusiasm for saving the souls of our neighbors or of all mankind, a government of this sort injects an ingredient, not of reason (how should we expect that?) but of the irony that is prepared to counteract one vice by another, of the raillery that deflates extravagance without itself pretending to wisdom, of the mockery that disperses tension, of inertia and scepticism: indeed, it might be said that we keep a government of this sort to do for us the scepticism we have neither the time nor the inclination to do for ourselves."[43]

Here Oakeshott has tried to visualize a political order which is precisely not the prize in a contest among men of differing dispositions. What is indispensable is that those who are recruited into it understand what they are there for, and this, in turn, presumably depends on the rest of us, in the midst of our "too much appearing passion," never entirely forgetting why we put them there. The governors are not to be despised nor overrated. We must all agree to

42. Thomas Hobbes, *Leviathan*, chap. 15.
43. Oakeshott, *R*, 193.

protect them from themselves and us. We abide by rules in order safely to allow free rein to the imagination in everything else.[44]

Under these circumstances a pursuit can be preserved where there are those who will undertake its preservation. Oakeshott thinks of the family, the school, the university, scholarship, arts, and all activities involving connoisseurship such as fishing, cooking, carpentry, horse-breeding, poetry, dance, music, baseball (cricket), and the like.

This view of political activity supposes the possibility of distinguishing the engagements of youth from those of maturity:

> Everybody's young days are a dream, a delightful insanity, a sweet solipsism. Nothing in them has a fixed shape, nothing a fixed price; everything is a possibility, and we live happily on credit. There are no obligations to be observed; there are no accounts to be kept. Nothing is specified in advance; everything is what can be made of it. The world is a mirror in which we seek the reflection of our own desires. The allure of violent emotions is irresistible. When we are young we are not disposed to make concessions to the world; we never feel the balance of a thing in our hands—unless it be a cricket bat. We are not apt to distinguish between our liking and our esteem; urgency is our criterion of importance; and we do not easily understand that what is humdrum need not be despicable. We are impatient of restraint; and we readily believe, like Shelley, that to have contracted a habit is to have failed. These, in my opinion, are among our virtues when we are young; but how remote they are from the disposition appropriate for participating in the style of government I have been describing. Since life is a dream, we argue (with plausible but erroneous logic) that politics must be an encounter of dreams, in which we hope to impose our own. Some unfortunate people, like Pitt (laughably called "the Younger"), are born old, and are eligible to engage in politics almost in their cradles; others, perhaps more fortunate, belie the saying that

44. Oakeshott, *R*, 195.

one is young only once, they never grow up. But these are exceptions. For most there is what Conrad called the "shadow line" which, when we pass it, discloses a solid world of things, each with its fixed shape, each with its own point of balance, each with its price; a world of act, not poetic image, in which what we have spent on one thing we cannot spend on another; a world inhabited by others besides ourselves who cannot be reduced to mere reflections of our own emotions. And coming to be at home in this commonplace world qualifies us (as no knowledge of "political science" can ever qualify us), if we are so inclined and have nothing better to think about, to engage in what the man of conservative disposition understands to be political activity.[45]

One cannot fail to notice in considering such passages as these that Oakeshott is engaged in the attempt to elicit the poetic intimations from the everyday. That the style is indicative of the thought is revealed by recalling that in current parlance this image of age and youth would be reduced to talk of generation gaps and subcultures. The difference is not just in the words but in the intimate connections established between the words to evoke the shape of a comprehensive and embracing world. A world not incidentally to be appreciated not as raw material for scientific reinterpretation, but as an arrangement of images whose composition is arresting. His writing increasingly is to be examined in light of what he has to say about poetry: "Poetry appears when imagining is contemplative imagining; that is, when images are not recognized either as 'fact' or as 'not-fact,' when they do not provoke either moral approval or disapproval, when they are not read as symbols, or as causes, effects, or means to ulterior ends, but are made, remade, observed, turned about, played with, meditated upon, and delighted in, and when they are composed into larger patterns which are themselves only more complex images and not conclusions. A poet arranges his images like a girl bunching flowers, considering only how they will appear together."[46]

45. Oakeshott, *R*, 195–96.
46. Oakeshott, *R*, 224.

On one hand, Oakeshott insists that the practical world is always a world governed by the distinguishing of "fact" and "not-fact." Hence, for him, the world of practice and the world of poetry are fundamentally different, if not estranged. Yet, on the other hand, their respective attributes are brought out by noticing how they differ. Thus, they cannot be merely different, or merely estranged. On the contrary, they know each other and themselves by the differences: what makes sense in the one is precisely nonsense in the other. To see things in this way is to see the irrelevancy of hostilities and refutations. The world can neither be reduced to practice nor to poetry. Perhaps, nonetheless, the poet might illuminate the practical without violating its premises.

The reverse is impossible—the practical world can never illuminate the poetic world—although the practical world can be the occasion for the poetic. However, this is not a cause for concern inasmuch as the practical world is secure in its prominence in our experience. This might seem implicitly to establish the superiority of the poetic over the practical, appearances to the contrary notwithstanding. Yet, in the conversation of mankind there is no hierarchy. Perhaps the superiority intimated here is the consequence of seeing the human situation as presented by a poetic voice instead of a practical voice: that voice to be true to itself necessarily preserves its integrity even while reaching out to its counterparts in the quest for self-understanding. One might say that the poetic voice attempts to transform the curse of the Tower of Babel into a blessing, making the confusion of tongues a momentary, but beautiful, harmony. It is hard, then, to avoid the conclusion that poetry, so to speak, adds something—but not something necessary since the practical world is complete in its abstraction as a world. Images that purport to perfect the practical world are mere ideologies, having only symbolic meaning, that is, propagandizing as particularly relevant some part of what we already know how to do. At most an ideology's "distorting mirror . . . will reveal important hidden passages in the tradition, as a caricature reveals the potentialities of a face."[47] And poetry certainly cannot lead us anywhere because in

47. Oakeshott, *R*, 125.

political activity (and indeed in every activity) "men sail a bound-less and bottomless sea; there is neither harbour for shelter nor floor for anchorage, neither starting-place nor appointed destina-tion. The enterprise is to keep afloat on an even keel; the sea is both friend and enemy; and the seamanship consists in using the re-sources of a traditional manner of behaviour in order to make a friend of every hostile occasion."[48]

Perhaps what poetry adds is the conversational possibility at its purest. The practical voice is a raucous, often stentorian, voice, and is, whatever else it may be, a tireless, intrusive voice which is never open to the argument that it has exhausted its stock of interesting and vital conversational gambits. The multiplicity of its expressions easily leads it to believe that it *is* the conversation of mankind, and that po-etry is merely an eccentric device for getting on. Practical activity tries to turn the historian's research into retrospective politics, the scientist's to technical applications, and the poet's image-making to a conveyance of familiar thoughts and emotions.[49] In short, it is hard to avoid the conclusion that the practical world is not only abstract but aggressively so.[50] According to Oakeshott, "A work of art is merely an image which is protected in an unusual degree from being read (that is, imagined) in an unpoetic manner."[51] Perhaps poetic images are more protected from practicality's aggression than historical or scientific images. If so, they are valuable guides to understanding the conversation of mankind. It is not that the conversation of mankind could never be discerned from the point of view of the other modes of imagining but that they are less secure from the misunderstand-ings to which all the modes alike are subject in some measure. One is thus drawn to the thought that what has replaced the philosopher seeking the whole unmodified, for Oakeshott, is the poet reflecting on his engagement and thereby preserving the spark by means of

---

48. Oakeshott, *R*, 127.
49. Oakeshott, *R*, 234–45.
50. "It is a very powerful world; it is wealthy, interfering and well-meaning. But it is not remarkably self-critical. . . . With amiable carelessness it assumes that whatever does not contribute to its own purposes is somehow errant." Michael Oakeshott, "The Idea of a University," *The Listener*, 43 (1950), 426.
51. Oakeshott, *R*, 225.

which to rekindle the conversation of mankind. The poet is the traveller who returns to his city in modesty. Refusing to seek the subduction of practicality, he hopes to avoid the corruption of the pretentious philosopher. Remaining true to his artistry he might inadvertently produce a composition that will enchant the practical world for a moment endearing it to a brief pause before it plunges ahead in the ceaseless quest to be undistracted by illusion.

IV

On Human Conduct attempts to clarify and summarize the major themes of a lifetime of reflection. It is divided into three lengthy essays each of which has some claim to stand alone, but, when taken together, compose a sustained reflection of astonishing quality. Some have described it as containing no argument whatsoever and have found it impossible to respond to it. Perhaps there is a question about how to read the book. For Oakeshott, "Philosophical reflection is . . . the adventure of one who seeks to understand in other terms what he already understands and in which the understanding sought (itself unavoidably conditional) is a disclosure of the conditions of the understanding enjoyed and not a substitute for it."[52] In other words, this is to be the exemplification of the thinker disclosing himself. It is an interior argument, the exploration of a character, a coming to know oneself, and, by that means, providing an occasion for a conversation. It is a self-exploration and it is argumentative only in the fact of its disclosure. Hence it is absurd to expect a refutation of alternative doctrines. This is not the defense of a doctrine. We might look at this self-refutation as a hermetically sealed argument in which everything is stipulated by definition. That, however, would be to notice it without penetrating it. To look at it the other way, as a self in argument with itself, reveals its consistency with all that Oakeshott has previously written, and illustrates how what he thinks actualizes itself toward a world of others. I think it not unreasonable to say that it is a work of art because protected, to an unusual degree, from being read in an unpoetic manner. It is the rendering of a fully explored

52. Oakeshott, *HC*, vii.

individuality within the "circumstantial frame of the covers of a book."[53]

Whereas Oakeshott summarized his thought in terms of "poetry" and "conversation" with the publication of the collection in *Rationalism in Politics*, he has subsequently transposed the same way of thinking into other images, namely, "conduct" as opposed to "behavior," "association" as opposed to "society," "law," and "authority." The first part of *On Human Conduct* sets forth Oakeshott's understanding of human affairs in terms of the postulate of individuality as self-disclosure and self-enactment. The phrase "human conduct" deliberately opposes the phrase "human behavior," pointing to the fundamental distinction between "nature" and "spirit" or "non-nature." To study the behavior of men is to study them as if they were the outcomes of processes involving no agency. When human beings are studied in this way they are seen as emanations of the physical-biological world or as the exhibitions of a "psychology." "A psychological process (or, indeed, a physiological, a chemical, or a mechanical process) may, of course be abstracted from every 'going-on' identified as human conduct, but wherever there is action or utterance there is an intelligent agent responding to an understood (or misunderstood) situation meaning to achieve an imagined and wished-for outcome, and this cannot be 'reduced' to a psychological process or a 'structure,' however gross the misunderstanding, however lunatic the imagination, however fanciful the wish, and whatever its similarity to the actions and utterances of others."[54]

To consider human beings in terms of their conduct is to see them as "reflective intelligences whose actions and utterances are choices to do or to say *this* rather than *that* in relation to imagined and wished-for outcomes. And the relationships between them to be investigated are recognized to be themselves expressions of intelligence which may be enjoyed only by their having been learned and understood and in virtue of an acknowledgment of the authority of

53. Oakeshott, *R*, 225. One might profitably consider here Matthew Arnold's reflections on Edmund Burke in "The Function of Criticism at the Present Time."
54. Oakeshott, *HC*, 23.

their conditions or of a recognition of their utility. The subject of enquiry in this enterprise of theoretical understanding is actions and utterances in respect of being subscriptions to procedures or 'practices' comprised of rules and rule-like considerations whose postulates are beliefs. It is a science of intelligent procedures, not processes."[55]

The second part presents what Oakeshott takes to be an "ideal" order for human beings who understand their engagements with each other in terms of "conduct" rather than "behavior." This order is called the "civitas" or "civil association" comprising individuals who think of themselves as "cives" or "citizens." They are associated in the recognition of a rule of law, but they are not bound by necessary interests, needs, wants, or dispositions in common. These individuals do not compose a "society" and they are not compelled by "social forces" which have the significance of independent variables. They are not obsessed with what their fellows are doing, they are not constantly frustrated by "relative deprivation," nor are they engaged ineluctably in a perpetual siege of their resources in order to indulge in an endless transformation of "wants" into "needs," or a ceaseless redistribution of their possessions according to some principle of comparability which the terms of their association will not ground. Such people understand that they are subscribing to, not obeying, a body of laws, which laws are the result of the deliberations of rulers or office-holders in authority. They cannot *obey* laws because laws do not exactly tell us what to do. Laws provide us with guides to conduct which must be constantly interpreted according to the contingent circumstances of selves among other selves. I cannot "obey" a red traffic light, but I can choose to observe the implication for conduct of its presence provided the contingent circumstances do not seem to me to require disregarding it (if I am driving an accident victim to a hospital for example). And "authority" here is not understood as some sort of "informal" or "tacit" power or influence but as the specific engagements to rule associated with an office of rule, exercised under agreed-upon terms, to produce rules to which citizens may subscribe.

55. Oakeshott, *HC*, 23–24.

As Oakeshott sees it, "power is not identifiable with authority and it is not even among the considerations in terms of which an office of government is recognized to have authority. The difference is categorial. The contingent features of its apparatus of power are neither formally nor substantively related to the constitutional shape of the office of rule."[56] Nor is authority to be designated in terms of building consensus. On the contrary, as Oakeshott understands the problem, authority is misunderstood and undermined when it is defined as the building of consensus, the proclamation of unifying goals, or gaining influence by advancing interests, because authority is appropriate precisely to an association of human beings whose terms of association have already ruled out consensus and common goals, and who have no fixed criteria of social importance. The muddled nature of our current understanding of authority, to give one example, insures the chronic nature of the "credibility gap": To understand the building of consensus to be a prerequisite to claiming authority insures that no claim to authority will ever satisfy its prerequisites. The reason we subscribe to a rule, according to this view of things, is not because we have been cajoled or paid off, not because it is in our interest, and not because we have been blackmailed with threats of all sorts, but because the rule proceeds from those who have been constituted to make rules, and who have been able to conclude that the crystallization of an important argument among citizens is sufficient to make an intelligent and workable rule possible.

Oakeshott believes that this "ideal" of "civil association" is not merely an ideal. It is an ideal deeply rooted in European historical experience of the past five hundred years, and the theorization of it in clear terms constitutes one of the great intellectual achievements of the modern European consciousness in its attempt to understand itself. However, this ideal has not held the field unchallenged because the historical experience of the modern world has generated an alternative ideal which is also very powerful.

---

56. Michael Oakeshott, "The Vocabulary of a Modern European State," *Politics Studies*, vol. 23 (June–Sept. 1975), 212–13.

Thus, Oakeshott turns, in the third part of *On Human Conduct*, to an interpretation of European experience in its slow and confused emergence from medieval to modern self-understanding. The struggle in modern times to find an adequate theorization of order has developed two fundamental ideal types. One he designates by the term "societas" and the other by the term "universitas." These terms refer to the question of the purpose or reason for the order in which an aggregation of human beings lives, that is, it refers to the terms of association themselves. Now, the terms by which an association of human beings understands itself will have great effect with respect to what it is thought that the government should do or not do. In a "societas" which is like what Oakeshott describes elsewhere as "civil association" there can be no charge to the government to pursue some corporate purpose because it is part of the terms of association that there is no such corporate purpose in the first place. Hence governors cannot be managers of an enterprise in which citizens are thought of as corporate workers or role-players. In a "universitas" the terms of association include corporate purpose and, correspondingly, governors can be entrusted with tasks that would be ruled out in the other case. However, none of this has anything to do with the shape of the government itself. There is no requirement that government be specifically "democratic" or "oligarchic," or whatever, in either "societas" or "universitas." That this vocabulary has remained vastly confused in modern European history is obvious. This careful attempt to sort out and systematically recategorize the terms of political discourse, which I have only hinted at, is the culminating project in Oakeshott's work. It is a task that is consistent with his own reflection that the object of study is "a science of intelligent procedures, not processes," and it presents yet another transposition in his conversation.

Oakeshott responds to the modern world as one who has paid careful attention to the flood of images to be found in it, and he has provided a partial key to the images, something of a manual of style. But with Oakeshott manuals are always suspect because they are abridgements of experience and no substitute for experience. This manual does not tell us how to write, or act, for profit. The world of practice remains a world of ideas of its own free to choose in its own terms how to live.

Moreover Oakeshott has not, to date, found any articulable resolution for the polarities of modern consciousness. The two ideals of order have never found a resolution in their historical evolution, and, consequently, there can be no philosophic articulation that resolves them into one. The purpose of philosophy is not to change the world but to explain it. What must be said is that the modern consciousness is a divided consciousness. Oakeshott calls its polarities "sweet enemies," and while he leaves no doubt as to his own inclination to the image of civil association, he pays respectful attention to the ambiguities of his civilization and its heritage. To articulate the alternatives is to render them, in terms of their postulates, mutually exclusive. Thus the philosopher in seeking to explain the world reproduces, at the level of thought, its exclusivities. Wherever efforts have been made to suppress one of these alternative ideals of order in favor of the other the effort has always, so far, failed to reach completion, resuscitating instead the flagging spirit of its antagonist. The unity of modern states is, in great measure, illusory. This condition is partly obscured by the immense growth of the techniques of control available to modern military and bureaucratic powers, indifferently available to regimes regardless of their ideological proclivities. The yearning for unity is, so far, beyond fulfillment. Reliance on the apparatus of control has served as much to remind us of that as anything else.

Over half a century Oakeshott has consistently sought to understand himself. There are many responses that might be made to being dragged out of the cave by the scruff of the neck. One is to transform this disruption into a beautiful composition that adds to the conversational resources of the world we all share. This I take to be the achievement of Michael Oakeshott.

The Sceptical Disposition
Montaigne, Hume, Oakeshott

I

MONTAIGNE HAS TOLD ME that reason is either mockery or a source of contentment. Reason to be good has to be an instrument for us to live well and at our ease. Pain and discomfort cannot be our goals. Even in pursuing virtue we are pursuing what we happen to find desirable; virtue is a kind of pleasure.

Those who try to characterize the pursuit of virtue as a painful struggle, redeemed only by actually attaining virtue, are hard to take. After all, no one ever perfectly attains virtue and thus the pursuit of it must, by itself, yield pleasure, or else no one would undertake the venture.

The principal benefit of virtue is disdain for death. "Death mingles and fuses with our life throughout." Such disdain yields "soft tranquility" without which all other pleasures are extinguished. Disdain of death is the key because no other difficulty is so inevitable. "Your death is a part of the order of the universe; it is a part of the life of the world." Indeed, the goal of our career is death; we move forward through time by necessity and design, going on to

Previously unpublished lecture prepared for delivery at the 1986 annual meeting of the American Political Science Association at the Washington Hilton in Washington, DC, August 28–31, 1986. Printed here by permission from Timothy Fuller.

new things as if we want to go toward death while really trying to go away from it. The paradox is clear. To overcome it we need virtue.

We are temporal beings with minds capable of imagining that we could leave the path of time. The remedy is the collection of the mind to recognize the path that cannot be escaped. We must seek to die as we were born, making a pilgrimage without fear, because it is the order of things.

The child comes naturally into the world. The adult through the activity of reason falls into disharmony with nature. The remedy is to acquire "virtue," which returns the adult to the natural where he is at home. Reason must reason to overcome itself in order to acquire virtue. Virtue makes compatible nature and thought. The mature human being combines nature, reason, and virtue in a disposition for which every day becomes equal—equally on the path of time, equally natural. "Why do you fear your last day? It contributes no more to your death than each of the others. The last step does not cause the fatigue, but reveals it. All days travel toward death, the last one reaches it." "Premeditation of death is premeditation of freedom. He who has learned how to die has unlearned how to be a slave. Knowing how to die frees us from all subjection and constraint."

Education in right habits thus is essential. Vice begins early. Proper habits acquired early will produce "a natural and unstudied propensity." Under their sway, we may find satisfaction. Habits insulate us from superstition about nature (miracles). Habit softens judgment once we recognize that reason is at work in all habits and all ways; custom is the mediation between reason and nature. There is nothing custom cannot do. Custom is the queen of the world.

On the one hand, then, we can, through our own habits, develop standards of taste and judgment by which we rank the world, often being horrified by those who do not do as we do. On the other hand, reflecting on the universality of this condition, we can learn to judge and reason freely in private and to conform to orthodox opinion in public. Innovation is always dangerous; the Reformation is a classic case.

Here we see the peril of preferring to be learned rather than able. Character is far more important than learning. We need to learn ways of thinking rather than precepts. We need to learn how to transform learning into our own distinctive idiom, to appropriate it to the formation of our individuality. "I study myself more than any other subject. That is my metaphysics, that is my physics." We should study character, not dates. We should aim at balance of judgment, tolerance, realism about what can be done.

Virtue is in moderation. Remember that "barbarism" is whatever *we* do not approve of or have the habit of doing. What is "wild" is not what Nature produces but the altered state of natural things produced in our various cultures. The less cultivated, the more natural; the more refined, the more unnatural. Art smothers Nature.

Consider the cannibals of the New World: they enjoy good health and abundant food; the day is spent in dancing. They hold two ethical precepts: Resoluteness in war and affection for wives. Their warfare is limited and noble; our European by contrast is barbaric in its imperialism. Who then is the actual "savage"? Abstract yourself from the perspective of your own customs and ask yourself, Who is noble and who is not?

Upon reflection, then, what should we expect in the world? First, discussion, not unison. Why should any proposition astonish me? Any belief offend me? "Our life is composed like the harmony of the world, of contrary things, also of different tones, sweet and harsh, sharp and flat, soft and loud. If a musician liked only one kind, what would he have to say? He must know how to use them together and blend them. And so we must do with good and evil, which are consubstantial with our life. Our existence is impossible without this mixture, and one element is no less necessary for it than the other. To try to kick against natural necessity is to imitate the folly of Ctesiphon, who undertook a kicking match with his mule."

Every opinion or fancy, no matter how lunatic, is a production of the human mind. Discussion should, therefore, be vigorous, even quarrelsome and contradictory. Opposition should make me attentive rather than angry, and I should have the courage to be corrected. I should make myself bow to the force of my adversary's reason. "We need strong ears to hear ourselves judged frankly; and because there are few who can endure frank criticism without being stung by it, those who venture to criticize us perform a remarkable act of friendship."

"By training myself from my youth to see my own life mirrored in that of others, I have acquired a studious bent in that subject. . . . I study everything: what I must flee, what I must follow. So I reveal to my friends, by their outward manifestations, their inward inclinations."

All I should require is order in argument. Let us avoid confusion and disorderliness, but let us admit any argument to the point as good. Let us remember also that sound argument is not sophisticated. Do not, therefore, hide behind footnotes. Learning suffocates dull minds and trains sharp ones to reason everything away into meaninglessness. If we condemn custom in others because it is custom, let us recall that we are condemning what is inevitably in us as well. It is in the discussing, not the winning or losing, that we find what we are looking for, what is most human.

"Scribbling seems to be a sort of symptom of an unruly age." "We dignify our stupidities when we put them in print." Writing increased in the Reformation and in the time of Rome's decline. Let us remember that vanity consists in increased shouting about the petty. How much better the essay than the monograph. How much better the "excusable" life that is neither a burden to oneself nor to others. Need one seek to manage things or to expound them? Is it not better perhaps to preserve the existing reign of habit? The blessed liberty is in overcoming vanity, diminishing entanglements, becoming our own resource, borrowing nothing and remembering that giving is also dangerous. Fortune is gentle to those who do not demand much.

All of these tentative conclusions are the product of the mind which has not reached a firm footing although it has reasoned its way out of the missteps of reason. "If my mind could gain a firm footing, I would not make essays, I would make decisions; but it is always in apprenticeship and on trial."

If I then had to deal with rulers, I would know what would constitute my greatest act of friendship. After all, "there is no class of men that has as great need as they of true and frank admonitions . . . since people have formed the habit of concealing from them anything that disturbs their plans; . . . Most of the duties of true friendship are hard and dangerous to attempt toward a sovereign; so that there is need, not only of much affection and frankness, but of much courage as well."

Nevertheless, though all this may be stated clearly, it does not stop the world from trying to decide everything. "I do not much like the opinion of the man who thought by a multiplicity of laws to bridle the authority of judges, cutting up their meat for them. He did not realize that there is as much freedom and latitude in the interpretation of laws as in their creation. And those people must be jesting who think they can diminish and stop our disputes by recalling us to the express words of the Bible. For our mind finds the field no less spacious in registering the meaning of others than in presenting its own. . . . [The number of laws] bears no proportion to the infinite diversity of human actions. . . . There is little relation between our actions, which are in perpetual mutation, and fixed and immutable laws. The most desirable laws are those that are rarest, simplest, and most general. . . . Men do not know the natural infirmity of their mind: it does nothing but ferret and quest, and keeps incessantly whirling around, building up and becoming entangled in its own work, like our silkworms, and is suffocated in it." But is it not clear that this multiplication of restraints is imprudent? Does prudence not lie in cultivating one's personal freedom? Does this not require letting others be? Invention outruns wisdom. It is better to be ignorant than to be excessively self-conscious. At times, it is necessary not to know.

II

In a series of remarkable portraits, David Hume sets out the dispositions of the "Epicurean," the "Stoic," the "Platonist," and the "Sceptic."[1] He makes clear that he does not intend to provide a precise historical account of the ancient sects. Rather, his aim is to show dispositions that "naturally form themselves in the world, and entertain different ideas of human life and of happiness."[2] Each disposition is presented in turn as if speaking for itself. The result is a

1. All references to Hume will be taken from David Hume, *Essays Moral, Political, and Literary*, ed. by Eugene F. Miller. (Indianapolis: Liberty Fund, Inc., 1985).
2. Hume, *Essays*, 138, n. 1.

conversation or symposium, reconstructed from life in a philosophically detached account.

The Epicurean sees the puniness of human reason and artifice when measured over against the artistry of Nature herself. He rejects the speculative pretensions of the schools of Greece. What nature has implanted within us is far greater than anything human reason can devise to impose upon us. The voice of Pride is subdued by the voice of Nature. At best Pride creates an exterior appearance of dignity which deceives the "ignorant vulgar."[3]

The effort to maintain philosophical appearances risks melancholic dejection. One must throw off this "violent constraint" and consult one's "own passions and inclinations." The "dictates of nature" must replace the "frivolous discourses" of the philosophers.[4] "Chearful [sic] discourses" outstrip "formal reasonings," and "the hollow debates of statesmen and pretended patriots." We shall enjoy the present, bewitched neither by vain reasoning nor by uncontrolled emotion, nor by the pursuit of glory which is but "the shadow of a dream." And if we are troubled by the shadow of mortality, let us remember "that if life be frail, if youth be transitory, we should well employ the present moment, and lose no part of so perishable an existence. Yet a little moment and *these* shall be no more. We shall be, as if we had never been. Not a memory of us be left upon earth; and even the fabulous shades below will not afford us a habitation. Our fruitless anxieties, our vain projects, our uncertain speculations shall all be swallowed up and lost. Our present doubts, concerning the original cause of all things, must never, alas! be resolved. . . . Be acquainted with this philosophy, in order to give an unbounded loose to love and jollity, and remove all the scruples of a vain superstition."[5]

The Stoic insists that nature has endowed man with "a sublime celestial spirit" urging art and industry to the utmost. The exemplary man is one of action and virtue. Nature decrees that man, unlike the other creatures, must exert himself. Beneficent nature "having given thee art and intelligence, has filled the whole globe

3. Hume, *Essays*, 140.
4. Hume, *Essays*, 141.
5. Hume, *Essays*, 142–45.

with materials to employ these talents: Hearken to her voice, which so plainly tells thee, that thou thyself shouldest also be the object of thy industry, and that by art and attention alone thou canst acquire that ability, which will raise thee to thy proper station in the universe."[6]

All human striving is to attain happiness. "For this were the arts invented, sciences cultivated, laws ordained, and societies modelled, by the most profound wisdom of patriots and legislators."[7]

History is the record of trial and error. In attending to this record and seeking remedies for our mistakes we may eventually arrive at rules of conduct. In fixing them we become philosophers, and in putting them into practice we are "sages." "This labour itself is the chief ingredient of the felicity to which thou aspirest. . . . Every enjoyment soon becomes insipid and distasteful, when not acquired by fatigue and industry." We are like the hunter seeking prey: "Having exerted in the chace [*sic*] every passion of the mind, and every member of the body, he then finds the charms of repose, and with joy compares its pleasures to those of his engaging labours."[8]

The pursuit of pleasure will pall and disgust. The result can only be increasing exposure to inconstant fortune and accident. "Happiness cannot possibly exist, where there is no stability; and security can have no place, where fortune has any dominion: . . . The temple of wisdom is seated on a rock, above the rage of the fighting elements, and inaccessible to all the malice of man."[9]

To achieve this detached height is to become a sage. But detachment must not become indifference and is prevented from doing so by the sentiments of sympathy and affection which cannot be obscured by sorrow at human misery or sensual pleasure. Beyond this, the social passions, when wedded to the quest for virtue, provide "transporting pleasures" in "laudable and worthy actions," extended to the "most distant posterity." "In the true sage and patriot are

6. Hume, *Essays*, 147.
7. Hume, *Essays*, 148.
8. Hume, *Essays*, 149.
9. Hume, *Essays*, 150.

united whatever can distinguish human nature, or elevate mortal man to a resemblance with divinity."[10]

"GLORY is the portion of virtue, the sweet reward of honourable toils, the triumphant crown, which covers the thoughtful head of the disinterested patriot, or the dusty brow of the victorious warrior. Elevated by so sublime a prize, the man of virtue looks down with contempt on all the allurements of pleasure, and all the menaces of danger. Death itself loses its terrors, when he considers, that its dominion extends only over a part of him, and that, in spite of death and time, the rage of the elements, and the endless vicissitude of human affairs, he is assured of an immortal fame among all the sons of men."[11]

The Platonist, contemplative, devoted to philosophy, seeks resolution in an irresolute world. The rational soul in mankind seeks the Supreme Being. The human heart is restless with every apparent pleasure that it encounters, not the least example of which is the false philosopher who seeks the "ignorant applauses of men, not the solid reflections of thy own conscience, or the more solid approbation of that being, who, with one regard of his all-seeing eye, penetrates the universe."[12]

All the works of man are the products of mind at work and only mind. Ultimately, we are led to the thought that the mind at work in us is the mind that structures and orders the universe itself, that "exquisite and most stupendous contrivance." "But it is our comfort, that, if we employ worthily the faculties here assigned us, they will be enlarged in another state of existence, so as to render us more suitable worshippers of our maker: And that the task, which can never be finished in time, will be the business of an eternity."[13]

The Sceptic begins his thinking upon the vast variety of the world. Philosophers notoriously attempt to reduce the variety to one or a few principles, thinking that the small portion of the vast variety they can see stands in for all the rest. The mistake is to assume that nature "is as much bounded in her operations, as we are in our

10. Hume, *Essays*, 152–53.
11. Hume, *Essays*, 153–54.
12. Hume, *Essays*, 157.
13. Hume, *Essays*, 158.

speculation."[14] It should be noticed that "The Sceptic" is longer than the preceding three essays put together. It comes last and begins as a critique of the claims of the various philosophical schools. In the order in which the essays appear, there is a movement from the pursuit of pleasurable repose in the present, to the pursuit of patriotic duty for the sake of posterity in the future, to the contemplation of the eternal which transcends the temporal dimensions, to a self-conscious reflection on the modes of philosophical thinking. If the movement is from the earthly to the heavenly, or from the bodily to the spiritual, the final movement is toward the problematic situation in which all of these ways of thinking coexist in the world. If each is a purported road to happiness capable of intelligent expression, and defended by appeal to features of our experience, one must consider the possibility that the best understanding is that of the sceptic who does not seek to refute the alternatives as irrelevant but merely juxtaposes them for all to see. Each of these alternatives is thus available to us. It is also true that we are quite likely to be inclined toward one rather than another. But the sceptic puts forward the possibility of distinguishing between our inclinations and our considered opinion. Presumably this is the purpose of a philosophical conversation: These alternatives are not matters for demonstrable proof or refutation but exemplifications of the variety that scepticism notices. Thus the sceptic begins to philosophize with a criticism of the philosophers. They are particularly prone to simplify and reduce the question of human happiness.

Nevertheless, if we follow this line of reasoning, we must consider that there may be nothing more to be said than that variety is all. Are there no preferences among courses in life? Is one man's conduct to be judged as preferable or not as another's?

First, there is a difference among men with respect to the prudence with which they pursue whatever ends they have chosen. The general maxims of prudence are found out through common sense. The philosopher has no special insight about these maxims. Do not,

14. Hume, *Essays*, 159–60.

therefore, come to the philosopher as if to a "cunning man" who has a magical device to impart.

But then what of the task of choosing the ends themselves? Here the philosopher is in danger of excessive strictness or excessive liberality. In any case what can be offered is only the philosopher's opinion. The philosopher holds it in little esteem, begging only that it be neither a source of ridicule nor of anger.[15]

The opinion is that "there is nothing, in itself, valuable or despicable, desirable or hateful, beautiful or deformed; but that these attributes arise from the particular constitution and fabric of human sentiment and affection."[16] It is true that the sentiments of the mind are more uniform than the bodily feelings. However, in actuality there are always disputes and no obvious means of reconciliation. Diversity of sentiment forces us to recognize that nature rules over us and that we cannot replace nature's diversity with our artificial uniformities. The common denominator of life is death, which treats fools and philosophers alike.[17] Thus we are either cast into the world of the diverse, or we are nowhere. We did not seek such diversity; we can barely effect any change in our own inclinations let alone those of others. "In a word, human life is more governed by fortune than by reason . . . more influenced by particular humour, than by general principles."[18]

Nonetheless, it will be argued, is there not a difference between the Ptolomaic [*sic*] and the Copernican systems? Is that difference not that the latter is a closer portrayal of the reality of the solar system than is the former? Is it not true that "though all the human race should for ever conclude, that the sun moves, and the earth remains at rest, the sun stirs not an inch from his place for all these reasonings; and such conclusions are eternally false and erroneous?"[19]

15. Hume, *Essays*, 161–62.
16. Hume, *Essays*, 162.
17. Hume, *Essays*, 180.
18. Hume, *Essays*, 180.
19. Hume, *Essays*, 164.

If we may grant this, we shall nevertheless see that in disputes over the beautiful and the ugly, or the hateful and the desirable, there is a sentiment arising from ourselves with respect to the object described as beautiful or not, desirable or not, that is not inherent in the object. This is more easily acknowledged in matters of power, glory, or vengeance. It is less easily accepted in regard to beauty (cf. *Euthyphro*, 7d).

But consider Euclid's circle: The geometric description of its properties says nothing about its beauty even if there are those who express such a sentiment about it. The properties may be comprehended as well by one who does not think of it as beautiful as by one who does. There is nothing to guarantee that someone with a perfect grasp of Euclid's geometry, or of the Copernican system, will experience enjoyment in consequence of that grasp. Enjoyment is evidenced in the passion with which one pursues an object and in the success enjoyed in the pursuit. Does this observation make a difference to the status of geometry? Is geometry undermined if we deny intrinsic beauty to it? Will people stop employing geometry if this doctrine gets about? Almost certainly not. A discovery in moral philosophy need make no alteration in the matter. Nor need the discovery of Copernicus alter action and conduct.[20]

One can suggest some maxims about enjoyment. They come down to moderation between tumult and lethargy, a preference for sociality over fierceness, cheerfulness over gloominess. Philosophy is perfectly capable of violating these generalities: "*Philosophical devotion*, for instance, like the enthusiasm of a poet, is the transitory effect of high spirits, great leisure, a fine genius, and a habit of study and contemplation."[21] Such a state cannot sustain itself. It must reattach to the actualities of common, historical existence: "business and action fill up all the great vacancies of life."[22]

What is to be recommended, then, is a virtuous temper. This can be given a general characterization whose helpfulness is open to doubt, however, since the sentiments and affections are little alter-

20. Hume, *Essays*, 166, particularly the footnote.
21. Hume, *Essays*, 167.
22. Hume, *Essays*, 167.

able. There is much opportunity for divergence between our senti- ments and affections on one hand and our circumstances on the other: "No man would ever be unhappy, could he alter his feelings. . . . But of this resource nature has, in a great measure, de- prived us. The fabric and constitution of our mind no more depends on our choice, than that of our body."[23]

This is the universal human condition. Philosophers are not ex- empt. So much the less is there any point in their counselling human beings to change themselves dramatically or at all: "The empire of philosophy extends over a few; and with regard to these too, her au- thority is very weak and limited."[24] In fact, human beings are born tending to aspire to virtue or not. Philosophers cannot elicit from others what is not there to begin with. When virtue is there, the philosophers have only a marginal role in enhancing its growth. Scep- ticism concludes that, for the ills of the human race, there is no philo- sophical cure. The study of the sciences and the liberal arts, and the acquisition of good habits will help, provided that the virtuous ten- dencies were already present: "To diminish therefore, or augment any person's value for an object, to excite or moderate his passions, there are no direct arguments or reasons, which can be employed with any force or influence."[25]

Reflection at its best "insensibly refines the temper" against the illusions of passion and tranquilizes the mind without inducing that indifference which would diminish the pleasures of the game of life. If there is no philosophical cure for the unsought human condition, there may be a philosophical cure for the philosophical ill: The philosopher has thought up the problems he cannot solve; he can think his way out of preoccupation with such problems by acknowl- edging their insolubility. In this way scepticism philosophizes about philosophizing, and the sceptic submits to the world. In so submitting, the philosopher rids himself of that greatest of all pre- tensions: that he should rule.

23. Hume, *Essays*, 168.
24. Hume, *Essays*, 169.
25. Hume, *Essays*, 171.

III

Michael Oakeshott, disciple of Montaigne and Hume, is a sceptic who would "do better if only he knew how."[26] He can offer some explanations of what political actors understand themselves to be doing. Such explanations are, however, not to be taken as warrants for the conduct explained. Politics is a self-contained manner of human activity; it does not require an additional theory to get it going, to maintain its momentum, or to carry out its self-chosen activities. A farmer does not first become an agricultural theorist in order to learn farming. If he has learned farming, he may then provide an abstract description of the activity. But does anyone think that the abstract description adds something not found in the activity of farming itself? So with politics, or any important activity. The philosopher of politics or of farming speaks indicatively. That is, he expresses in words what is already to be found in the activity; if it is an intellectual activity, he expresses in other words what has already been expressed in words. The activity's practitioner does not require this service from the philosopher; nor is it clear how much benefit may be derived from partaking of it. The practitioner is no less sensible for ignoring the philosophic expression altogether.

Speaking indicatively, we may say that politics is an "activity of attending to the general arrangements of a set of people whom chance or choice have brought together."[27] More specifically, we usually mean "the hereditary co-operative groups" called "states." Such entities have come into being long before us and are likely to persist long after us. There is never a blank slate on which we may write what we want. To think otherwise is to suffer an illusion. This illusion is nonetheless evident in the world and must be noticed as a feature of the rhetoric of politics.

In the nature of the case, however, "politics springs neither from instant desires, nor from general principles, but from the existing traditions of behaviour themselves."[28] "Arrangements," in short, are

26. Michael Oakeshott, "Political Education," in *Rationalism in Politics* (New York: Basic Books, 1962), 111. Hereafter cited as *RP*.
27. Oakeshott, *RP*, 112.
28. Oakeshott, *RP*, 123.

neither merely desires nor merely principles. They are a manner of living, a way of life, composed over time by the myriad choices of individuals in the society of each other, establishing practices through which they render their association concrete and humanly possible.

Such arrangements, of course, have consequences. They are the product of intelligence responding to its surrounding circumstances according to its understanding of those circumstances. In responding, human beings discover "intimations" or possibilities which are neither necessary nor unimportant. There are always more such intimations than can be followed up at any moment. Choices among the possible avenues of exploration must be made. Political debate makes its appearance here: "relevant political reasoning will be the convincing exposure of a sympathy, present but not yet followed up, and the convincing demonstration that now is the appropriate moment for recognizing it."[29]

There is no logically implied direction to be discovered, no right intimation among all the intimations that may come in for consideration. Human beings find their purposes in life in constructing purposes by response to their circumstances. All such responses, no matter how far removed from our own sympathies, are equally exhibitions of intelligence at work. We cannot specify our final goal or *the* final goal. We may be able to minimize the chance of disaster "if we escape the illusion that politics is ever anything more than the pursuit of intimations; a conversation, not an argument."[30]

A conversationalist is the agent of a flow of sympathy, not the purveyor of the naturally right. A philosopher may certainly be a conversationalist. One might expect that the philosopher would be a particularly good conversationalist, provided that he did not lose a healthy sense of his own unimportance. The philosopher might well be able to accept this unimportance with poise, becoming all the more engaging.

Yet for some the philosopher may have a depressing effect. In politics, the philosopher is obliged to say, "men sail a boundless and

29. Oakeshott, *RP*, 124.
30. Oakeshott, *RP*, 125.

bottomless sea; there is neither harbour for shelter nor floor for an-chorage, neither starting-place nor appointed destination. The en-terprise is to keep afloat on an even keel; the sea is both friend and enemy; and the seamanship consists in using the resources of a tra-ditional manner of behaviour in order to make a friend of every hos-tile occasion."[31]

With regret the philosopher puts aside the possibility of superhu-man wisdom, but with relief points to the traditions without which we would fall into a morass of equalized choices. The emphasis is on the capacity of human intelligence to continue to use the resources of its history. There is confidence that intelligence is not likely to be exhausted. In our moment, the responsibility is ours. It is not likely to be the final moment, and, in any case, we cannot act as if it were. We do not and cannot know that. Nor can we unmake the inheri-tance we have. History cannot be taken back. Thus we must go on.

Tradition "is not susceptible of the distinction between essence and accident, knowledge of it is unavoidably knowledge of its detail: to know only the gist is to know nothing."[32] Intimacy with tradition may yield tranquility without rest. Politics is best conducted in the attitude of energetic sobriety. Who is better suited to this than the accomplished conversationalist? Such a one is eager for the dialogue but not impatient of its endlessness. This attitude results from having grown up hearing the already ongoing voices of one's world, and hav-ing learned to speak with them. The study of history, properly con-ducted, will introduce us to the detailed, concrete nature of our way of life, and will illustrate on a broader scale what is true of our own experience. The lesson will be that a manner of living indicates how we may conduct ourselves but not what we are required to do, nor where we are required to go. We may gain inspiration from "thinkers and statesmen who knew which way to turn their feet without knowing anything about a final destination."[33]

---

31. Oakeshott, *RP*, 127. One will note that the postulate of this view is ex-pressed in Montaigne's advice about making a friend of death.
32. Oakeshott, *RP*, 128–29.
33. Oakeshott, *RP*, 131.

Political philosophy may help us to think straighter about the concepts we employ. Here and there it may reduce the incoherency of our thinking.

It has no capacity to increase our success in political activity. All of the foregoing reflections may be seen as the effort of a political philosopher to escape from his own occupational illusions by looking directly at the object of his investigation, namely, politics itself.

There we see what political actors actually succeed in doing: they pursue the intimations of the traditions of which they are a part. They may deny this and seek to do something else. In the end, they cannot do anything else. Of course, they can sometimes persuade others that they have escaped this limitation. They can rename the Tower of Babel and vary its architectural nuances. They can attempt to pursue perfection as the crow flies. They can become cynical graspers after power for its own sake. What, finally, they cannot do is to fend off the reassertion of the human condition as it has always been.

Fortunately, the death of false ideas is not identical to the death of the human spirit. It arises from its own ashes. Nevertheless, it would be to the good to avoid recipes for the production of ash heaps where possible. Sensible politicians will do so. Philosophers do not produce sensible politicians. Philosophers will be fortunate if they notice sensible politicians and speak their praises simply by describing them. In so doing, they perform a not altogether useless task.

Political philosophers are thus of a conservative disposition. This is not to be confused with what is currently discussed as "conservatism" paleo- or neo-. The reference is specifically to a disposition from which no obvious generalization about views on specific policy questions may be drawn. The political philosopher is not in the business of determining of which ideas it may be said that their time has come, or gone. This conservative disposition reveals the nature of the sceptic's enjoyment. There is something known today as the "programmatic conservative." The latter, whatever it reveals, does not reveal the conservative disposition. Plans to end all planning, or to "give the government back to the people," suggest something far removed from what is intended here.

If one of the disposition in question should be asked, "Why ought governments to accept the current diversity of opinion and activity in preference to imposing upon their subjects a dream of their own? it is enough for him to reply: Why not? Their dreams are no different from those of anyone else; and if it is boring to have to listen to the dreams of others being recounted, it is insufferable to be forced to reenact them. We tolerate monomaniacs; it is our habit to do so; but why should we be *ruled* by them? . . . Government . . . does not begin with a vision of another, different and better world, but with the observation of the self-government practised even by men of passion in the conduct of their enterprises. . . . The intimations of government are to be found in ritual, not in religion or philosophy; in the enjoyment of orderly and peaceable behaviour, not in the search for truth or perfection."[34]

Ruling involves the making and enforcing of rules of conduct. Rules of conduct are not prescriptions for how we ought to live. They are adverbial conditions, specifying that, whatever we choose to do, we must do it under certain conditions. Such conditions may help or hinder us in the pursuit of our aims. The function of the rules of conduct, however, is neither to help nor to hinder, neither to pronounce in favor of nor against particular self-chosen pursuits of individuals.

Governing provides a *vinculum juris*. When successful, it will reduce the number of unfortunate collisions among interests. It will insure compensation for injuries. It will punish those who refuse to abide by rules of conduct. But government is "not the management of an enterprise, but the rule of those engaged in a great diversity of self-chosen enterprises . . . not concerned with concrete persons, but with activities . . . not concerned with moral right and wrong . . . not designed to make men good or even better."[35] Such a government seeks only "necessary loyalty" because it is indifferent to truth and error alike. Such a government may expect "respect and some suspicion, not love or devotion or affection."[36]

34. Oakeshott, *RP*, "On Being Conservative", in *RP*, 187–88.
35. Oakeshott, *RP*, 189.
36. Oakeshott, *RP*, 192.

Rules of conduct will have to change over time, of course. Such modification as is necessary "should always reflect and never impose, a change in the activities and beliefs of those who are subject to them, and should never on any occasion be so great as to destroy the *ensemble*."[37] Even armed with this disposition it will not necessarily be an easy or simple task to act in accord with it: "To rein-in one's own beliefs and desires, to acknowledge the current shape of things, to feel the balance of things in one's hand, to tolerate what is abominable, to distinguish between crime and sin, to respect formality even when it appears to be leading to error, these are difficult achievements."[38]

Here is maturity: coming to be at home in the world. As with Montaigne, we discern a pattern of movement from natural harmony at birth to the disharmony of youthful exuberance, to the reflective return to the world which we must inhabit and which differs from the one of our poetic images and political fancies. There is no rule enforcing this upon us. We may experience this with greater or lesser grace, but it is the capacity to find the days of age equal to the days of youth which qualifies us for undertaking political activity.

There is a parallel between the wisdom of the philosopher and the practical insight of the mature politician. But they do not need each other to come to them. Let us be thankful if they can live safely together in the same polity.

---

37. Oakeshott, *RP*, 190.
38. Oakeshott, *RP*, 195.

Authority and the Individual
in Civil Association
Oakeshott, Flathman, Yves Simon

I

IN THINKING ABOUT AUTHORITY, two ways of structuring
the modern political situation must be kept in mind. The first
meditates on the tension between understanding man as a self-
determining being and the residually present understanding of
the Classical-Christian outlook. The thesis that civilization may
advance materially while declining spiritually is, to many, vividly
dramatized by the circumstances of our time. The rhetoric of progress is less compelling now. Many wonder what utterances or actions can qualify as authoritative.

The second affirms an ideal of civil association, emphasizing
individuality and diversity, presupposing that human beings are intelligent agents. This is a world of selves among selves, disclosing
themselves to each other in pursuing their self-chosen aims. The
conduct of affairs can be intelligible and manageable without trying to answer questions about the *summum bonum* or *finis ultimus,*
provided only that there are some mutually recognized procedures

Reprinted with permission from *Nomos XXIX: Authority Revisited*, eds.
Roland Pennock and John W. Chapman (New York: New York University
Press, 1987), 131–51.

or practices to impart modest stability to the restless transactions of individuals with each other. The self-sufficiency of this civil association precludes a search for authoritative pronouncements about the spiritual conditions of life. From this perspective, the function of authority is severely circumscribed and certainly does not extend to any assessment of the "spiritual condition" of mankind.

In both of these, however, there is a positive and affirming conception of the function of authority. We will see both the convergence and divergence between them in considering Yves Simon and Michael Oakeshott.

On the other hand, what I shall call "resolute irresolution" is a noticeable feature of contemporary liberal politics. This attitude, which I shall illustrate by consideration of the work of Richard Flathman, arises out of reluctance to pay any tribute to authority. Authority is treated with ambivalence as a negative necessity to be exercised with apology and regret. To commentators like Flathman, the continued necessity of authority shows a failure of human ingenuity to have devised means to achieve a social spontaneity that would circumvent relations of authority or at least diminish them to a barely perceptible presence.

II

To Oakeshott, the focal feature of the civil condition is association in terms of noninstrumental "moral practice": "In respect of this practice *cives* and subjects are not joined as comrade expeditionaries in a communal adventure . . . or in some notional and banal agreement to be equally advantaged or not unequally disadvantaged . . . but in that relation of somewhat 'watery fidelity' called civility."[1] His aim is to show the logic of an association that is specifically civil and not anything else. In this he follows, at least in part, Aristotle when he distinguishes the civil association as a relationship obtaining only among human beings, more or less equal, subscribing to some constituting instrument, altogether composing a complete, self-sufficient structure.

1. Michael Oakeshott, *On Human Conduct*, 147.

Within this association, the interaction of agents appears in two modes. The first, "enterprise association," involves "intermittent transactional association of reciprocity in which agents . . . seek the satisfaction of their wants in the responses of one another. . . . It is a relationship of bargainers."[2] This sort of relationship does not describe association in terms of "civility" or "civil association." Civil association is association in terms of the conditions of a practice illustrated principally in "a common tongue and a language of moral converse."[3] A practice does not "prescribe choices to be made or satisfactions to be sought; instead, it intimates considerations to be subscribed to in making choices, in performing actions, and in pursuing purposes . . . it postulates 'free' agents and it is powerless to deprive them of their freedom."[4]

Individuals in civil association are agents who mediate between their particular circumstances and the generally acknowledged procedures. Practices are not principles from which we could derive courses of action.

No particular actions define human conduct. Individuals must always choose, from among alternatives that occur to them, what they take to be fitting illustrations of acknowledged moral practices in responding to contingent circumstances. Practices qualify, but do not determine, actions. Relationships arising from common subscription to a practice without specification of a joint purpose, product to be produced, or end to be reached, suggest what *civil* association is.

Oakeshott wants to describe a relationship among individuals that does not override their self-identification. Following Hobbes, he imagines how orderliness may come to be among selves who inevitably measure the world according to their own lights.

The ideal expression of civil association is derived from setting out a consistent interpretation of the requirements of order for human beings jealous of their individuality (in themselves what they are for themselves). Citizenship is association in the recognition of

2. Oakeshott, *On Human Conduct,* 112–13.
3. Oakeshott, *On Human Conduct,* 119; 59.
4. Oakeshott, *On Human Conduct,* 79.

a rule of law, not of necessary interests, needs, wants, or common dispositions.

Authority is found in the exercise of the duties of an office, under agreed-upon terms to make rules to which the citizens may subscribe. This categorically distinguishes power from authority. The associating aim of citizens is to establish and maintain authoritative rule. It is the commitment, existing in the thinking of individuals, to conduct themselves as *cives* in a *civitas,* that supersedes relations of mere power. For Oakeshott, the high achievement of modern Europe is the replacement of systems of command and obedience by arrangements of rules, adjudication, and voluntary subscription—relations of authority and acknowledgment in civil association.

Practically speaking, the categorical distinction of authority from power is not a fixed and final achievement. The distinction is hard to establish and easy to lose. But even though individuals do not perfectly act in accord with the distinction, the distinction is indispensable to conceive civil association. To perceive power and authority as separable and, as a consequence, to exercise ingenuity in making the distinction a practical reality, is the realization, albeit imperfect, of the ideal civil association.

The categorical distinction vanishes when authority is defined in terms of building consensus, proclaiming unifying goals, or constructing coalitions of interests. To make consensus prerequisite to the establishment and exercise of authority is to fail to see that authority is required by the absence of consensus and cannot be employed to create or recreate consensus.

Setting out the ideal expression of civil association, and the authority that goes with it, clarifies what we are already seeking (for Oakeshott philosophizing is saying in explicit terms what is already implicit in our experience). In the process, some things we think we are pursuing have to be set aside. It is the austerity of the conception of authority and civil association that constitutes a barrier to its acceptance far more than anything else. Moreover, the question of how to achieve civil association and relations of authority and subscription is entirely left aside. Their possibility (reminiscent of Plato) depends fundamentally on the clarity of our vision of them.

III

Despite Oakeshott's effort at clarification of the elements of modern political order in terms of civil association and relations of authority and acknowledgment, there remains a strong tendency to explain or ground these relationships in some more material, tangible way, rejecting Oakeshott's position that human order is an interpretation of circumstances, a form of self-understanding or self-interpretation alone. To speak of human order any other way is to speak of something categorically different or to disguise what is distinctively "human" and hence "civil" or "political." At best one may construct an amalgamation of elements from different categories of understanding. An example of this is to be found in the extensive analysis of authority in the recent work of Richard Flathman.

In *The Practice of Political Authority*,[5] Flathman embarks upon his own effort to distinguish the exercise of authority from the exertion of coercive power, to distinguish "authority" from the "authoritarian." To do so, Flathman reviews and summarizes the literature on authority as falling into two large categories: the first theorizes authority in substantive purposive (S-P) terms and is exemplified, in his view, by Plato's *Republic;* the second theorizes authority in formal-procedural (F-P) terms and is exemplified by Hobbes's *Leviathan.* In the by now well-established formulation, the distinction is between "an authority" and "in authority." Flathman's primary interest lies with "in authority" since that is the dominant concept within modern liberalism.

In earlier works as well as in this one, Flathman has discerned an impasse between claims of rights and the exercise even of "in authority" relationships.[6] Flathman's preference for what we may call self-critical traditionality is endangered by the disordering effects of rights claims in conflict with the discretionary judgments of

5. Richard Flathman, *The Practice of Political Authority* (Chicago: University of Chicago Press, 1980).
6. See Richard E. Flathman, *The Practice of Rights* (Cambridge: Cambridge University Press, 1976).

office-holders. The balance of "order" and "progress" developed by
J. S. Mill as a proper conception of social balance in a free society,
and in a different vocabulary expressed by Flathman, is thought by
him to be close to falling apart. Furthermore, Flathman does not
find any clear resource to employ in maintaining the symbiotic relationship between these contending factors of social life.

Flathman addresses himself directly to the problem in his discussion of "authority and the 'surrender' of individual judgment."[7] By
"surrender of individual judgment" what is meant is that an individual, in submitting to someone's exercise of authority, withholds his
own assessment of the merits of what is proposed to be done in favor
of the assessment emanating from whoever is in authority. The submitting individual does not at this point demand a justification that
would move him to act in the prescribed manner on his own in the
absence of an authoritative pronouncement. In short, the exercise
of authority by A must be presumed to have altered the conduct of
B from what it would have been had A not exercised authority.

Now, if I understand Flathman correctly, he wishes to show that
a relationship of authority between A and B cannot properly be understood in terms of the debate over whether B surrenders judgment
and whether that surrender is good or bad. For Flathman, A can exercise authority in relation to B without B surrendering his "judgment" even if B's conduct alters from what it would have been.
Flathman is trying to mediate an abstract dichotomy between the
proponents of extreme claims of rights for whom "surrender of judgment" is *prima facie* wicked, and the proponents of unquestioning
submission to authoritative pronouncements for whom the exercise
of authority is the only salvation from the war of all against all.

If B submits to the pronouncement of A, thereby altering his conduct, he may be thinking that A is authorized to pronounce to this
effect on B but B may still think that what A pronounces is not good
and should not have been pronounced. B may act in conformity with
A's exercise of authority while not "believing in it." For B to submit
to the pronouncement of A is not to be taken as a sign that B now
believes something to be "true" or "good" whereas he formerly

7. Flathman, *Practice of Political Authority*, chap. 5.

believed it to be "not true" or "not good" (or perhaps "indifferent" or "uncertain"). All that may be said is that whereas B's conduct might have gone one way it will now go another.

But does this analysis relieve the earlier impasse? Even if the alteration of conduct does not require a surrender of judgment, what can be the ground of altering one's conduct without changing one's judgment if not the calculation that order is preferable—in this case—to disorder? And what basis is there for any B to continue to make this calculation in favor of order? One is strongly tempted to answer this question by resort to an argument from habits. Bs will either accept, or not accept, as authoritative, pronouncements from As, as the case may be. Moreover, perhaps the exercise of "in authority" takes on, through habits of compliance, the appearance of "an authority" until some jarring eventuality reminds people of the arguments against "an authority." One might say, on behalf of the argument that to submit to authority is to surrender one's judgment, that it forthrightly acknowledges the tenuousness of all political order and the paradoxical basis upon which the indispensability of authority is established. It has the force of Hobbes's clarity as opposed to the appealing indecisiveness of Locke.

Flathman has provided a strong argument for the possibility of maintaining one's "spiritual autonomy" while submitting to authority. So far then we have an incipient defence of the political order as a "necessary evil," but do we have Tocqueville's "common belief" from which social well-being may spring? Flathman has defended authority from a prima facie charge of wickedness, but it remains to this point a burden to be borne: "Is the fact that a rule or command carries *in* authority itself a conclusive reason for B qua B to have an obligation to conform to the rule or to obey the command?"[8]

Flathman's answer here is that the obligation to conform obtains when the command is "valid." Questions of validity, however, "do not decide themselves. They are decided through the exercise of judgment by parties to the *in* authority relationship."[9] Moreover, the basis for such judgments consists in "some array of values and

8. Flathman, *Practice of Political Authority,* 104.
9. Flathman, *Practice of Political Authority,* 104–5.

beliefs that has acceptance in the society or association of which it [authority] is part. For values and beliefs to give such support, a kind of congruence must be thought to exist between them and the actions and requirements of authority. The initiatives, the leadership, in maintaining such congruence may indeed rest largely with the As. But the Bs must believe that the congruence exists, and this belief requires judgments on B's part."[10]

The difficulty with this is that it tends to duplicate authority. Behind A lurks something even more authoritative than A's authoritative pronouncements. As Flathman states it, B may appeal to the authoritative background as well as A. Indeed, B must do so in order to exercise judgment on the pronouncement of A. However, if it is the very meaning of the authoritative background which is at issue (as in principle it must be in every case of A's judgment and pronouncement) then there must always be an incipient crisis of authority, as Hobbes would surely have seen immediately. Is Flathman not in danger of reintroducing a disguised natural source of authority?

It would seem that the genius of Hobbes's solution to the duplication of authorities, which in his time manifested itself in the conflict of theological and political authorities, and which Hobbes saw would show itself in eloquent appeals to private revelatory experiences, has been overthrown by Flathman. The appeal to the authoritative background is Flathman's up-to-date restatement in secular, historical terms of Locke's "appeal to heaven," which anyone can exercise at any time. In a way, then, Flathman seems close to admitting that the relationships of political life can be recorded as the endlessly evolving pursuit of intimations of the authoritative— it is human responses to their sociology. Who, then, is authoritative with respect to the authoritative background? Why cannot B go beyond the question of whether A holds the office of authority, to the "substantive merits" of A's pronouncements? Is not B entitled to claim that he is "an authority" on the exercise of "in authority"? Indeed he is, as Hobbes would say, if he is willing to put himself back into the state of nature.

10. Flathman, *Practice of Political Authority*, 106.

Thus, B must choose to surrender his judgment in some important respect. B must do so in the sense of separating his private opinion from his public conduct. This is unavoidable. Those who object to the exercise of authority as demanding surrender of judgment correctly perceive that, in the relationship between "in authority" As and the objects of authoritative pronouncements, the Bs, there is a genuine inhibition on Bs externalizing their contrary beliefs in action. Flathman wants to defend this inhibition as necessary, but he equally does not want to be seen in the uncomfortable role of hard-headedly defending real, perhaps painful, restrictions on self-determination. He criticizes theorists who do not mind that role, most notably Hobbes and Michael Oakeshott:

> The argument for self-discipline in effect contends that for purposes of action Bs confronted with an A or an X must proceed as if B is the only role they play and as if the characterization "an A" or "an X" is the only characterization that they may consider. This is not "implausibly circumspect" (Oakeshott), it is impossibly limiting. There is no such thing as a person who is nothing but a B, and there is no such thing as a formulation that is nothing but an A or an X. In thought and action the several roles that any person plays and the several characterizations of which any formulation allows inevitably coexist and interact in a variety of ways. As important as they are, role conceptions and distinguishing characterizations do not and cannot (if only because they are commonly defined in part by reference one to the other) form hermetically sealed compartments or windowless monads that are or could be altogether isolated from one another.[11]

The latter is a rhetorically powerful statement but it does not dispose of any of the difficulties. It is precisely because no one is ever only an A or a B, and because no role is ever invulnerable to the nuance of meaning given to it by anyone who plays it, that the elucidation of the authoritative relationship between As and Bs is among

11. Flathman, *Practice of Political Authority*, 107–8.

the hardest of accomplishments and the most easily eroded. The erosion works both ways. On the one side, the office-holder is in danger of either overstepping his bounds or failing to exercise the duties of his office when they are painful; on the other side, the one who must submit to authority is in danger of wanting someone in authority to be an authority (thus relieving B's ordeal of being conscious and self-enacting) or of "appealing to heaven" merely by being a clever enough sophist to know that A's interpretation of the "authoritative background" of social life can always be made to look arbitrary in some respect.

The problem is not whether we need the "ideal type" of the relations of authority. We do need it inevitably if we are to clarify what we understand to be the requirements of political life. On Flathman's own terms it would seem that we need to know how to recognize when we are acting toward the implementation of the ideal of authority and of citizenship and when we are not. But Flathman, in my opinion, fears that to put the issue this way is to come perilously close to acknowledging that the preeminent requirement is the exercise of authority by the office-holder and not the claim of independent judgment on the part of the individual who will be subjected to the authoritative pronouncement. Common sense suggests that the hallmark of the civic order in a liberal society would be self-discipline or self-regulation. The alternative that forces itself upon us is self-assertion or demand for support on our own terms, or refusal to accord legitimacy to any exercise of authority that does not have prior approval from our point of view (which would be tantamount to making ourselves authorities on the exercise of authority, or making *ourselves* the authoritative background of the exercise of authority).

Flathman states that many are convinced "that citizens have a positive *duty* to make continuing assessments of the substantive merits of X's [requirements emanating from authorities] and a positive duty to make action on these assessments an integral part of *in* authority relations."[12] No doubt this is a widely held view. What foundation it has other than that it is widely held is by no means

12. Flathman, *Practice of Political Authority*, 108.

clear. Why does any B have this duty? Who may impose this duty? Who may assess the manner of its discharge? Can there be a "positive duty to take action on these assessments" in an "in authority" relationship? Can someone "in authority" command us to assess the pronouncements he issues in the form of actions that will exhibit our attitudes toward them? Does he not have to insist that we resound by acting in accord with such pronouncements? If not, then what is his authority for?

Because the issue of whether continued allegiance to authority depends on our independent assessment of the fruits of its exercise has not yet been unequivocally settled, Flathman acknowledges that he has not so far provided "a conclusive argument for or against rejecting authority as such."[13] This is the case because so far all we have as means to settling our attitude to authority are our calculations of its advantage or disadvantage for us. This seems to be a consequence of the fact that, for Flathman, no substantive determination of good for a society is possible. The latter would require articulating a nonarbitrary (the right) opinion on what is good or just amidst the myriad opinions that present themselves. Failing "an authority" we are led to philosophical skepticism on the question of "good," and to "in authority" as the skeptic's solution. But if any "in authority" is arbitrary (i.e., its pronouncements are not the right opinion but only putatively the rule), would it not be better to have no authority? What of the one who willingly submits to the "condition of mere nature" and the possible "war of all against all"?

So far, I think, Flathman has absolutely no answer to such a person. Like Locke, once he has accepted the "appeal to heaven" (B's appeal to the authoritative background values against A's interpretation of them in rules), he can only hope that people will generally feel no compulsion to appeal to heaven. Thus, like Locke, Flathman would have it two ways at once: the threat of the appeal to heaven will help keep the authorities skittish about the exercise of authority, and most people will perhaps find it to their advantage to be governed by those who are skittish about governing.

---

13. Flathman, *Practice of Political Authority*, 109.

This may be clever but it is ineluctably contingent: "widespread and continuing approval, or at least the absence of overly emphatic and insistent disapproval, of the X's is a condition of *in* authority (and hence of any 'surrender of judgment' thereto). In short, the existence of *in* authority is a condition of decisions to obey X's is a condition of the existence of *in* authority."[14] Is this remark different in its actuality from the following: "The constitutional histories of European states have some brilliant passages; but, for the most part, and not unexpectedly, they have been the stories of somewhat confused and sordid expedients for accommodating the modern disposition to judge everything from the point of view of the desirability of its outcome in policies and performances and to discount legitimacy."[15]

Nor does even building civil disobedience into the system of "in authority" relations resolve the dilemma. After a lucid account of how the civil disobedient proposes to remain a B while nonetheless refusing to obey the authorities, Flathman concludes: "A showing that the idea of civil disobedience is compatible with *in* authority can be justified."[16] What is clear is that such a complex version of the "in authority" relationship (one making room for civil disobedience) is acceptable to Flathman personally. This version pays its respects to the anarchist and to the Hobbesian simultaneously.

Does Flathman wish authority to disappear altogether? Perhaps it would be more correct to say that he would like to see it totally transformed. The general tendency of his discourse assumes that there is something embarrassing at least, ominous at worst, about the exercise of authority. Although he sees a necessity for authority, he thinks that there is always an incipient illegitimacy in its exercise, or at least that people will tend to perceive authority as suspect. The prescription might be to democratize authority, yet "restricted forms of democratization are likely to diminish the value of the authority itself while reproducing, in what may seem to be only minimally altered forms, the very difficulties that the devices are intended to

---

14. Flathman, *Practice of Political Authority*, 114.
15. Oakeshott, *On Human Conduct*, 193.
16. Flathman, *Practice of Political Authority*, 122.

remedy."[17] Any radical democratization, while "intended to induce participation that is more widespread, vigorous and efficacious than is encouraged or even allowed by more restricted modes of democracy" and thus to "reconcile authority and individual agency," will "in an association of any size" cause conflict between the two: "Either the participation is intense but less widespread and the arrangement becomes hard to distinguish from restricted democracy, or it is widespread but lax or thin, thereby failing to enliven identification with and acceptance of substantive outcomes. And in both cases its formal properties leave the association subject to the veto power that the scheme puts at the disposal of all members."[18]

Even if democratization would have value for making the exercise of authority more palatable (which is certainly not obvious), the issue of the substantive merits of the outcomes of exercising (democratized) authority would remain. In short, even here under conditions of democratization Flathman insists on maintaining a distinction between the authoritative background values and the pronouncements of officials as to the meaning of the authoritative for purposes of action. Any claim to merge authority and the authoritative must be rejected.[19]

But the point must be raised again: Is this position not reintroducing the criterion of substantive merit as the means to assess the exercise of authority (the criterion of self-interest, rhetorically projected as an elucidation of authoritative background values)? Can the civil disobedient claim to remain a B while seeking to establish an alternative authoritative interpretation of the authoritative? Flathman insists on this because he thinks that to do otherwise is to open oneself to "imposition and domination seeking to clothe itself in the normative garb of authority."[20] If I understand this, it seems to lead to the proposition that the best way to prevent "imposition and domination" is to invite clashes over the substantive merits of the actions of those holding offices of "in authority." This confusion must

17. Flathman, *Practice of Political Authority*, 195–96.
18. Flathman, *Practice of Political Authority*, 199.
19. Flathman, *Practice of Political Authority*, 205.
20. Flathman, *Practice of Political Authority*, 124.

arise to the extent that Flathman both wishes to have moral progress (see p. 241) bespeaking some concrete actualization of good, and also fears every concrete determination of good that is in fact brought forward.

In fact, Flathman's is a theory of the inevitability of clashes over substantive merits of governmental action. As such, it is a real denial of the "in authority" relationship as primary, or, to put it differently, it is a revisionist interpretation of the theory of "in authority" in the form of a politicization. So far the politicization does not have any clear programmatic content. But it seems reasonably obvious that for Flathman the pure theory of "in authority" is distasteful because it sharply distinguishes the exercisers of authority from those upon whom the exercise will fall, or at least it seems to do so (see pp. 241–43). On the other hand, Flathman cannot dispense with "in authority" because of the fundamental philosophical skepticism that underlies his conception of, and commitment to, the liberal political tradition. His aspiration is that the distinction between As and Bs should ultimately collapse.

It would seem that the pure theory of "in authority" accepts this conclusion as well. After all, theorists like Hobbes and Oakeshott do not argue that the historical background of a society is definitively explicated by those who exercise authority. What they argue is that we can only rescue ourselves from the arbitrary and the capricious by reliance on some exercise of authority to avoid the war of every interpretation against every interpretation. Thus, it is difficult to see that Flathman has any solution to the problem posed by the ever available "appeal to heaven." He has to maintain the possibility of such an appeal while urging every effort to mitigate authority's offensiveness to those who know that they can appeal to heaven.[21] "As a response to most if not all of what has been accepted as political authority in human history, the judgment that 'it is not as bad as might be thought' is about the most that could be sustained."[22] Even more startlingly: "the conclusion Rousseau drew in the eighteenth century remains correct in our own day; political

---

21. Flathman, *Practice of Political Authority*, 218–19.
22. Flathman, *Practice of Political Authority*, 220.

authority is in principle a justifiable human practice, but at present that practice is nowhere actualized in justifiable form."[23]

It is hard to avoid concluding that for Flathman what is "authoritative" is the impasse from which he started and to which he seems continually to return. Flathman's key to political life is resolute irresolution.

IV

Resolute irresolution is a noticeable trope of contemporary liberal politics. To be sure, this is not how Oakeshott understands authority. To the contrary, for Oakeshott relations of authority and acknowledgment in civil association are the high-water mark of the political imagination. Yet to other commentators, such as Flathman, there is an unresolved question of the right or the just coupled with a desire for some, as yet undefined, spontaneity of relationship that would circumvent the need of relations of authority, or diminish them to a barely perceptible presence.

To this Oakeshott might reply that an association of agents may create and protect a sphere of spontaneity only by way of establishing relations of authority, and agree with Hobbes's "brisk and decisive" answer that "authentic *lex* cannot be *injus*. This does not mean that the legislative office is magically insulated from 'unjust' law. It means that this office is designed and authorized to make genuine law, that it is protected against indulging in any other activity and that in a state ruled by law the only 'justice' is that which is inherent in the character of *lex*."[24]

It is clear that the "authoritative" of which Flathman speaks resolves no issues of the "jus" of "lex" and may only exacerbate them in the clash of interests to which debate over the "jus" of "lex" gives rise. Nonetheless, the questions of purpose or of the goals or ends of life do not disappear. It may be objected to Oakeshott that, while he has an affirming view of authority, his affirmation is merely of a

23. Flathman, *Practice of Political Authority*, 229.
24. Michael Oakeshott, "The Rule of Law," in *On History and Other Essays* (1983), 130–31.

circumstantial achievement, an appreciation of a certain relationship for its own sake. Let us consider, then, a theorist of authority who explicitly seeks an unequivocally positive theory of authority, Yves Simon.

Simon's thinking on authority is conditioned by his structuring of the modern political context from a perspective formed from sources outside it, the natural law tradition as it thinks in terms of the ascent of the soul as opposed to the progress of society: "Political and social consciousness, in modern times, evidences an obscure belief that the progress of freedom is synonymous with social progress . . . that social progress is identical with the progress of liberty . . . conceived as implying a decay of authority, so that three terms, social progress, the progress of liberty, and the decay of authority, are currently identified."[25]

One may note that this describes an unmistakable tone in Flathman's analysis. It cannot describe Oakeshott insofar as Oakeshott rejects in toto "progress" as a meaningful theoretical concept. It touches Oakeshott too, however, insofar as Oakeshott is a modern individualist, which Simon is not. Yet even if Simon is not a modern individualist, he assumes the reality of the individual in the Aristotelian-Thomistic tradition: Authority is exercised "through a practical judgment to be taken as a rule of conduct by the free-will of another person . . . no authority can ever take the form of an impersonal necessity."[26]

It is exactly here that many begin to distrust authority in either the Oakeshottian or Simonian versions. There is something arbitrary about practical judgments since it is always possible that they could go some other way. In other words, one way of assessing authority is to say that it only substitutes for an as yet undiscovered certainty that surmounts "practical judgment" in the Aristotelian sense.

Simon objects to this on the ground that it mistakenly interprets political authority as if it is the prelude to scientific or theoretical

25. Yves Simon, *The Nature and Functions of Authority* (Milwaukee: Marquette University Press, 1948), 5–6. See also Yves Simon, *A General Theory of Authority* (South Bend: University of Notre Dame Press, 1980).
26. Simon, *Nature and Functions of Authority*, 6–7.

wisdom, thus failing to remember Aristotle's insight in maintaining the separateness of practical and theoretical wisdom. But beyond this, such a view obscures the discovery of any essential function of authority, i.e., some function important to human beings which can be fulfilled in no other way. If such a function can be sighted then it will be possible to circumvent the view that authority is only a necessary evil, perhaps a temporary necessity of civilization's development so far, but ultimately dispensable. The latter view encourages attacks on authority as if the attacks were a sign of enlightenment long after, following Oakeshott, authority has successfully replaced coercion as central to political order. Or, to put it another way, the continued necessity of authority comes to be seen as a deficiency: "It means that the amount of authority necessary in a society is inversely proportional to the perfection reached by that society . . . the law of progress would take the form of an asymptotic curve at whose unattainable term there would be a complete elimination of authority."[27]

In search of this essential function of authority, Simon proposes a thought experiment. Let us imagine "a community of adults, intelligent and of perfect good will" and let us consider what is required for the common life of such a community. If we do not assume inevitable unanimity (not a logical necessity even with "perfect" good will), how will this community assure unity of action?

Simon's response is that unity even under these ideal conditions requires authority; even the perfectly "enlightened" society will require authority. The correct direction of action cannot be demonstrated "because we are unable to overcome the mysteries of contingency."[28] Moreover, a decision that is perfectly valid (to travel by car to a vacation resort) may be undermined (by an unforeseeable car crash). The truth of a practical judgment does not "refer to its conformity with the reality of things," but to "conformity with the requirements of a will which is supposed to be sound, healthy, honest . . . not the truth of a cognition but the truth of a direction."[29]

27. Simon, *Nature and Functions of Authority*, 15.
28. Simon, *Nature and Functions of Authority*, 23.
29. Simon, *Nature and Functions of Authority*, 24.

An association of individuals of perfect good will can never avoid this limitation even with the best will in the world: "it can never be shown evidently that this or that practical judgment, to be taken as a rule for our common action, is the best possible one."[30] With respect to practical judgment it is possible to act in a better or worse state of awareness of the requirements of judging well in contingent circumstances, but it is in principle impossible progressively to master and transcend the precarious and variable relation of judgment to the reality of things. Thus in the temporal succession of human experience good judgments are not perpetuated and they do not accumulate. A movement from sound judgment to sound judgment cannot be a movement in the form of better to better still. The latter is wishful thinking.

Those associated in perfect good will cannot depend on unanimity, and as the number increases, the experience of unanimity should decline in frequency. But action must be taken. People of good will must acknowledge the need of authority and establish it. It is a function of good will to do so. It is, one may say, the natural consequence of adequate human reflection on human relations. It is not "defectives" or "primitives" who require authority, but those most fully and self-consciously human.

These most fully human beings, being real individuals, have both the inclination to associate and also to accomplish their own ends. But these ends include that of association. What is good from an individual's perspective may or may not be received as good by others. Conflict over goods to pursue is not a symptom of wickedness (for we are still supposing individuals of perfect good will), but the natural consequence of the limited perception of the possibilities of good that is available to any individual. Individuals of good will must see this and thus the very desire of their own good carries them beyond themselves toward the others for confirming or qualifying response. The effort to confirm that individual goods are not incompatible with the larger range of goods is a continuous development from the desire for particular goods to the desire for good. What is good is neither merely abstract, because the first intimations of it

30. Simon, *Nature and Functions of Authority*, 27.

are in particular material desires of real individuals, nor merely particular, since the desire is for something "good," it is not just desiring, and that it may be good depends on common acknowledgment in some degree of more or less.

But since unanimity is not only precarious and infrequent but also overrun by the fecundity of possible goods, where individuals are recognized to be real, authority will be required. It will be required not so as to suppress the spontaneous diversification of individual perceptions of good, but to establish some manageability where every good thing cannot be pursued simultaneously. One imagines here an inversion of the Hobbesian notion of the *bellum omnium contra omnes*.[31] Thus the natural movement toward identifying one's good and thence good as such brings forth the desire for authority as the practically necessary condition of fulfilling the quest for one's good and the good. Authority, so far from standing in opposition to human diversity, is *essential* to its rational ordering in qualifying as an attribute of the good itself. Some putative "progress" beyond the need of authority is, in fact, a retrogression masquerading as an abstract "ideal."

To avoid misunderstanding, however, it must be added that it would be entirely mistaken to take this as an argument merely in service to the "powers that be" as if every existent exercise of rule exemplified authority. Pursuit of good carries to sight the need, if good is to be rendered practicable in a really existing polity, of authority, that form of rule which responds to what underlies and constitutes it and may be acknowledged by its subjects as referable to what they require (which is not saying they must "approve" or "agree" with everything it says or does even if they observe it). What is carried to sight is not the "authoritative" (although historians and sociologists may think they are discovering this retrospectively) but a practical judgment determining the "good" for purposes of

31. "That virtuous people, as a proper effect of their very virtue, have the common good and subordinate their choices to its requirements is an entirely unquestionable proposition. Thus, *in a certain way at least*, the volition and intention of the common good are guaranteed by virtue itself, independently of all authority." Yves Simon, *Philosophy of Democratic Government* (Chicago: University of Chicago Press, 1953), 39.

practical action. If anything is "authoritative," it is this judgment and it cannot be subordinated to a "condition" of its appearance.

V

To conclude just here would perhaps suggest to the careful reader a convergence, despite idiomatic differences, between Oakeshott and Simon in their positive affirmations of authority when its function is lucidly set forth. But significant divergence must be mentioned and it will return us to the point with which we began.

While it is true that both Oakeshott and Simon begin from the reality of the individual and the individual's "free will" (Simon) or capacity for intelligent response to contingent circumstances (Oakeshott), their conceptions of the "liberty" enjoyed by this individual ultimately diverge in a way that affects their theories of authority. Simon follows Jacques Maritain in distinguishing "initial" from "terminal" liberty, or the capacity to choose from the attainment of choosing good as opposed to evil. Here we must recall the difference between "progress of society" and "ascent of soul."[32] "Initial liberty" is akin to Oakeshott's "intelligent response," but for Oakeshott there can be no meaning to "terminal" liberty apart from "self-enactment" in an individual agent. "Self-enactment" means, in effect, the attempt on one's part to live one's life in a manner consistent with the direction one has chosen for it. This is separable from "self-disclosure," which is the series of actions and utterances of one perceptible to others and which they may or may not take to be consistent with one's self-enactment so far as they have awareness of both.

For Oakeshott, no common meaning of "self-enactment" can be established. Selves cannot become simply transparent to each other. Efforts to achieve this must tend to fall into ideology or at least misunderstanding. Thus Oakeshott maintains the absolute dichotomy between good and what agents pursue in their "imagined and wished-for outcomes." Authority cannot therefore operate as a coparticipant in the lives of individuals, guiding them, however indirectly, to that

32. Simon, *Nature and Functions of Authority*, 40.

enactment which would no longer be strictly a *self*-enactment. No such thing lies in the capacity of anyone exercising authority. Indeed, for Oakeshott, this would be tantamount to reintroducing a command which one must obey even though its implementation might continue to have features of practical judgment. And even if this command were associated with a divine revelation emanating from a sovereignty that is not constituted by our consent, the belief that such a sovereign command is possible *is* constituted by consent.

Insofar, then, as Simon, who has traveled a long way down the road of modernity with Oakeshott, subtly reintroduces a notion of the "progress of society" in the form of a "spiritual ascent," articulated through authority which would assist us to move from "initial" to "terminal" liberty, he must diverge from his travel companion. Of course, it is clear that what Simon (and Maritain and, lately, John Finnis) has in mind is not at all what Flathman means by the "authoritative." The latter can never be other than the cultural conditions of society in some epoch of its temporal progression. Equally clear, to an Oakeshottian, would be the danger, or likelihood, that the conditions of terminal liberty could never be extricated from the "authoritative" of Flathman. The point, then, is not to deny the possibility of universal, spiritual good. The point is never to forget what the limitations of earthly authority are. To my knowledge, Oakeshott has never denied the former nor forgotten the latter. To put it another way: as against Simon's Thomism, one may array Oakeshott's Hobbesian version of Augustinianism. In either version, authority is the creative achievement of the human spirit which "redeems" the liberty of choosing or the procedure of intelligent response to contingency.

Here is where the philosophical conversation on authority might approach the profundity it deserves. Oakeshott brings forth what might be called the pure theory of authority, disengaged in the farthest degree from considerations which mask its categorical attributes. In many respects Simon, and other representatives of his tradition of thought, need not quarrel with Oakeshott's achievement. Nor would Oakeshott fail to appreciate Simon's desire to establish a substantive meaning for good, not as cultural "behavior" but as a natural inclination toward fulfillment which could be translated into "ends" to aid us in the pilgrimage of life. Nevertheless, for Oakeshott, the pilgrimage is a "predicament" and not a "journey." This is not Oakeshott's attempt to refute the alternative but an attempt to say indicatively what can be said. To speak indicatively is to remain consistent with his theory of civil association and of authority and to keep other reflections in the realm of the private.

To Oakeshott, the inclinations which "by nature" move all human endeavor can only be understood as imagined and wished-for outcomes in a state of constant revision in the sequences of individual experience, and authority offers a certain stability of procedure but no independent criteria of enactment pertinent to preferences among self-enactments. Simon, in his emphasis on the essentiality of practical judgment, converges with Oakeshott in upholding the procedural achievements of modern democratic polities. They may agree to disagree, as friends occasionally do; they disagree on the metaphysical premises of the conduct to which they mutually agree to subscribe.

Memorial Service at the London
School of Economics, May 17, 1991

I DISCOVERED MICHAEL WHEN, as an undergraduate, set to write
a paper on Hobbes, I discovered his introduction to the *Leviathan* in my college library. This solidified my decision to take up an
academic career; I hoped I might write an essay like that someday. I
still hope to do so.

Michael and I first met in September 1974 when he came to Colorado College to inaugurate a series of lectures on liberal learning
that were to celebrate the college's centenary. His lecture, "A Place
of Learning," now reprinted with his other remarkable essays on education in *The Voice of Liberal Learning*, electrified an audience of
four hundred. For years thereafter members of the college talked of
the event. We here today will understand; for we have been lucky to
be present on other occasions to witness Michael speaking, in a way
uniquely his, with an extraordinary combination of tranquil reflec-
tiveness and piercing illumination.

He stayed at Colorado College for a week, talking to students and
faculty and exploring the Colorado Rockies with me. He particularly
was taken with our trip to the Cripple Creek gold camp, nearly a
ghost town, where we clambered around the old mines, looked out at

Printed with permission from Timothy Fuller. Title appeared originally as
"Remembering Michael Oakeshott: Memorial Service at the London School of
Economics, May 17, 1991."

the Collegiate Range of fourteen-thousand-foot peaks from the sum-mit of Mount Pisgah, and had a beer together at the hundred-year-old bar in the Imperial Hotel where every summer the overheated melodramas of the nineteenth century are reproduced for tourists.

Since we had not met before then, I asked him what made him accept my invitation. He said he had had an uncle who migrated to California at the end of the previous century to grow tomatoes—this had excited in him an interest in reading about the Old West—and that the idea of pioneers crossing the great prairie to Colorado in covered wagons, carrying the Bible, Shakespeare, and other great works of our civilization was irresistible. He had followed this through Adams's *The Log of a Cowboy* and such great American novels as Willa Cather's *My Antonia*. I, of course, had long since fallen in love with England in a somewhat antiquarian way, and fallen under the influence of his writings. Henceforth our friendship was sealed, and I began my series of annual visits to London and to Dorset to bring him news of the part of the world I inhabited and to refresh myself with the wisdom of whatever books he was currently reading and thoughts he was currently thinking. He particularly enjoyed it when I brought my family, and he sent cards every Christmas to my wife Kalah and to my daughters Margaret and Amy.

He made one more visit to Colorado in 1982 to receive an honor-ary degree from Colorado College. My last conversation with him was in May 1990 at the Letwins, and my last letter from him came in the late fall when he assured me that, as soon as his current mal-adies improved, he would respond in detail to the issues we had been most recently considering.

There are many things I remember, but for now I shall remember him as the great teacher that he was. I believe his writings in political philosophy will survive long into the future, but it is his remarkable impact on students that we must sustain through our recollection. I am happy to say that a dozen or so of my own students had the privilege of studying at the London School of Economics in his His-tory of Political Thought program. Many of them have gone on to successful academic careers of their own, forever touched by him.

I have not personally known anyone who could feel the beauty of youth more intensely, even at the end of his days, than Michael. The sense of his being alive to the possibilities of existence was with him even to the end, and it was the secret of his effect on students. He never forgot what it was like for them even though he knew that one cannot remain in the youthful dream: "For most," he said, "there is what Conrad called the 'shadow line' which, when we pass it, discloses a solid world of things, each with its fixed shape, each with its own point of balance, each with its price; a world of fact, not poetic image, in which what we have spent on one thing we cannot spend on another; a world inhabited by others besides ourselves who cannot be reduced to mere reflections of our own emotions."

In 1963, he was asked to address the new students here at LSE and so he wrote a short address called "On Arriving at a University," letting, as he put it, "my imagination play round the experience of being a first-year undergraduate." He told the students they were not here "to learn how to be a more efficient cog in a social machine." "You are here," he said,

> to educate yourselves, and education is not learning how to perform a social function. . . . You have come here to get acquainted with truth and error, not merely with what is and what is not serviceable to a productivist society. Secondly, almost everything that has happened to you since you arrived here, and much of what was told you beforehand, has tended to turn you into self-conscious "Students," people with many rights, a few duties, and a special status in society. Indeed, some people seem to think that being a "student" is a sort of profession. Forget it.
>
> You are certainly card-carrying members of something— but of what? The cards are certainly useful; they let you into special exhibitions at the Tate for half-price, and they give you the run of the youth hostels of Europe. But I hope you will not let them make you feel that you have joined something like a trade union. What the cards signify is that you are members of something much more like a confraternity of strolling players—to which I, also, am glad to belong. The police sometimes move us on; but we are tolerated, and to live in an area of toleration is much pleasanter than having a

niche in society. Half the world prays that it may be forgotten by the system that surrounds us; we are the happy few who are more nearly forgotten than anyone else. Let us enjoy it.

One can list the essential works: *Experience and Its Modes* (1933), *Rationalism in Politics* (1962), *On Human Conduct* (1975), *Hobbes on Civil Association* (1975), *On History* (1983), *The Voice of Liberal Learning* (1989).

But as I list these, I remember that one of Michael's favorite stories was of the Chinese wheelwright who could not, at seventy, turn over his craft to his son because his son could not get the hang of it. The wheelwright generalized from his failure to inculcate into his son more than the abstract rules of his craft when he remarked to his Duke, who was reading the words of the sages, that books are "the lees and scum of bygone men." "All that is worth handing on," the wheelwright said, "died with them; the rest, they put in their books."

One thinks too of Socrates who refused to write philosophy down. But then one remembers also Plato who devised a method for writing philosophy down without writing it down. The intent of Michael's writing was like that. In the lees and scum there is, after all, a lingering presence which is a blessing in disguise.

Assessing Oakeshott's Political Thought

I

MICHAEL OAKESHOTT (1901–1990) is among the preeminent political philosophers of our time. His major works span a period from the 1933 publication of *Experience and Its Modes* to the 1989 publication of his essays on education in *The Voice of Liberal Learning*. In between, the most notable works are *Social and Political Doctrines of Contemporary Europe* (1939), Introduction to the Blackwell Edition of Hobbes's *Leviathan* (1946), *Rationalism in Politics* (1962; New and Expanded Edition, 1991), *On Human Conduct* (1975), *Hobbes on Civil Association* (1975), *On History and Other Essays* (1983).

Oakeshott's academic career was essentially divided between his time as a Cambridge history don—he was a life fellow of Gonville and Caius College where his portrait now presides over the faculty dining room—from the mid-1920s to 1949, and his professorship at The London School of Economics and Political Science (LSE) from 1951 to his official retirement in 1968. He was in the British Army during World War II. He spent a brief period at Oxford between 1949 and 1951. He continued to preside informally over the Tuesday semi-

Reprinted by permission from "Symposium: Morality, Politics, and Law in the Thought of Michael Oakeshott," *Political Science Reviewer* 29 (Spring 1992): 1–14. Title appeared originally as "An Introduction: Michael Oakeshott's Achievement."

nar of the History of Political Thought Program at LSE, an MSc degree program he had founded, from 1968 through 1980, presenting annually his papers on the nature of historical inquiry, the latter being finally published in *On History* in 1983. Thereafter, he gave up his flat in Covent Garden and retired to his cottage on the Dorset coast.

His education was at St. George's School, Harpenden, and at Cambridge. In the mid-1920s he attended lectures on theology and philosophy in Marburg and Tubingen. It is uncertain whether he heard Heidegger lecture at Marburg in 1926. Some have the impression that he said he did; others that he said he did not. It is certain that in the 1920s in Cambridge he belonged to a small society of Cambridge dons (never more than eight or nine) called the "D Society" which met regularly to read papers on theological subjects. One of his papers, "Religion and the Moral Life," was published in 1927. He has recalled to me in a letter how he and others of this group went to hear Schweitzer, whose *Quest for the Historical Jesus* he much admired, play the organ at Trinity College Chapel in 1925. In the last years of his life he returned to this field reading such works as Jaroslav Pelikan's *Jesus through the Centuries*.

In "Religion and the Moral Life,"[1] Oakeshott rejects the idea that religion and morality are identical, proposing, rather, that "morality is a condition of religious belief," having to do with "honesty with oneself." "Religion," he argued, "if it is an activity of human beings must be the activity of moral personalities; and no religious doctrine or notion can properly be called 'religious' if it does not accord with the requirements of moral personality. . . . Since religion is a relation between God and moral persons, all notions of irresistible grace operating mechanically are impossible, for the characteristic of moral personality is its autonomy."[2] The moral and the religious, in short, are intertwined, and it is in our self-enactment that we discover the way they go together in our particular circumstances. It follows both that a religious community can never be fully articulated in abstract rules or catechetical exercises, and also that the boundaries

1. See Michael Oakeshott, *Religion, Politics, and the Moral Life*, 39–45.
2. Oakeshott, *Religion. Politics, and the Moral Life*, 40.

between the "church" and the "world" will always be uncertain. The boundaries will vary and will depend a good deal on the moral imagination.

In the moral dimension as such we will always face the ordeal of living up to one "ought" after another; no success in one case guarantees success in the next; no success in one case precludes another case for which we may or may not find adequate ways to respond. Moral life is an endless series. "In religion," Oakeshott says, "we achieve goodness, not by becoming better, but by losing ourselves in God. For goodness is never achieved by becoming better: that is the self-contradiction of morality that always runs the risk of being self-defeating. Religion, then, is the completion of morality, not in the sense of a final end to an historical series, but as the concrete whole is the completion of all the abstractions analysis may discover in it. Religion is not the sanction of morality, but the whole of which morality is an aspect, and in which mere morality perishes, that is, is discovered as an abstraction." Those familiar with *Experience and Its Modes* will perceive the embryo of its argument here.

Oakeshott thus concluded that the absolute independence of the moral personality is the condition of knowing the absolute dependence upon God, where such dependence does not and cannot mean blindly obeying God's will. Otherwise, the moral would not be the moral, and a defining characteristic of the human would be excluded. But, Oakeshott goes on, the formal autonomy of the moral personality has to be connected to a moral content: "Free action is not moral action unless it is also wise. . . . A concrete moral action is the autonomous, free, *and adequate* reaction of a personality to a situation." Morality, in short, inevitably issues in a history of actual conduct as it reveals a feature of the universal character of the human. We cannot be religious without enacting a pattern of moral practices; we cannot enact a pattern of moral practices without being driven, implicitly or explicitly, by a desire for that completion in goodness which can never be captured fully in the particular decisions we take in the effort to do what we think it our duty to do.

This early essay suggests a way to grasp Oakeshott's life-long interest in theology and early church history which is little known to most of his readers because, after the early 1930s, he wrote virtually nothing overtly on these topics. Toward the end of his life he often remarked on his intention to have written more but that it was now "too late." Discerning readers of his essays will note passages in his essays, and one four-page section of *On Human Conduct*, that allow this interest to break through.

He was always reticent on this subject (he thought reticence was an appropriate acknowledgment of inevitable limitation), feeling that ours was not an age of much capacity for profound theological discussion. He thought it would be neither easy to state theological issues satisfactorily nor for readers to think with imagination on such matters. For him, theologizing required an imaginatively powerful construction of human experience as the encounter with the eternal in the midst of the ineluctable temporality of our existence. He thought that St. Augustine enjoyed the greatest religious imagination within our tradition and after him Pascal. A clue to his religious sensibility may be found in his admiration for Walter Pater's novel, *Gaston de la Tour*, wherein is depicted the pilgrimage of a character who seeks beyond formalities the experience of the divine in all things, but who does not forget the necessity of practical judgment and skepticism toward claims made on behalf of personal "insights" and "revelations." J. H. Shorthouse's romantic *John Inglesant*, was another of Oakeshott's favorites. He once told me that, as a young man, he often made excursions to Little Gidding "just to see it." Indeed, in the last several years of his life, we conversed more often than not on topics like these; his exegeses of classic theological writings were remarkable and sometimes startling. It is a genuine loss that we shall not have them in written form. Oakeshott could strike one as an eccentric religious pilgrim with a sometimes stoic, but always a strongly romantic, if not bohemian, streak. Life for him was an adventure, a quest that, as with Don Quixote, was often uncertain of its direction. But as an intellectual adventurer, Oakeshott did not find that an uncertain destination left him with no sense of how to proceed. It is a pervading theme in his work that one need not understand everything that is going on in order to find an intelligible place for oneself.

His political philosophy, with its preference for a "civil association," maximizing the opportunity for individuals to find their own adventures, and his rejection of "rationalism," as a perversion of the medieval quest (a move from slaying the dragons that cross one's path to defining the world as a single great dragon to be put right), are intimately tied to this religious-philosophical attitude. One can also see that his critique of rationalism is akin to his rejection of the idea of morality as a completable, cumulative series of human actions. One needs to notice these features to see him whole.

There lurks also a connection to intellectual developments that run from Coleridge to T. S. Eliot, a connection that would have been difficult for him to accept insofar as its expression was too explicit. We find a clue in his admiration for Michael Foster's writings, particularly *Mystery and Philosophy*, which emphasize the contingency of existence. All of these catalysts for his thought, no doubt surprising to many of his readers, move in the context of the influence on him of the ancient quest for the whole, of Hobbes's theological perspective which, to our misfortune, he expounded only briefly in "Leviathan: A Myth" (1947), and of Hegel's and Bradley's philosophy of religion. We can find parallels in the stories of Joseph Conrad and of Isak Dinesen, for both of whom he had the utmost admiration. It was evident in his conversation that these thinkers and writers fit together to him whereas many would find them jarringly inapposite.

II

The essays in the present collection[3] mark the first sustained effort, following his death in December 1990, to assess his contribution to contemporary political philosophy. It is also the first collection of essays by political philosophers devoted to him since the special issue of *Political Theory* in 1976. The essays herein address several issues central to contemporary debates in political philosophy. They help clarify what the issues are and show the originality of Oakeshott's contribution. Each author is thoroughly acquainted with Oakeshott's writ-

3. I am referring here to the essays in "Symposium: Morality, Politics, and Law in the Thought of Michael Oakeshott," *Political Science Reviewer* 29 (Spring 1992): 1–14.

ings as a whole. Several of them studied under him as graduate students at LSE, two of them wrote their dissertations on his work, one was a colleague of his for twenty years. Readers will discover that, typical of "Oakeshottians," these essayists do not engage in hagiography; they create a conversation with Oakeshott and among themselves. This collection does not take up every relevant topic—there are no essays on Oakeshott's philosophy of education or on his interpretation of Hobbes. But there is more than enough here to show the direction that discussion of Oakeshott's thought is likely to take.

Paul Franco's essay offers a virtual summary of the middle period of Oakeshott's work as encapsulated in the collection of essays, originally written between 1947 and 1960, in *Rationalism in Politics* (1962). The new, expanded edition (1991) adds six more essays, extending the period covered from 1932 to 1975, but shows the consistency in Oakeshott's thought that Franco suggests, even over that much longer period. *Rationalism in Politics* will probably remain the principal point of entry into Oakeshott's work. It will continue to be the best way to make acquaintance with his work.

Franco explains in careful detail how Oakeshott's attack on "rationalism," while occasioned in part by opposition to the collectivist character of post-war British politics, was much more, and decisively, developed from his long-standing philosophical skepticism going back to *Experience and Its Modes*, and to essays criticizing Bentham and Mannheim in the 1930s. Franco argues that the single "passionate thought" unifying Oakeshott's work from early to late is his expression of the distinctively human as the ceaseless endeavor to bring all experience into coherency by means of immanent critique and reflection. The always-to-be-sought, never-quite-to-be-achieved unity of experience as a whole is the driving force of human life; in this all human beings, qua human, participate.

Moreover, one could add that one form of the expression of this "passionate thought" was Oakeshott's regular resort to the ancient story of man's prideful aspiration to join the divine and the punishment for it, induced by a misunderstanding of our "autonomy." As Franco points out, Oakeshott, contrary to many modern thinkers, distinguishes the liberal tradition, which he wishes to defend, from rationalism and progressivism.

Oakeshott denies the transparency of the social order to individual reason and insists instead that the liberal aspiration has to do with limiting and dispersing power. The liberal tradition is, for Oakeshott, constituted in opposition to the politics of uniformity and perfection. The universal passion for the coherency of the whole of experience overwhelms claims to uniformity and perfection precisely because such claims will always caricature the whole, settling for an imitation, and thus must become barriers to the apprehension of the whole that is sought. Eventually, all putative perfections and uniformities will be burst apart by the neverending development of the human spirit in its quest for fulfillment. Oakeshott's very idea of what the human spirit seeks (shared with Plato, Augustine, and Hegel) leads him to a critique of all claims to have completed, or to know how to complete, that search.

Oakeshott's invocation of the Tower of Babel connects to Franco's demonstration of the centrality for Oakeshott of the concrete universal, showing that freedom, the prime value of the liberal tradition, cannot have a merely abstract definition; freedom finds its rationality in coming to terms with the structure of a historically evolved world of practices and procedures, and ultimately with the formal expression of the intersection of this free play of the human spirit with its contingent conditions through a rule of law in a "civil association." In this, Franco prepares the way for the discussions of Oakeshott's remarkable contribution to the philosophy of law and the modern state in the essays of Richard Friedman and David Mapel.

Robert Orr covers much the same ground as Franco, but sees the character of Oakeshott's work very differently. Whereas Franco insists on subtle transpositions within a framework of strong consistency, Orr finds unresolved tensions in Oakeshott's intellectual development. Orr also prefers the Oakeshott of *Rationalism in Politics* over the Oakeshott of *Experience and Its Modes* and especially of *On Human Conduct*.

What Orr prefers is the Montaigne-like, skeptical Oakeshott who knows that all intellectual constructions inevitably fail to manage and hold together the diversity of experiences they try to encompass. This is the Oakeshott—an authentic Oakeshottian character without doubt—who seeks rather humbly and unassumingly to be at home in that corner of the world which is his allotted portion, and who is not seduced by efforts at systematic philosophic construction. This Oakeshott appeals as one who combats rationalism precisely by refusing to speak or to act in a manner that concedes anything to the rationalists. This is the Oakeshott of the "voice of poetry in the conversation of mankind," who looks for the delightful in the midst of the drab and who is sufficiently intrigued by his own circumstances to find adequate adventure at home and in quiet conversation with friends.

Orr brings this out by sharply delineating the antagonism between Aristotle's earthy, animal human being who barely peeks out from nature, and the abstract Oakeshottian agent, divorced from nature, portrayed in *On Human Conduct.* The late work of Oakeshott, as Orr argues, defined human beings as "agents" extricating themselves from the natural in favor of the realm of purely human, purely intellectual reflection (a reintroduction of Kantian elements he earlier seemed to have set aside). Thus, Orr shows that there is an unresolved, perhaps unresolvable, conflict in Oakeshott's thought.

This tension may well be related to a decision on Oakeshott's part that we are so far gone from the ability to appreciate traditionality that it became necessary to recast his earlier arguments in language appropriate to the prevailing intellectual idioms. But if so, Orr would argue that Oakeshott was mistaken to do so because it diluted the protest against modernity that was central. In contrast to Franco, then, Orr would argue that Oakeshott's "concrete universal" was finally lost from sight in his later work in favor of the expression of an abstract "ideal" of "civil association."

The dialogue between these two interpretations is a consequence of a complex effort on Oakeshott's part—reminiscent of Hegel, or more recently Gadamer, to mediate between the formalities and the contingencies of existence. For example, while Oakeshott was perhaps not, philosophically speaking, interested in the natural world, as Orr points out, he was in his personal life a devoted gardener, and in his personal relations forever a man of local and habitual affections. Thus, one might read *Rationalism in Politics* as an essay on civil society and *On Human Conduct* as a formal development of law and the state, seeing the two works in dialectical tension, qualifying and constraining each other.

Richard Friedman's essay expounds Oakeshott's idea of law in the context of contemporary legal philosophy. Friedman develops this topic, central to Oakeshott's thinking, in a way that should shape critical discussion for some time to come. What comes to light is that Oakeshott was one of the most remarkable philosophers of law in our time.

We can see in Friedman's discussion part of an answer to resolving conflicting tendencies, revealed by Franco and Orr, in terms of a theory of law and political authority. Friedman's essay shows how human beings, understood as subjects of law, continually reconcile agency with particularity: Oakeshott could respond to the quite reasonable dissent posed by Orr, that Aristotle did, in this sense, foreshadow his own work on law, authority, and civil association.

In Friedman's account, Oakeshott's agent is one who can always act otherwise, but who must act. As Hegel said, ideas are not so impotent as to remain only ideas: they have consequences. An agent is a human being with an idea of himself—a self-understanding—which unavoidably makes itself manifest in actions and utterances in the world. An answer to the alleged abstraction of the agent, in short, is to say that agency must realize itself concretely; it cannot avoid doing so. The agent must make a history and cannot remain only in the realm of ideas, while equally the history, even in its particularity, is the exhibition of the universal human capacity for self-conscious agency. Agents must seek their actuality according to some limiting conditions of doing so. Agents may be able always to act otherwise, but they also have their specific identities as they put themselves into action. They make themselves something in particular, and this is not lost but embedded in their actual lives. In a sense, agents are always "solving" the problem of their own abstractness, but never solving it once and for all. For this and other reasons, Horst Mewes will remind us in his essay that for Oakeshott it is crucial that a human being is a continually emerging, self-enacting dramatic identity, not a closed character. Self-enactment is not mere behavior, it is an interpretation for action of one's life.

Law and authority, then, are necessary elements in arranging our-selves in relation to each other so that whether taken as agents overcoming our own abstractness or as self-disclosing, self-enacting dramatic identities, we can live together cooperatively and not merely in self-defeating antagonism. In explicating how he conceived this, Friedman's is the best and most accurate account known to me of Oakeshott's intentions regarding the definitions of law and political authority.

Friedman distinguishes "neutrality" from "non-instrumentality" so clearly as to change the direction of subsequent discussions of this matter on the part of Oakeshott's critics. He also shows that Oake-shott's now widely known distinction between "civil association" and "enterprise association" is a distinction between that sort of com-pulsory association which is consistent with the freedom human be-ings enjoy in understanding themselves as agents of themselves—i.e., civil association—and that sort of association proper only when it is voluntary: enterprise association. The emphasis on law as non-instrumental, rather than as neutral, refers to the way in which a subject of law, who is an agent, is actually subject to law. One dis-covers how it is possible to be rule-governed and still autonomous. This will lend support to John Coats's essay which discovers strong affinities to republicanism in Oakeshott's opposition to the tenden-cies of democratic cultures, obsessively concerned to satisfy bodily desires, to seek compulsory enterprise associations.

David Mapel's essay complements Friedman's by comparing Oakeshott's thought on law and the state to the work of H. L. A. Hart and Lon Fuller. Oakeshott's legal philosophy falls on neither side but rather, using elements characteristic of arguments of each, mediates among the tension-ridden strands of the efforts to define the char-acter of the law. Mapel shows that for Oakeshott there is both a dis-tinction between "moral duty" and "legal obligation," and also that there is an "inner morality of the law" and also "justice."

Mapel also takes up the question of the non-instrumental law rightly showing that, for Oakeshott, the responses necessitated by legal rules are not specified by the rules themselves. But he goes on to show that, in the act of subscribing to rules in particular circumstances, individuals do balance and weigh competing norms of moral duty and do consider external consequences of their actions even though under the constraints they have accepted in the law. The adequacy of the rules will depend on the adequacy of our action in specifying what the rules do not themselves initially specify. Thus, to Mapel's way of thinking, a pure non-instrumental civil association is neither possible nor desirable.

Mapel concludes that "if civil association must have purposes, there is no set of purposes it must have." There is a sort of constrained instrumentality. He gives a qualified assent to Oakeshott's effort to theorize a special kind of civil order in which the operation of the laws comes from our "specification," not from deduction, weighing, or balancing, but which yet does not free us from having to draw rough and ready lines, depending on our diagnosis of current political life, between too much purposiveness and too little. Herein Mapel reminds us of Orr's conclusion about the problem of defining unambiguously what is an "adverbial background" condition of action and what is an expression of purpose.

Finally, Mapel shows that Oakeshott's originality is to depart from most current political theorists who merely debate which purposes they want to pursue, who do not ask themselves seriously whether pursuing purposes is the most significant undertaking, or whether civil association could ever be coherently organized merely by debating alternative purposes.

John Coats's essay breaks new ground by illuminating an implicit connection between Oakeshott's political philosophy and the theory of republicanism. He points out, as do Franco, Friedman, and Mapel, that Oakeshott does not defend individualism by resort to a doctrine of rights but by appeal to the authority of law. This leads Coats to compare an ideal republican character to an ideal democratic character.

As Coats understands the republican tradition, it honors an association based on mutual deference among genuinely diverse talents. Such an association defines as virtues discipline and civility, and encounters liberty not in "the silence of the laws," but in the "generality of the laws." Mature republicans are self-dependent, have no felt need or desire for "political leadership," and think of themselves as creating a rational order for themselves in terms of their own resources and traditions, neither looking to outsiders for guidance, nor expecting outsiders to affirm their self-chosen way of life. Political activity in a republican order consists in continually revising and exploiting traditional knowledge or, as Oakeshott famously put it, politics is there known to be "the pursuit of intimations."

By contrast, democratic characters understand themselves to be pursuing power for the purpose of controlling the distribution of goods. They define their pursuits in tangible, bodily ways and are prone to egalitarianism under the influence of the dominance of the body. Politics is reduced to competition for the same basic goods at the expense of the appreciation of true diversity, and is driven by the experience of relative deprivation and the hope of relief through leaders. There is a powerful temptation to assume the universality of this outlook, to assert prejudices as trans-prejudicial, and to claim to leap from ignorance to certainty by means of technique (to rely on the "rationalism" Oakeshott opposes).

Finally, Horst Mewes breaks important ground by providing, so far as I know, the first major, direct comparison of Oakeshott with Hannah Arendt and Leo Strauss based on thorough and equal conversancy with the writings of all three. Mewes does so by emphasizing Oakeshott's concern for the religious dimension of self-enactment as the overcoming of contingency contrasted with self-disclosure as the mere finding of one's place in the contingent. This is significant since most previous commentary on Oakeshott has not seen this nor put him into the context of his contemporaries in political philosophy.

Mewes shows that the questions of "agency" and "autonomy" are, for all three thinkers, fundamental questions of political philosophy. All three thinkers place the question of "the status of individuality," and their fear of individuality's tendency to self-destruction, at the center of their thinking. All three are struck by the banality of modern, democratic culture, all have republican tendencies (either Greek or modern), all are classically educated. Yet only Oakeshott, despite agreeing with Arendt and Strauss on much of the modern pathology, thinks that autonomy is not illusory. He thus embraces the modern liberal tradition, while Arendt and Strauss, each in a different way, express grave doubts.

Mewes shows that Oakeshott's individualism is not a "doctrine" of the individual: "Oakeshott's notion of individuality precludes a self based on any purely 'internal' principle, instinct, normative intuition or inspiration attempting to assert . . . claims." The Oakeshottian self makes itself in and through "intelligent engagement" with the world and is "expansively adventurous."

While Oakeshott rejects all doctrines of human nature, contra Strauss's neoclassicism, he does not reject the possibility of a focal meaning of the human. Doctrines of human nature, for Oakeshott, are crystallizations of specific congeries of interrelated historical experiences, in all of which the faculty of human self-consciousness has shown itself in multifaceted ways. As such, these doctrines of human nature are enlightening and to be examined philosophically, but they cannot adequately capture and define once and for all the inexhaustible play of the human spirit in its universal, perpetual quest for self-understanding.

Oakeshott carries this far enough to assert that, again contra Strauss, even the apparent primacy of the practical is only apparent. All forms of human understanding are conditional. Practical understandings are limiting intepretations of the possible ways to act responsibly toward the widely varying circumstances of time and place.

For Oakeshott, the defining, permanent character of the human cannot be realized once and for all, definitively or paradigmatically. Autonomy is not, then, to be sought by imagining that one is bringing oneself into conformity with a perfect model. Rather, autonomy is realized in the artfulness of a life, in that intellectual and emotional maturity that enables one to discover the nuances of possibility in the situations in which one finds oneself. Excellence lies in the formal perfection of action vis-à-vis one's associates in instances of opportunity for action, but never once and for all; it is the adornment that accompanies freely chosen action despite the limits of one's resources for responding to the demands of contingent situations.

But what Oakeshott takes to be real, Arendt, expounding much the same experience, finds to be an illusion. For her the central feature of human action is the endless endeavor to extricate ourselves from the merely natural—toward what? Toward greatness and glory. In doing this, however, the action always will exceed the understanding so that the human will never know what it really is. The modest solidity of Oakeshott's world, its inhabitants confident of reaching some modicum of self-understanding, and thus a degree of flexible stability in the midst of contingency, dissipates in the mystery with which Arendt surrounds the human effort to be fully—purely—human. Thus, although Oakeshott understands human action as the creation of a dramatic identity, he resists defining, as Arendt does, the dramatic as the ineffable, the endless overcoming of human emptiness. At the same time, he finds Strauss's return to ancient concepts of human nature too restrictive for the full play of human consciousness. This will also explain why it is that Oakeshott, in his critique of modernity, shows neither nostalgia for the ancient alternatives, nor a sense of excessive futility about the present.

Oakeshott's is a quasi-traditional notion of character as situated between nothingness and eternity, capable of self-enactment as an encounter with eternity, as autonomy within the dailiness of life, wherein religious sentiment is both a completion and admission of a limit.

III

We have, then, a set of independently developed essays which cohere in noticing salient features of Oakeshott's thought: his critique of modern rationalism, his theory of human agency and human knowing, his theory of autonomy and of the distinctively human, his concept of law and of political authority, and his exposition of the way we live now with civil association as the appropriate ordering of such lives as we have learned to lead.

It was Oakeshott's view that philosophy is an accidental discovery we make when we break into conversations questioning our assumptions only to discover the conditionality of all human knowing. This leads some contemporaries to imagine that he was, after all, a post-modernist thinker. We do not know what he would have thought about this argument; it came too late in the day for him to respond.

In fact, however, he learned from Socratic inquiry, from the Augustinian assault on Babelian pridefulness, from the skepticism of Montaigne, Hobbes, and Hume, from the confrontation with our unresolved inbetweenness in Pascal and Hegel, and from other lesser sources. He could be and was amused by the antiquity of contemporary philosophical prejudices. He was aware that the modern world regularly promotes itself on the grounds of its supposed novelty. He saw Towers of Babel forever being built under disguise and with clever circumlocutions so as to obscure to ourselves that the way we live now resembles the way we have always lived. In opposing stories of our greatness with stories of our littleness, he nonetheless affirmed the imaginative power of the human spirit. In our end is our beginning, he could have said. The details of political debate he judged in the light that wisdom begins in knowing that we do not know.

The Poetics of the Civil Life

MICHAEL OAKESHOTT WAS BORN on December 11, 1901, in the county of Kent, and died on December 19, 1990, at his nineteenth-century quarryman's cottage, on the edge of the Purbeck marble quarries, in the tiny village of Acton on the Dorset coast. His academic career began at Cambridge in the early 1920s. He was a Life Fellow of Gonville & Caius College where his portrait now presides over the faculty dining room, and he remained a university lecturer in history until the end of the 1940s with an interlude of military service in the Second World War. Following a brief time at Oxford he took the Professorship of Political Science at the London School of Economics in 1951.

The latter appointment, at the time, was a matter of much political gossip. The Churchill government had been thrown out of office in 1945, but then the Tories and Churchill regained power just as the chair in political science, previously held by the very prominent and socialist Harold Laski, became vacant. The appointment of the conservative Oakeshott to a post at the heart of the university in Britain most famous for its association with Sidney and Beatrice Webb and the Fabian Socialists, was a scandal among the intelligentsia. For years, many British academics disdained Oakeshott as a political

Reprinted by permission from Timothy Fuller, *The Achievement of Michael Oakeshott*, ed. Jesse Norman (London: Gerald Duckworth, 1993), 67–81.

appointee. And they were not reassured by his inaugural lecture, "Political Education," which has become a celebrated example of the sceptical attitude to politics reminiscent of the essays of David Hume or Michel de Montaigne. In that lecture, Oakeshott rejected the politics of infinite progress through the propagation of ideological programmes for the radical transformation of the human condition. In particular, he insisted it was not the vocation of the political philosopher to change the world but to understand it.

In saying this, Oakeshott was challenging Marx's dictum in the "Theses on Feuerbach" that the purpose of modern thought was not to explain but to change the world. Marx had set himself up as a court of appeal, ruling on philosophic schools as to whether they were revolutionary or good as opposed to reactionary or bad. From the perspective of a Marx-influenced intellectual environment Oakeshott inevitably was seen as a reactionary.

What has become clear since then, however, particularly as the influence of Marxist categories has been increasingly challenged, is that Oakeshott was not at all interested in going back to an earlier state of affairs. His conservative disposition was quite far removed from any nostalgic reaction, or from any neo-conservative or neo-liberal counter-ideology. Thus he never really became the guru of Thatcherism as some who lack subtlety have alleged.

What he meant was that each generation must do the best it can with the resources it has in responding to circumstances it did not choose but cannot avoid. The idea that we are better than our forebears he thought pretentious and proved largely by self-affirmation. In his view of the human condition, the delights of life are seldom to be found by continually seeking to transpose everything into a goal-oriented project. Conservatism to him meant enjoying the possibilities of the present, the only time one has actually got to do something with. He deplored, for example, the politicisation of the universities because he saw that it would rob students of the one brief interval in life when they could explore the delights of learning for its own sake without the burdens of immediate practical responsibility.

He had little brief for the current preoccupation with "leadership" and "problem-solving," and little praise for the lingering influence of Benthamite calculation. The view that life's meaning is always to be found in the quest for some future condition, putatively superior to the present, he found a sad misunderstanding of what it means to be human.

For years after his inaugural, critics accused him of pessimism or even nihilism. This response signified to Oakeshott that we live in a peculiarly faithless age. He meant that the nihilism is actually lodged in those who cannot find value in the present life, or anywhere but in politics, but must always seek some other world. This represented to him a deep-seated denial of life's meaning expressed paradoxically as a quest for a meaning which is not yet. By contrast he lauded the poet for delighting in the beauty of images, the composer who thinks in melodic lines. I shall soon try to illustrate this idea of his a bit more.

Oakeshott was the most significant British political philosopher of our century and yet, like Montaigne, for whom he had the greatest admiration, a man of specific locality and an idiosyncratic turn of mind. Oakeshott was in the modern world, and one of its most profound analysts, but not of it. His cottage had no central heating or television and only recently a telephone. The advantages of these amenities he thought exaggerated, perhaps not altogether good for us. To the last, he corresponded in a tiny, rather elegant script, disdaining the typewriter, much less the word-processor.

Oakeshott surveyed the world without feeling compelled to roam it. He had a great attachment to certain places in the world—the France of Montaigne, Siena, the mountains of Colorado, Cambridge, or Winchester Cathedral which he sometimes stopped to visit when travelling between London and Dorset—but he felt no necessity to go to them. He had a clear vision of these places from afar, and that was sufficient. He had no interest in photographs, and to my knowledge never took a snapshot in his life.

Seeking to understand himself, he welcomed travellers to his cottage whose conversation would complement his own and check his observations. In writing, his genre was the essay which in his case, as Emerson said of Montaigne's essays, was the transfer of conversations to the written page. What he wrote he saw as invitations to his readers to respond conversationally, not as arguments seeking to end all argument. He thought his essays merely revealed the reasons he had come to accept for the views he took. He easily admitted that others might see things differently. Civility, the mark of humanity, was the acknowledgment of the uncertainty of all human knowing. His essays carry on a tradition in English letters we associate with the names of Bacon, Hume, Macaulay, and John Stuart Mill.

He was a shrewd judge of character and yet he had a romantic streak. His judgments seldom turned judgmental, and he regularly preferred to serve those who might reasonably have been expected to serve him. He did not look for reasons to be negative.

Friendship and love were central to his life. The relationship of friends, he said, "is dramatic, not utilitarian." Loving is not doing good, nor is it a duty, but the communication of one unique self to another: "Neither merit nor necessity has any part in the generation of love; its progenitors are chance and choice—chance because what cannot be identified in advance cannot be sought; and in choice the inescapable practical component of desire makes itself felt."[1]

Encounters with him were dramatic but not melodramatic, memorable but not at the price of one's composure. He led his life as if he knew friendship and love were to be found, and yet he was always joyfully surprised when they came his way. It is hard to imagine that he ever appraised anyone in terms of their potential usefulness to himself.

The phrase "chance and choice" occurs elsewhere in Oakeshott's writings only in relation to his definition of politics as attending to the arrangements of a set of people "whom chance or choice have brought together." The connotations of the phrase differ from love to politics, but what is implicit in both is his view of life as an adventure fraught with contingency and encompassed in mystery. He transposed the idea of pilgrimage in the religious and chivalric senses into the drama of self-discovery. Biblical language was never far from his thought, particularly those myths which most vividly and imaginatively evoked the human condition.

Most powerful for him was that Genesis story on which, in fact, he published two different essays thirty-five years apart (1948 and

1. Michael Oakeshott, "The Voice of Poetry in the Conversation of Mankind" (1959) in *Rationalism in Politics* (1962), 244.

1983), calling both "The Tower of Babel." This was the biblical source of his scepticism. He found that story a most relevant comment on modern rationalism which he disdained not alone by comparison to Platonic and Scholastic rationalism, but especially by comparison to his view that life is a traveller's tale. There is a course to follow, but with no simple or certain destination. His models were as diverse as *Sir Gawain and the Green Knight, Amadis of Gaul, Don Quixote*, Montaigne's *Essays*, Shakespeare's romances, J. H. Shorthouse's *John Inglesant*, Walter Pater's *Gaston de la Tour*, Willa Cather's *My Antonia*, Joseph Conrad's sea stories, cowboy stories of the Old West, and the tales of Isak Dinesen.

In a little-read essay, "Leviathan: A Myth" (1947), Oakeshott revealed the tie of his lifelong interest in Hobbes—the one major thinker on whom he wrote extensively—to the religious imagination that was distinctively his:

> The myth of the Fall of Man, says Berdyaev, "is at bottom a proud idea. . . . If man fell away from God, he must have been an exalted creature, endowed with great freedom and power." But in the myth of our civilisation as it appears in *Leviathan* the emphasis is on the opposite pole; it recalls man to his littleness, his imperfection, his mortality . . . what makes *Leviathan* a masterpiece of philosophical literature is the profound logic of Hobbes's imagination, his power as an artist. Hobbes recalls us to our mortality with a deliberate conviction, with a subtle and sustained argument. He, with a sure and steady irony, does what Swift could do with only an intermittent brilliance, and what the literature of Existentialism is doing today with an exaggerated display of emotion and a false suggestion of novelty.[2]

It is a mark of Oakeshott's originality to have seen Hobbes as a brilliant contributor to the organising myths of our civilisation and not merely as the prototype of modern secularism and rational choice.

2. Michael Oakeshott, "Leviathan: A Myth" (1949) in *Hobbes on Civil Association* (1975), 153ff.

Oakeshott thought egalitarian politics fallacious, but he was a spiritual democrat: he did not think anyone could gain exemption from the limits of mortal human existence; he was Augustinian, not Pelagian. He thought Hobbes a touchstone for our era which needed to be recalled both to the contingent character of its knowledge and to an admission of its mortality:

> The pursuit of perfection as the crow flies is an activity both impious and unavoidable in human life. It involves the penalties of impiety (the anger of the gods and social isolation), and its reward is not that of achievement but that of having made the attempt. It is an activity, therefore, suitable for individuals, but not for societies. For an individual who is impelled to engage in it, the reward may exceed both the penalty and the inevitable defeat. The penitent may hope, or even expect, to fall back a wounded hero, into the arms of an understanding and forgiving society. And even the impenitent can be reconciled with himself in the powerful necessity of his impulse, though, like Prometheus, he must suffer for it. For a society, on the other hand, the penalty is a chaos of conflicting ideals, the disruption of a common life, and the reward is the renown which attaches to monumental folly.[3]

While rejecting talk of a "human nature," Oakeshott none the less affirmed the abiding presence of something categorically human that does not differ now from what it was in the past. Like Aristotle, Oakeshott insisted the distinctiveness of being human manifests itself in the faculty of conversation:

> As civilised human beings, we are the inheritors, neither of an inquiry about ourselves and the world, nor of an accumulating body of information, but of a conversation, begun in the primeval forests and extended and made more articulate in the course of centuries. . . . It is the ability to participate in this conversation, and not the ability to reason cogently, to

3. Michael Oakeshott, "The Tower of Babel" (1948) in *Rationalism in Politics*, 59–79.

make discoveries about the world, or to contrive a better world, which distinguishes the human being from the animal and the civilised man from the barbarian.[4]

In short, we have been fully human from that primeval moment when human beings discovered their humanity by sitting down to talk. The civilised are those anywhere who know this; the barbarians are those anywhere who resist knowing it. Yet, as conversational beings, we are endlessly implicated in an engagement of self-discovery and association; we have a history, he thought, not a nature. Doctrines and orthodoxies are always to be adjusted to new conditions; ideologies come and go, for they are momentary coagulations in the fluid sea of human utterance, caricatures of a complex reality. They crystallise only to dissolve, and they will never satisfactorily substitute for, nor exhaust the revelations of, the masterpieces of religious, political, poetic, and scientific thinking. The latter, in their probing revelations of the human predicament, resist all efforts to be reduced to textbooks or "solutions" to "problems."

Similarly, human beings are in principle free: to be human, Oakeshott thought, is to be a reflective intelligence interpreting the surrounding circumstances and responding in accordance with what one understands or misunderstands the character—the possibilities and the limitations—of those circumstances to be. Human beings must learn everything. We are what we learn to become. We find ourself born into a world already shaped by those who came before us and who seem to understand what we have yet to understand. We must appropriate that world to ourselves as best we can, and no one can do it for us.[5]

In elaborating Oakeshott's political outlook, it is necessary to see what is often missed by commentators: his outlook is suffused with a religious character that yields no easy doctrinal formulations because its motive is not to construct propositions. His inspiration is the pre-Reformation religious imagination of popular Christianity filtered through the romantic expression of nineteenth-century poetics:

4. Oakeshott, "The Voice of Poetry" (1959) in *Rationalism in Politics*, 199.
5. Michael Oakeshott, *On Human Conduct* (first essay); Michael Oakeshott, "A Place of Learning" (1974).

Religious faith is the evocation of a sentiment (the love, the glory, or the honour of God, for example, or even a humble *caritas*), to be added to all others as the motive of all motives in terms of which the fugitive adventures of human conduct, without being released from their mortal and their moral conditions, are graced with an intimation of immortality: the sharpness of death and the deadliness of doing overcome, and the transitory sweetness of a mortal affection, the tumult of a grief and the passing beauty of a May morning recognised neither as merely evanescent adventures nor as emblems of better things to come, but as *aventures*, themselves encounters with eternity.[6]

In passages such as these, Oakeshott's distinctive appreciation, and affirmation, of the human shines through. His view of politics, numerous critics of a certain kind notwithstanding, bespoke neither pessimism nor nihilism. The most often quoted passage on this point is this:

In political activity, then, men sail a boundless and bottomless sea; there is neither harbour for shelter nor floor for anchorage, neither starting-place nor appointed destination. The enterprise is to keep afloat on an even keel; the sea is both friend and enemy; and the seamanship consists in using the resources of a traditional manner of behaviour in order to make a friend of every hostile occasion.[7]

Juxtaposing the latter with his evocation of the encounter with eternity, one sees that, fascinated though he was by the study of politics, Oakeshott found the heart of life elsewhere. Oakeshott is the preeminent antagonist of all those today who wish to reduce the meaning of life to political action. The fatality of the political life, he thought, is that it is always tempted to think of acting once and for all, perhaps for the last time. In the nature of things, however, this is what politics can never do, and what it would hate if it ever actually verged on

6. Oakeshott, *On Human Conduct*, 85.
7. Michael Oakeshott, "Political Education" (1951) in *Rationalism in Politics*, 127.

doing it. Politics must thrive on its own dissatisfaction, seeking that completion which would be the final contradiction of what makes the activity attract to begin with.

If this is not precisely the Augustinian doctrine of the two cities, it is nevertheless a comparable imagining of the fault-lines of our existence: we are caught between contemplation and delight on the one hand and the "deadliness of doing," "the *danse macabre* of wants and satisfactions," on the other. Insofar as this differs from Augustine's formulation, it is because Oakeshott derived from Hegel the engagement to avoid the appearance of dualism in characterising human experience, believing, as did Hegel, that the modern world was distinguished by the task to refuse the estrangement of the spiritual and the material. For Oakeshott, this meant that the modalities of experience were encompassed in the unity of experience as a whole; every way of knowing is a way of being in the world—we are in ourselves what we are for ourselves. To grasp historical existence—the meeting of time and eternity—would involve comprehending Hegel chastened by Augustine. This is a project, ultimately theological in nature, which Oakeshott long thought of pursuing but never undertook.

Politics is a necessary evil, neither to be despised nor overrated. That Oakeshott did not take his bearings there is a deficiency only for those who do not share his quest for the poetic intimations of life amidst an otherwise drab activism.

It is in this sense that Oakeshott was willing to call himself a "conservative." All the important activities, he argued, are inherently conservative because they depend not only on acquiring an abstract technique but also on apprenticeship to practitioners who exhibit in their work the background lore or art of the activity which cannot be written down in books or summarised in manuals. The mistake of modern rationalists was to think that the technical part of knowledge could stand by itself, and here he took a view reminiscent of Michael Polanyi's explorations of tacit and personal knowledge.

He was often criticised for insisting on the importance of tradition, and criticised in some quarters as an historicist. Others have asserted that he could not distinguish between the mere givenness of a background and the affirmation of it as good, that he drifted off into some sort of traditionalist mysticism. Oakeshott was seldom given to responding to these criticisms. He might have said that the issue of what is virtuous in our heritage arises out of a discussion conducted in terms of that heritage and by appeal to it. How else is this to take place? He did not see this as a "problem" to which there may be a "solution," or no solution. It is a description of being human that our resources are both inspiring and limiting at the same time.

Thus a conservative disposition followed from recognising what the human situation is. Oakeshott was not urging us to be conservative—he was arguing that we could not help but be so. To deny this is not only to disguise the truth about ourselves, but also to lead us into ill-considered projects for transforming the human race. He sought to derive no specific political programme from this disposition, and he was often sceptical of those programmatic conservatives and neo-conservatives whom he characterised as devising "plans to end all planning." Here he remained consistent with what he understood to be the philosopher's vocation to speak in the indicative, not the hortatory, mood: "Thinking is at first associated with an extraneous desire for action. And it is some time, perhaps, before we discern that philosophy is without any direct bearing upon the practical conduct of life, and that it has certainly never offered its true followers anything which could be mistaken for a gospel."[8] "A philosophical essay," he said, "does not dissemble the conditionality of the conclusions it throws up and although it may enlighten it does not instruct. It is, in short, a well-considered intellectual adventure recollected in tranquillity."[9]

As a political sceptic he could accept the principle that that government is best which governs least. His best government would be one which devised procedural rules, adjudicated disputes when necessary, and had few or no economic resources to distribute, thus leaving it with little power to preach instead of govern.

He thought that the main obstacle to enjoying such a government was the unavoidable and continuous preparation for war that im-

8. Michael Oakeshott, *Experience and Its Modes*, 1.
9. Oakeshott, *On Human Conduct*, vii.

posed upon all modern governments the undertaking to organise society in terms of uniformity of goals, reinforced by infatuation with technology, and the belief that human beings could not be entrusted to take care of themselves unless directed by an extrinsic goal or purpose, an ideology.

Yet he has also been called a classic "liberal."[10] There is much warrant for this view in that it points to his belief in the importance of the individual, of self-reliance, of property rights, of dispersal of governmental power and of the rule of law.[11]

In fact, Oakeshott combined elements of both conservatism and liberalism in his thought. He was not a doctrinaire thinker. He thought he dwelled in a tradition of thinking comprising many nuances. It did not occur to him that one should choose among abstract positions. He was both an individualist and a traditionalist, finding them essential complements. The most careful working out of this is the second essay of *On Human Conduct* wherein he explicates how individuals, by subscribing to "practices," associate themselves with others in terms of a manner of thinking and doing—a language—which gives them an idiom in which to express their talents, but not a command as to what they are to do or to say.

The most famous distinction to emerge from Oakeshott's culminating work, *On Human Conduct* (1975), is that between "enterprise association" and "civil association." Briefly, the former is a voluntary agreement among individuals to associate in the pursuit of a common purpose or purposes. In this sort of association, the individuals become role-players, subordinating themselves to the requirements of succeeding in the chosen pursuit, usually under a manager whose function is to coordinate a division of labour effectively. For Oakeshott, enterprises are intrinsically private activities— even if they involve many or all of the people in a society—because they are associations organised in terms of someone's chosen goal or purpose which is not what others might choose. In principle, then,

10. Most recently by Paul Franco in *The Political Philosophy of Michael Oakeshott* (1990).

11. Michael Oakeshott, "The Political Economy of Freedom" (1949) in *Rationalism in Politics*; and Michael Oakeshott, "The Rule of Law" in *On History and Other Essays* (1983).

it should be voluntary precisely because what it chooses as its organising principle cannot be what everyone would choose, and it must exclude other possible pursuits that do not fit its ambitions.

Civil association, by contrast, is "an intelligent relationship enjoyed only in being learned and understood, distinguished (for example) from relationship in terms of propinquity, kinship, genes" and in which citizens would be associated "neither in respect of a common enterprise nor in procuring the responses of others in seeking the satisfaction of their individual wants, but in terms of a practice or language of civil intercourse which they have not designed or chosen but within the jurisdiction of which they recognise themselves to fall and which, in subscribing to it, they continuously explore and reconstitute."[12]

Oakeshott's ideal commonwealth is "not itself an enterprise, an undertaking, an 'economy,' or an educational or therapeutic organisation, and not enterprisers or groups of enterprisers associated in seeking recognition or advantage for themselves in their undertakings, but an association of *cives*; a relationship of equals, and a self-sufficient condition in being relationship in terms of the conditions of a practice which are not used up in being used and not in terms of a substantive purpose or purposes to be pursued."

In developing these ideas, Oakeshott had also to turn his attention to the nature of authority, of law, and of civil obligation as they would appear in such an ideal civil association. The civil association requires someone to occupy an office of authority that is acknowledged as the source of authoritative pronouncements by those who have subscribed to it. The occupant of an office like this is not privileged with special insight or knowledge, and is certainly not warranted in defining the *summum bonum.* The one who exercises authority is to establish and clarify rules or laws in what Oakeshott called the adverbial form: they are considerations to be taken into account in choosing how to conduct ourselves with each other. "They are not the rules of a game" for that would imply we are already engaged in a common pursuit and more or less repetitive performance. They are not the rules of an enterprise because the rules of an enter-

12. Oakeshott, *On Human Conduct*, 182–83.

prise "specify conditions alleged to be instrumental to the pursuit of what is already recognised as a common purpose."[13] They are rules which "prescribe the common responsibilities (and the counterpart 'rights' to have these responsibilities fulfilled) of agents and in terms of which they put by their characters as enterprisers and put by all that differentiates them from one another and recognise themselves as formal equals—*cives*."[14]

Thus there will always be disputes as to how to subscribe to the rules in the specific actions we choose in our particular circumstances. There must be authority to make rules and to adjudicate disputes over the rules. But none of this implies for Oakeshott development toward common purposes or the elaboration of a managerial policy for relating people to each other efficiently. Adjudication presupposes adherence to the rule of law in the sense defined and is to amplify our understanding of what the law says. This must be done significantly in that it furthers our understanding; justifiably in that a decision must be connected to the law which the adjudication presupposes; appropriately in being the resolution of a specific contingent uncertainty as to what adequate subscription to the law means in a specific case; and durably because it enters into the system of law intelligibly for citizens in deciding their future conduct.[15] Obligations, as opposed to actions taken out of a sense of moral duty, derive from the recognition of the law as authentic, and the law's validity "is a matter to be decided in terms of the resources for decision" provided by the law,[16] and by the continuous reaffirmation of its validity over time on the part of citizens who can distinguish between calculations of personal advantage or disadvantage and relating to each other in a strictly moral or civil relationship: as mutual subscribers to a system of rules that qualify their conduct without imposing specific actions. This is the public realm strictly speaking, detached from distraction by the numerous private pursuits of enterprise relationships.

13. Oakeshott, *Human Conduct*, 128.
14. Oakeshott, *Human Conduct*.
15. Oakeshott, *Human Conduct*, 133.
16. Oakeshott, *Human Conduct*, 151.

But all of this docs not fully reveal his commitment to and felicity in teaching. The original impetus to his academic career was his admiration for his teachers at St. George's School in Hertfordshire. He always thought of himself, first, as a learner, but those of us who saw him at work lecturing or in seminars knew that here was an extraordinary teacher. Even in his seventies, when he limited himself to attending the general seminar in the History of Political Thought at the London School of Economics, and occasionally reading papers on the idea of history, he could identify with students in a special way. He was less put off by the machinations of student politics than many an academic who would be thought to be more "liberal." In a way, he operated as if the university were the civil association the modern state has never quite become.

He had an enormous appreciation of the young and never forgot what it was to be young: "Everybody's young days are a dream, a delightful insanity, a sweet solipsism. Nothing in them has a fixed shape, nothing a fixed price; everything is a possibility, and we live happily on credit. There are no obligations to be observed; there are no accounts to be kept. Nothing is specified in advance; everything is what can be made of it. The world is a mirror in which we seek the reflection of our own desires . . . urgency is our criterion of importance; and we do not easily understand that what is humdrum need not be despicable. We are impatient of restraint; and we readily believe, like Shelley, that to have contracted a habit is to have failed."[17]

I have not personally known anyone who could feel the beauty of youth more intensely even at the end of his days than Oakeshott. The sense of being alive to the possibilities of existence was with him to the end, and it was the secret of his effect on students. He never forgot what it was like for them even though he knew, what too many teachers recently have avoided knowing, that one cannot remain in the youthful dream: "For most there is what Conrad called the 'shadow line' which, when we pass it, discloses a solid world of things, each with its fixed shape, each with its own point of balance, each

17. Michael Oakeshott, "On Being Conservative" (1956) in *Rationalism in Politics*, 195.

with its price; a world of fact, not poetic image, in which what we have spent on one thing we cannot spend on another; a world inhabited by others besides ourselves who cannot be reduced to mere reflections of our own emotions."[18]

The essential works to read are *Experience and Its Modes* (1933), *Rationalism in Politics* (1962; new and expanded edition 1991), *On Human Conduct* (1975), *Hobbes on Civil Association* (1975), *On History and Other Essays* (1983), *The Voice of Liberal Learning* (1989).

As I list these, I remember that one of Oakeshott's favorite stories was of the Chinese wheelwright who could not, at seventy, turn over his craft to his son because his son could not get the hang of it. The wheelwright generalised from his failure to inculcate into his son more than the abstract rules of his craft when he remarked to his Duke, who was reading the words of the sages, that books are "the lees and scum of bygone men." "All that was worth handing on," the wheelwright said, "died with them; the rest, they put in their books." One thinks too of Socrates who refused to write philosophy down. But then one remembers also Plato who devised a method for writing it down without writing it down. The intent of Oakeshott's writing was like that. In the lees and scum there is, after all, perhaps a lingering presence which is a blessing in disguise.

18. Oakeshott, "On Being Conservative," 196.

Jacques Maritain and Michael Oakeshott on the Modern State

FOR PRESENT PURPOSES I shall stipulate that the object of investigation of classical political philosophy is the ancient city and that the object of investigation of modern political philosophy is the modern European state. Jacques Maritain in *Man and the State* investigates the character of the modern state but also proposes a third possible object of investigation, the world political society.[1] Michael Oakeshott, on the other hand, explores, especially in *On Human Conduct*, the character of the modern European state as it has come to be, without speculating on what it may become in the future.[2] Maritain is proposing something that might be called post-modern, in a peculiar sense of the term, though he expresses this in terms of a philosophy of history that has ancient roots and an evolutionary character. Michael Oakeshott is a modern in seeking to understand the premises upon which the modern state has been conceived and modern politics have operated, and in distinguishing those premises from ancient alternatives. Both Maritain and Oakeshott recognize the emergence of the individual as a defining feature of the

Reprinted by permission from Timothy Fuller and John P. Hittinger, eds., *Reassessing the Liberal State: Reading Maritain's "Man and the State"* (Washington, DC: American Maritain Association, 2001), 24–33.
1. Jacques Maritain, *Man and the State* (Chicago: The University of Chicago Press, 1951).
2. Michael Oakeshott, *On Human Conduct*.

modern situation, although Oakeshott does not make the idea of natural rights central to this and Maritain does.

To speak somewhat loosely, one might say that Maritain engages in philosophizing that is idealistic in suggesting to us what we ought to be doing and what we ought to be aspiring to based on his analysis of what he finds to be the providential lessons of history, while Oakeshott philosophizes in the indicative mood: he seeks to explain what we have been doing and what we understand ourselves to be about, refusing to prescribe, because he does not think that one can, as a philosopher, prescribe a direction to take.

Maritain, although speaking within the Catholic tradition, is in many respects rooted in a nineteenth-century liberal progressivism reminiscent at times of both Immanuel Kant and John Stuart Mill, leavened by a Wilsonian internationalism preoccupied with the advent of the cold war and the bipolarity of the nuclear age; Oakeshott is conservative and a political realist, less willing to take his philosophical understanding of politics from the events that were immediately contemporary to both Maritain and himself. He did not, for example, think that the atomic bomb was a revelatory experience. I am not seeking to make a judgment of better or worse at this point, but rather to highlight what seems to me to be obvious differences in their understanding of the philosophical task and its relation to contemporary events, and to set them in dialectical relation. Maritain is a neo-Thomist progressive while Oakeshott is an Augustinian skeptic. What I propose to do is to set out the thesis of each on the modern state to see what we may learn from the comparison.

I

From the outset in *Man and the State,* Maritain wishes to characterize the idea of the modern state correctly, thereby establishing the scope, and thus the limits, of the modern state. He does this by putting the state in a grand historical context that is for him nothing less than the materialization of the Gospel in world history, with the emergence of natural rights in modern times as the articulation of what was implicit in the medieval natural law tradition, indeed in the very being of humanity. In this way, modernity at its best would be the implementation of the Christian recognition of the dignity of all persons.

For Maritain, the modern state is the topmost element of the body politic.[3] It represents the whole but, as an instrument in service to the whole and as a symbol of unity in the complex arrangements over which it presides, cannot be a substitute for or superior to the whole. The state is not the whole, but a representation of the whole.[4] At the same time, the state is to enact defense against foreign threats and is to be the means by which social justice is to be achieved, yet without being paternalistic. The state's activity is to be limited with respect to business, arts, culture, science, and philosophy, but it is to be a welfare state. The aim of the body politic is "to better the conditions of life itself" to seek a proper, civilized life for every member through the establishment of civilization and culture and the cultivation of faith, righteousness, wisdom and beauty."[5] The state must serve this aim in giving formal articulation to the body politic.

To make this clear, Maritain sets out to criticize and reject the concept of sovereignty, because sovereignty involves attributing to the state the character of a separate and transcendent whole which it cannot have. Only God is sovereign. No earthly power can claim the divine attribute. The state, he says, has supreme independence and power only with regard to the other parts of the body politic, subject to its laws and administration. To understand the modern state, then, requires one not only to identify its character but also to define the scope of its power. It is the organizer of the constituent elements of the body politic, but it cannot supersede them or substitute for them. The state is not absolute—no political institution can be absolute—but is comprehensive procedurally, supreme within its scope, but having no natural right or transcendent power, and it is always accountable to the people since its legitimacy depends on their acknowledgment of its authority.

For Maritain, the closest approximation to the right understanding of the state appears in the western democracies where there is

3. Maritain, *Man and the State,* 13, 15–19.
4. Maritain, *Man and the State,* 12–13.
5. Maritain, *Man and the State,* 54–55.

participation in governance of both rulers and ruled, and where in principle there is possible a collaborative relationship between liberal democracy and Christianity, the former being the practical matrix within which the aspirations of the latter are to be realized, to the degree possible, on earth. For Maritain there is an evolution in thought and aspiration to be traced from Aristotle through Aquinas to liberal democracy. As he says, "democracy is the only way of bringing about a *moral rationalization* of politics. . . . Democracy is a rational organization of freedoms founded upon law."[6] This is an unmistakable reference to the Kantian aspiration to replace political morality with moralized politics, or to solve once and for all the Machiavellian problem.

Moreover, the road to moral rationalization is "the highest terrestrial achievement of which the rational animal is capable here below . . . the only way through which the progressive energies in human history do pass."[7] For Maritain, democracy is the use of means worthy of the end sought, in which rulers and ruled participate jointly in self-governance. The evolution is toward practical truths coming to universal recognition in acknowledging the "rights possessed by man in his personal and social existence."[8]

Yet, at the same time, the process of materializing the Gospel message is ambiguous because modernity is not simply Christian; is indeed in many respects anti-Christian and secularizing. At best, then, we enjoy an emergent agreement on some practical truths in the midst of powerful metaphysical and theological oppositions.[9] There is, Maritain says, "notable progress in the process of world unification" at the level of practical formulations, but no theoretical position can "claim to establish in actual fact universal ascendancy over men's minds."[10] The most important "factor in the moral progress of humanity is the experiential development of awareness which takes place outside of systems."[11]

6. Maritain, *Man and the State*, 59.
7. Maritain, *Man and the State*, 59–60.
8. Maritain, *Man and the State*, 76.
9. Maritain, *Man and the State*, 76.
10. Maritain, *Man and the State*, 79.
11. Maritain, *Man and the State*, 80.

Yet, there are problems. The increasing recognition of natural rights, which is a necessary feature in Maritain's scheme, has been deformed by the failure to remember that natural law is the foundation of the rights of man. By losing that insight we moved toward abstract ideas of autonomy and then to disillusion over the conflicting abstract claims. We must, Maritain says, will to act in conformity with what is appropriate for our fulfillment. Moral law involves recognizing what is best for us as what is established independently by nature. This means that visions of an "ideal order" are generated out of our responses to the natural human character under varying historical conditions. To articulate an ideal order is to respond to the disposition in all human beings to live as they should. If this is universal, one might still expect that it would yield considerable, if not infinite, variety of response. But according to Maritain, "there is, by the very virtue of human nature, an order or a disposition which human reason can discover and according to which the human will must act in order to attune itself to the essential and necessary ends of the human being. The unwritten law, or natural law, is nothing more than that."[12]

There is a developing, not a finished, moral conscience because knowledge of the law is imperfect, and that development is necessarily toward "essential and necessary ends."[13] Natural law has to acquire the force of law, inclination has to be clarified and made specific. This has been happening through time and thus explains why there is both commonality and variability in the moral understanding. Maritain asserts that the "progress of moral conscience is indeed the most unquestionable instance of progress in humanity."[14] Unfortunately, however, rights now overshadow obligations in the common understanding. Thus the moral progress is vitiated by the way in which it has been understood and pursued in practice. The rights of human beings emerged by inclination, but the discussion and specification have been defective. Despite this, Maritain insists "there is a dynamism which impels the unwritten law to

12. Maritain, *Man and the State*, 86.
13. Maritain, *Man and the State*, 91.
14. Maritain, *Man and the State*, 94.

flower forth in human law, and to render the latter ever more perfect and just in the very field of its contingent determinations."[15]

It is difficult to know how to respond to Maritain's tension-ridden argument. It is by no means self-evident, even if we accept the idea that there is an evolving materialization of the Gospel message, that the materialization or practical realization of that message can or will have a necessary and unambiguous temporal outcome that approaches the ever more perfect and just. Dialectically speaking, Maritain seems to share with Hegel—I do not mean of course that Maritain is an Hegelian—a particular sort of incarnational theology in which the Idea, as Hegel would say, is not so impotent as to remain only an Idea, but he does not accept that what actually happens in the process is all that can happen, that it is open-ended and contingent, and that we may either fail to realize our aspirations or realize them in ways that are not at all what we expected or had hoped for, that, so to speak, our successes may turn into our failures. To posit "essential and necessary ends" is to say that there is an ideal or correct unfolding of moral conscience through time that is not alterable by its actualization in time. This evolution is thus a revealing of what is not subject to time and is supra historical. History is supposed to confirm the faith expressed.

On a different Christian outlook from Maritain's, the historically experienced combination of success and failure, of gain and loss, might be exactly what we should expect because it is what it means to be temporal beings. This does not mean that there are no better and worse results, better and worse regimes; but it may well mean that judgment in these matters will always be arguable and argument interminable; stipulating what is progressive is by no means self-evident.

Earlier, I mentioned the link of Maritain's outlook to the liberal tradition of Kant, Mill, and Woodrow Wilson. We must return to this in light of the fact that Maritain criticizes the liberal tradition in this context. He laments that faith no longer unites us, and that we now see that reason alone cannot successfully replace faith. Religion, to be sure, has not disappeared, but it has become plural, and

15. Maritain, *Man and the State,* 100.

there is no religious expression which can claim successfully to be authoritative for us all. As we have been moving from a "sacral" age to a "secular" age the integrating force of Christianity has been constrained or excluded even while its residual, leavening effects remain. We are in a post-Constantinian age.[16] It is obvious why Maritain would not accept this outcome as a realization in practice of the Gospel message, unlike some Protestant theorists or those theorists of secularization who believe that secular democracy is, in fact, a realization of the truth contained in the Christian tradition. But here again Maritain is unclear about whether, or in what sense, there can be in practice any such thing as the ideal order on earth. Of course, he accepts that the heavenly kingdom is not of this world, but does he fully explore the implications of this for earthly political life?

Maritain does recognize this insofar as he speaks of the need for Christian fortitude in a democratic society, and insofar as he commits himself to what he calls long-term success, rejecting what he calls the Machiavellian "illusion of immediate success."[17] What he is proposing is to be taken as an ideal of permanent, inspirational value. We might choose to acknowledge this without expecting ever to enjoy anything but an ambiguous and arguable practical result. But the question remains as to how much this view is contingent upon our response to the actual historical conditions we experience. The ideal may be maintained apart from our view of our rising and falling fortunes in history, but the very assessment itself will be subject inevitably to endless debate and argument. Given the joint participation in governance of rulers and ruled, the limitations on any claims to political authority, and the plural character of religious expression, it is hard to see how practical consensus on defining the true fulfillment of our destiny, so far as it is earthly, is to be achieved. One may admire the nobility of Maritain's aspiration but wonder whether he has fully absorbed, or was willing to admit, the true implications of the emergence of individuality in the realm which Hegel described as that in which all are free. The realm of

16. Maritain, *Man and the State*, 162.
17. Maritain, *Man and the State*, 71.

universal freedom invests human beings with the responsibility to determine for themselves what is essential and necessary to them.

Social structures, Maritain says, must constantly be altered to allow the full emergence of the articulation and exercise of rights that are always present awaiting a forum for realization. The end is predetermined, and it is only our awakening to that end and full understanding of it that is still to be achieved. Yet there are also constraints on how this may happen—recognizing the need to use means worthy of the end sought—in preserving the rights of property, of education, constitutional dispersion of power to prevent claims of sovereignty, and so on. The manner in which we conduct our affairs is crucial. That has to be part of the end, constraining any determination of what the end is for us, since it has to be for us. But it would seem that the end has to be grasped as we can grasp it, that we must participate in defining the end in order to guide our action. Under these circumstances, Maritain might be seen as a sober progressive, like John Stuart Mill, continually seeking to reconcile order with innovation, and, as also with Mill, believing that ultimately there would be a convergence on truth.

The largest political innovation would be the establishment of Maritain's world political society under the moral leadership of a supreme advisory council to "organize international opinion," to articulate a common good that will supersede the common good of each body politic, and to subordinate the state as the principal unit of politics and world history.[18] This would presumably constitute a concrete manifestation of the growing moral unity of mankind. One might describe this as the restatement of the Kantian ideal of the cosmopolitan point of view and perpetual peace as the solution to the Hobbesian problem, namely, how to gain a covenant without the sword. Yet it remains unclear, as in previous explorations of this ideal, how to achieve the covenant without the sword by means of agents of world history which inevitably employ the sword. At this point, one might think of the Augustinian critique of efforts to transform politics by means of politics within world history. And here I shall turn to Michael Oakeshott.

18. Maritain, *Man and the State*, 215.

II

Oakeshott famously has said that "in political activity, then, men sail a boundless and bottomless sea; there is neither harbour for shelter nor floor for anchorage, neither starting-place nor appointed destination. The enterprise is to keep afloat on an even keel; the sea is both friend and enemy; and the seamanship consists in using the resources of a traditional manner of behaviour in order to make a friend of every hostile occasion."[19] Oakeshott described himself as a skeptic who would do better if only he knew how. Politics, an object of lifelong philosophic investigation for him, especially aroused his skepticism. In this he followed that strain of the Augustinian tradition which sees politics as a necessary evil for fallen humanity, something we cannot do without but also something not to be overrated, and certainly not a source of salvation. He was skeptical of all ideologies, including schemes for world government or perpetual peace; more generally, he criticized the modern rationalism we associate with the legacy of Francis Bacon and René Descartes, first because he thought it promoted, especially in those less adept than Bacon and Descartes themselves, a philosophically mistaken understanding of human reason and how it works, and derivatively because he thought it magnified the dangers of political misjudgment in assuming that we can know where we are going and how to get there, what he called the pursuit of perfection as the crow flies. The political manifestation of this rationalism is to be found in the progressive and utopian tendencies of modern thought, not only in the extreme case of totalitarian regimes, but also the less obvious perfectionist idealism within the liberal tradition itself. Oakeshott's use of the term "rationalism" corresponds to Eric Voegelin's use of the term "gnosticism" in describing a misplaced claim of the autonomy of human reason, when armed with "appropriate methods," to remake the world according to our independently premeditated goals.

This rationalism and utopianism Oakeshott called the "politics of faith."[20] His point was that a *politics* of faith is contrary to faith

19. Michael Oakeshott, "Political Education" in *Rationalism in Politics* (1991), 60.
20. Michael Oakeshott, *The Politics of Faith and the Politics of Scepticism.*

as Christianity understands faith because it is faith in the things of this world. Oakeshott thought that what he called the "politics of skepticism," which tends toward minimalism in government because it thinks the primary issue is to constrain the use of governmental power rather than to expand it, is more appropriate to the human condition. At the same time, he thought that modern politics was a polarized field of tension between the "politics of faith" and the "politics of skepticism," that these dispositions emerged at the same time at the start of the modern period, roughly four hundred to five hundred years ago, and that they counterbalance each other, although the politics of faith has dominated in our era. It is this continuing polarity that constitutes the field of modern political life. Arguments over the scope of the state's activity, what it should or should not try to do, are shaped by this underlying field of tension within which we operate.

For Oakeshott, philosophy is the effort to understand in other terms what we already understand, to explain not to prescribe, to discern and describe the premises that clarify why we think and act as we do. Philosophical examination of politics led Oakeshott to formulate the explanation of modern politics as the tension between the politics of faith and the politics of skepticism. Yet this philosophical explication of modern politics cannot prescribe an ideal or generate a plan for improving the world. Oakeshott did not think that exploring politics philosophically could produce a simple, unified doctrine. He did not think we have access to a plan or a vision for reconciling the tension between the politics of faith and the politics of skepticism. His analysis seeks to clarify the way we live, but it leaves that as it is. The philosophical study of politics, as he saw it, is not a higher, more abstract way to advocate policies. In wanting to understand politics philosophically Oakeshott sought to examine politics in detachment from the specific issues which, at any given moment, dramatize or reveal the character of political activity. To understand politics in this way is to adopt a stance that is difficult, perhaps impossible, for political actors to take up so long as they remain political actors.

Equally, the philosophic inquirer, if drawn to one side or another in political debate, can only present that inclination by disclosing the reasons he finds persuasive, exposing his position to further philosophic investigation. In this, Oakeshott was unquestionably influenced by Socratic dialectic and accepted the limitations that dialectical inquiry imposes on equipping oneself for political action. To seek more is to abandon philosophic reflection, favoring persuasion and action over prolonged, unfinished conversation. One cannot simply unify philosophic understanding with practical action. The attempt to do so will necessarily sacrifice the philosophic endeavor, and corrupt political action insofar as it takes on a misplaced sense of certainty that it can leap over the contingency and uncertainty inherent to political action. On these grounds, an Oakeshottian would be bound to say that Maritain has mixed politics and philosophy, and has justified the mixture by stipulating a shape and direction of world history through a particular reading of the implications of Christianity.

What Maritain asserts, therefore, would become for Oakeshott an invitation to a conversation of questioning. Among the questions that might arise from an Oakeshottian standpoint are these: Is it definitive for Christianity that there be an evolving materialization of the Gospel message in world history? Is it not likely that to think in such terms is to engage in stipulating the revelatory significance of one's own historical era, even to claiming to have an authoritative insight into what is relevant and irrelevant to the advance of world history?

At the same time, there is no doubt that Oakeshott and Maritain would agree on the validity of the western polities. But Oakeshott would put less emphasis on the democratic element, and, rather than exalting rights, he would find the greater achievement in the rule of law and the constitutional limits on power that derive from a deep-rooted skepticism about politics that is itself prompted by Augustinian Christianity. He would see an error in thinking that one could advocate rights and also control the evolving understanding of what they mean to those who exercise them. For Oakeshott, the defect in the realization of rights, lamented by Maritain, is inherent to the idea of rights when rights are abstractly rather than locally and customarily understood. Maritain then could not assert that there is a "correct" realization of rights available to us. In this sense, Oakeshott acknowledges more fully the open-endedness of existence in world history, and did argue that Christian faith is not tied to the episodic character of historical existence. Like Maritain, Oakeshott would say that the state is not an independent entity but rides atop a complex whole that could never be comprehended in formal expression alone. Let us say that in practice they could be in friendly tension.

Maritain recognizes something that we surely cannot ignore: the universalism of thought that dominates our time. One may wonder whether Oakeshott adequately absorbed this phenomenon for he surely did not speculate on what could or might supersede the modern state. To understand philosophy as Oakeshott did, precludes speculation of this sort because it falls into the realm of the "ought to be" rather than the "is." Speculation on the future is an inevitable part of political activity, and there it makes a difference whether such speculation is sober and cautious or expansive and utopian, whether it is confident or alarmist, and so on. Thus to introduce such speculation into philosophical analysis is to confuse what, for Oakeshott, are two categorically different activities, amounting to carrying on politics by other means. Politics can overtake philosophy, but philosophy cannot overtake politics.

How then did Oakeshott characterize the modern state? In simplest terms, he articulated an ideal type of the modern state that he thought to be implicit in the actual practices of modern European states. It is a procedural state, largely intent on the tasks of minimal legislation and adjudication of disputes. In principle, it has at its disposal very little to redistribute. It is not the representative of a world historical purpose, or, perhaps, of any purpose but civil peace. Modern bodies politic, to use Maritain's term, are brought together by chance or choice, and are basically coercive associations bringing together people who need not and often do not agree on what their lives are for, but for whom exit is seldom a likely alternative. They are not voluntary associations which may be animated by a common purpose or a specified goal, and which one may enter and also exit. The civil condition is one in which many are bound together without agreement on common purposes or specified goals.

Moderns understand themselves as individuals entitled to recognition from each other, who are "in themselves what they are for themselves." The last thing people with such self-understanding want is to have a common purpose, justified as essential and necessary, imposed upon them. Nor is it likely that an agreement on the essential and necessary would arise spontaneously from the endless exchanges among them. Nor is there an agreement on anyone's claim to the authority to articulate such an agreement on behalf of the participants in the body politic. In short, the modern state in this view does not, and could not have, a telos. The modern state is organized precisely for people who do not think they can have such a thing. From the Oakeshottian perspective, one would ask Maritain if he is not confusing Christianity with an historicized neo-Aristotelianism.

In a way, the difference between Maritain and Oakeshott, to a degree, illustrates the distinction between the politics of faith and the politics of skepticism, as Oakeshott developed that distinction. It is clear that Maritain is not simply an exponent of what Oakeshott would call the politics of faith since that would mean the collapsing of the sacred into the secular. This clearly is not the case with Maritain as an orthodox Christian. Maritain appears in some measure to be drawn to the politics of faith. On the other side, insofar as Oakeshott would be in practice an exponent of the politics of skepticism, even though philosophically speaking he cannot advocate either position, he could be questioned as to whether he has grasped sufficiently the need to respond to what are thought to be the unprecedented conditions of the twentieth century.

The point is, however, that here we enter into political discourse within the range of what has characterized our politics for several centuries. Philosophical reflection on these matters has both clarified some features of the situation and also led us into the uncertainty that philosophy imposes upon us when we seek its aid in deciding what we mean to ourselves.

On the Character of Religious Experience
Need There Be a Conflict between Science and Religion?

Michael Oakeshott rarely acknowledged specific intellectual debts. In *Experience and Its Modes* (1933), however, he cited as major influences on his thinking G. W. F. Hegel's *Phenomenology of Spirit* (1807) and F. H. Bradley's *Appearance and Reality* (1893). Oakeshott was invoking the tradition of Hegelian/British idealism, knowing that he was swimming against the tide of philosophic fashion. What did he get from this philosophic tradition? Human experience is our world: "Experiencing and what is experienced are, taken separately, meaningless abstractions. . . . The character of what is experienced is, in the strictest sense, correlative to the manner in which it is experienced. These two abstractions stand to one another in the most complete interdependence; they compose a single whole."[1] For Oakeshott "there is nothing whatever which is not experience," and "there can be no experience which does not involve thought or judgment."[2]

Originally printed in *Zygon* 44 (March 2009): 153–67. Reprinted by permission of John Wiley & Sons–Books. Title appeared originally as "Oakeshott on the Character of Religious Experience: Need There Be a Conflict Between Science and Religion?"
1. Michael Oakeshott, *Experience and Its Modes,* 251.
2. Oakeshott, *Experience and Its Modes,* 251.

A number of things follow, for Oakeshott. He sought to understand arguments by uncovering the assumptions or postulates on the basis of which each party to an argument seeks a coherent understanding of experience, thereby clarifying how each makes sense of its experience. He pursued not refutation or advocacy but rather descriptions that show the assumptions at work to support conclusions reached on each side; he preferred to turn debate toward conversation and to treat arguments as conversational gambits. Talk is interminable so long as there are human beings. The aim of the philosophic inquirer is to understand better the voices offering accounts of what is already given in experience. The philosopher does not resolve disputes but gives an account of why they are the way they are, and also why from the perspective of each participant the alternatives may seem mistaken or irrelevant. He did not think that victories inevitably deepen insight or that defeats reveal lack of insight. The philosophic quest is for experience as a whole "unmodified." "Thinking," he said, "is not a professional matter. . . . It is something we may engage in without putting ourselves in competition; it is something independent of the futile effort to convince or persuade."[3]

Oakeshott was of a stoic disposition, disinclined to engage in quixotic ventures to change the world or set it right, whatever that might mean. He once remarked to me that Don Quixote was the prototype of the modern rationalist, that Cervantes' great work was both the anticipation and the critique of modern rationalism. Oakeshott did not always attain detachment, but his disposition was to do so. He saluted Montaigne, who had seen that reasoning is the faculty that makes us human but also produces the ordeal of consciousness that makes us problematic for ourselves. We self-conscious beings impose snares and traps on ourselves and then have to figure out how to deal with them. We continually interpret—well or ill—the world. Our reason leads into difficulties and then to contrivances to escape them. There is no reliable definition of *progress.*

3. Oakeshott, *Experience and Its Modes,* 7.

Thus Oakeshott identified himself as a skeptic: one who would "do better if he only knew how."[4]

He recognized as unending the task of comprehending the whole of experience. Given that, grasping the order of reality would ever elude us. We usually settle for abridgements—interpretations of experience through which visions of order from various perspectives may be attained. Some of these interpretations (arrests in thought) get sufficiently elaborated—even equipped with a method of inquiry that may be taught and learned—to turn into modes of experience. A *mode* is a powerful human invention (although its emergence may take a long time) for making sense of the world to its adherents, binding together individuals in associations that explore the world from their chosen modal perspectives. Each of these modes makes sense in its own terms but can at most achieve the appearance of universality by marginalizing experiences that threaten the coherence (and thus the satisfaction) of the understanding its adherents have come to defend. The coherence of each is abstract—that is, abstracted from the whole it seeks to understand. Imperial tendencies lurk among the adherents of each of these modes, tempting claims of methodological competence to assess critically the alternative modes and experience as a whole; each mode will tend to explain all of experience in terms of its own assumptions.

In *Experience and Its Modes* (1933) Oakeshott discussed the "historical," "scientific," and "practical" modes of experience. He thought they currently "represent the main arrests or modifications in experience," coexisting as abstractions from the whole of experience, attempting, each in its own way, to abate the mystery of human self-understanding.[5] The historical mode knows experience as past experience; the scientific mode knows it as stable, quantitative relationships; the practical mode lives by the tension between what is and what ought to be.

---

4. Michael Oakeshott, "Political Education" (1951), in *Rationalism in Politics* (1991), 44.
5. Oakeshott, *Experience and Its Modes*, 84.

As long as a mode remains content within itself it remains coherent to itself. When it steps out into other realms it begins to confront its own abstractness:

> It belongs to the nature of an abstract world of experience to be self-contained, sovereign, and to lie beyond the interference of any other world of experience, so long as it confines itself within the limits which constitute its character. Of course, if it oversteps itself, an abstract world of experience immediately becomes vulnerable, and of course, in the end, it must overstep itself, demand to be judged as embodying a complete assertion of reality: but so long as it remains faithful to its own explicit character, even the concrete totality of experience itself cannot compete with it on its own ground. History, Science, and Practice, as such, and each within its own world, are beyond the relevant interference of philosophic thought.[6]

In short, as long as a mode enters no dialectical engagement with other modes, or with a philosophic inquirer, it is protected from subversion by excluding what it wants to consider extraneous.

Oakeshott concentrated on these particular modes, but his point is applicable generally. He did not think that these modes exhausted the possibilities. "Indeed, my view is that there can be no limit to the number of possible modifications in experience. And the business of philosophy, in so far as it is concerned with these modes at all, is not to anticipate or suggest arrests in experience, but to consider the character of those which actually exist."[7]

He did not think that philosophic investigation added something to a mode that was not already there or that philosophy could "improve" the character of a mode by making it "less abstract." If anything, philosophic examination does not relieve but rather dramatizes the abstractness of a mode of experience: "It is my business to insist equally upon the incapacity of philosophy to take the place of any abstract world of experience, and in particular its

---

6. Oakeshott, *Experience and Its Modes*, 332.
7. Oakeshott, *Experience and Its Modes*, 331.

incapacity to take the place of historical, scientific or practical experience."[8] The philosopher cannot rule the modes or bring them to completeness but can only liberate himself from their seductiveness when he sees that they are barriers to experience as a whole.

In the 1950s Oakeshott discerned a "voice of poetry" that was separable from the practical mode where he had once thought poetry to be located. He transposed it to the status of an independent mode of experience in *The Voice of Poetry in the Conversation of Mankind* (1959). He never attributed modal status to religion; religion remained where he had located it in 1933—in practical life. Yet he reflected on religious experience throughout his life. He did not think that there was a specific way to be religious, as there might be a distinct way to be a historian, a scientist, a politician, or a poet. He denied that there was a sustainable distinction between the professionally religious and the laity, a distinction inherited from medieval times that he thought to have been superseded, the "belief that the true, unhindered service of God was possible only to members of a religious order or officials of the Church (that is, to those who made a profession of it) [which] promoted a false and irreligious division between those who were called to serve God, and those who were not, and gave a false importance to the former."[9]

Nor for Oakeshott is philosophy itself a mode, because experience as a whole is never identical with any mode of experience. Every mode is an abstract account of the whole of experience, and so a philosopher can never be at home in any of the modes; like Odysseus, he is restless for another home no matter how charming the local Calypso might be. The attractiveness of a mode of experience as a resting place for thought is a siren song distracting one from thinking without arrest, tempting one to abandon thought's odyssey. Wherever the philosopher's home may be, there can be no urgency to get there—because there is no plan, program, or map that we can consult to speed us on our way. "Philosophy is merely experience

8. Oakeshott, *Experience and Its Modes*, 354.
9. Michael Oakeshott, "The Claims of Politics" (1939), in *Religion, Politics and the Moral Life*, 92.

become critical of itself, experience sought and followed entirely for its own sake."[10]

Oakeshott was Socratic in finding himself committed to the examined life, to the dissolution of the certainties abstractions offer. All undertakings involve knowledge affected by ignorance. Each mode of inquiry specifies methods for reducing ignorance and criteria for defining knowledge. Thinking unconstrained by modal assumptions is "radically subversive" in its refusal to be satisfied with an "arrest" of inquiry.[11]

What Oakeshott has to say about religious and scientific experience needs to be seen in light of these considerations. Religious experience is a manner of being in the world, but it is not a mode, let alone the mode of modes. Religion has affinities with the poetic aspect of life but retains practical import, whereas Oakeshott came to see poetry as a contemplation of images that delight but do not point beyond themselves. Poetry is imagination liberated from practicality. He knew, of course, that many people attribute practical meaning to poetry and the arts, but what he meant to identify was what makes poetry poetry. He knew that many defend science for its technological fruits but that technology is not what makes science science. He knew that for many religion is uplifting and salutary for social well-being. But to him, all of this showed how preoccupation with practical life muddies thought. The incursion of science into the world of practical experience

> causes no less error and confusion in the world of practice
> than that which follows, in the world of science, from a
> similar incursion of practical thought . . . it is not easy for the
> modern mind to accept this view. We have too long been
> accustomed to the notions that science is a guide to life, that
> science is the only true guide to life, and that the world of
> practical experience (and particularly moral and religious
> ideas) must submit themselves to the criticism of scientific
> thought, for any other view not to appear false or reactionary

10. Oakeshott, *Experience and Its Modes*, 82.
11. Michael Oakeshott, "Political Philosophy" (1940s), in *Religion, Politics and the Moral Life*, 140.

or both. But there is little in the history of folly to which one may compare the infatuation which the modern mind has conceived for "science." . . . In so far as economics, or psychology or biology belong to the world of scientific experience, they must surrender all claim to be a guide to life.[12]

Oakeshott clearly is criticizing not science but "science"—popular notions of what science is in terms of what we hope science can do for our practical desires and concerns. Even if we allow practical concerns to dictate areas of scientific research, scientific findings, if they are to be scientific, cannot be defined or corrected by practical desires.

Religion, by contrast to both poetry and science, does not separate from our practical, mortal existence. Rather, it visualizes life's completion or perfection, the reconciliation of what is with what ought to be; it is an imaginative response to the arduous task of living consciously. Oakeshott did not see how religious experience could appeal if it were separated from the practice of living. Religion is not philosophy. Religion to him must be *practical* (in a special sense of the word, as I shall explain) or it has nothing to offer:

> Religious truths are those which are necessary to practical existence, without which practical existence falls short of coherence; they are those which attempt to satisfy the furthest claims and largest needs of practical life. Yet religion . . . has claimed that its truths are not merely practical but belong to the world of concrete truth. But, were this so, their practical value would at once disappear. . . . If religion has anything to do with the conduct of life, then the ideas of religion—ideas such as those of deity, of salvation and of immortality—are practical ideas and belong to the world of practice. And an idea which serves this world can serve no other.[13]

Religion for Oakeshott is not a kind of philosophy. What philosophy may have to say about religion is not directly pertinent to faith. Theology may have the appearance of philosophy, but because it is

---

12. Oakeshott, *Experience and Its Modes*, 312–13.
13. Oakeshott, *Experience and Its Modes*, 309.

generated by and serves faith it does not escape its grounding in practical life. Philosophy is indifferent to the practicalities of living; to pursue experience as a whole is to leave behind the world of practice; to be faithful to thinking is not the same as having religious faith; thinking passes beyond the limits of particular modes of inquiry—it is, practically speaking, "useless." Philosophy

> depends for its existence upon maintaining its independence from all extraneous interests, and in particular from the practical interest. . . . Few, perhaps, will be found willing to surrender the green for the grey, but only those few are on the way to a philosophy. And instead of a gospel, the most philosophy can offer us (in respect of practical life) is an escape, perhaps the only complete escape open to us.[14]

Oakeshott often spoke of the "deadliness of doing" and of the "*danse macabre* of wants and satisfactions." Philosophy escapes, is detached from, the practical life. Religion rescues us from the deadliness of doing and the frenzy of the *danse macabre,* but it does so by evoking experiences of fulfillment or completion in practical life.

How do these reflections affect thinking about religion and science?

The so-called conflict of religion and science is a prominent feature of contemporary debate. For Oakeshott, this is misleading because science and religion are of different modes of experience; one cannot absorb the other without unbearable contradictions in which unavoidable questions have to be disdained or explained away. There is no mode of modes—that is, no mode that can incorporate the other modes while maintaining its own coherence. Science is not a mode that explains all the modes. Science, no less than the other modes of experience, must make limiting assumptions in order to maintain its own coherence. According to Oakeshott, "The question of the character of scientific experience is not itself a scientific question,"[15] it is not a question scientists need take up before they can start to do what they do. Science's characteristic modification of

14. Oakeshott, *Experience and Its Modes,* 3.
15. Oakeshott, *Experience and Its Modes,* 173.

experience "is its attempt coherently to conceive the world, under the category of quantity; the explicit purpose in science is the elucidation of a world of absolutely communicable experience."[16] Further:

> The world of scientific experience is, then, created by a transformation of our familiar world; in science there is no attempt to elucidate the character of this world of perception in which we live, what is attempted is the elucidation of a world of absolutely stable experience . . . science can borrow and use no component of that world which it has not learnt how to transform. Scientific knowledge is not "organized common sense"; it is a world of knowledge which begins to exist only when common sense and all its postulates have been forgotten or rejected. Experience becomes scientific experience when it is a world of absolutely communicable experience. Scientific experience is based upon a rejection of merely human testimony; its master-conception is *stability*.[17]

This sort of critique Oakeshott applies to every mode. For example, the historian's reverence for past experience is the enemy of decisions that practical life demands. History remembers what the politician would forget. Historians sometimes imagine that we can avoid mistakes in the present if we remember the past, but, as Hegel said, what we learn from history is that we never learn from history—it is too easy to see in the past what we already take the present to demand. The history of science reminds us of the open-endedness of scientific inquiry, and thus science's imperialism can never succeed in subduing experience as a whole to itself; neither can the historical, the political, the poetic, or the religious understanding achieve such a triumph. "Science, history and practice, as such, cannot collide; they are merely irrelevant to one another," asserts Oakeshott.[18] For this reason he came to celebrate the "conversation of mankind," which accepts that we are already fully human and cannot progress toward perfection by a putative

---

16. Oakeshott, *Experience and Its Modes*, 243.
17. Oakeshott, *Experience and Its Modes*, 171.
18. Oakeshott, *Experience and Its Modes*, 316.

comprehensive integration of knowledge or by synthesizing the ways of knowing.

Oakeshott wanted to purge dualisms from his thinking, beginning with overcoming the distinction between experience of the world and the world itself. He emphasized that human beings have access to nothing independent of their experience. The distinction between experiencing and what is experienced cannot stand. The something outside our experience is a thought within our experience. The experience of transcendence is a form of self-understanding. "Revelation" is an aspect of experience and must be within our experience or it is nowhere. Nothing comes to us unmediated by thought; everything must be in experience—there is no unthought experience. Meaning comes in the endless effort of human beings to interpret the world and respond according to their understanding of what it is they are responding to.

Although this certainly shows Hegel's influence, Oakeshott was also affected by Augustine, whom he often called the most imaginative theologian in the Western tradition. Oakeshott was taken by Augustine's meditation on the radically temporal, mortal character of human existence, which in our consciousness of it gives rise to the thought of that which is not temporal. That is, the idea of the eternal emerges in the capacity of human thought to imagine the negation of the temporal, to imagine the eternal as the not-temporal (see *The Confessions*, Book XI). But Augustine thought that the capacity to conceive the nontemporal revealed that the eternal preceded and presided over the temporal, drawing the temporal to it, leading him to faith that he could converse with God. Oakeshott remained reticent about this affirmation. Like Hegel, he thought that the unfolding of thought had shown us that the Sun that enlightens is not above us but within us, it is human intelligence at work. For Oakeshott, Plato's "Allegory of the Cave" is an essay in self-discovery and self-understanding, not a divine illumination drawing us to itself from beyond.[19] We are, he said, self-making beings who are "in ourselves what we are for ourselves." To be a human being is to be a

---

19. See part 1 in Michael Oakeshott, *On Human Conduct*.

"for itself," we are what we "learn to become."[20] We pursue the intimations of our existence, continually making ourselves into what we imagine we want to be. Religious experience does not rescue us from this temporality. Rather, it is a response of varying intensity to this unsought and unavoidable but necessary "evil."

The following passage shows how Oakeshott adapted elements of Augustinian and Hegelian thinking to say something about religious experience:

> Religion, indeed, as I see it, is not a particular form of practical experience; it is merely practical experience at its fullest. Wherever practice is least reserved, least hindered by extraneous interests, least confused by what it does not need, wherever it is most nearly at one with itself and homogeneous, at that point it becomes religion . . . religion is practical activity, and religious experience is practical experience; and that in religion practical experience realizes its full character, religion is the consummation of practice. . . . What is important for religion has always been the profession which is contained in the actual conduct of life.[21]

Oakeshott had expressed himself on what he meant by the "conduct of life" in his "Religion and the World."[22] In that essay, Oakeshott took up the following issue: Our religious (specifically Christian) legacy demands other-worldliness. But we live in and for the world, so this legacy demands negation of our existence. We cannot deny that religion has always had this other-worldly aspect. Does this mean that religion must be irrelevant save for a few eccentrics who willingly cultivate separation from life? That is, are we irreligious if we continue to take life in the world seriously?

This is one of those dualisms Oakeshott wanted to dissolve. He cared about religion, but he also was of the world. What was he to do? The opposition of worldliness and other-worldliness was, stated

20. Michael Oakeshott, "A Place of Learning" (1974), in *The Voice of Liberal Learning* (1989), 19.

21. Oakeshott, *Experience and Its Modes*, 292.

22. Michael Oakeshott, "Religion and the World" (1929), in *Religion, Politics and the Moral Life*, 27–38.

thus, unacceptable to him. He was seeking to understand the problem of worldliness. Intellectually, he was convinced that human
beings are implicated in only one world of experience. The question, then, is not about being in the world or out of the world but
rather of different ways of being in the world. "For, should our interest lie with religion at all, we shall scarcely be content with the
dogma that it consists in an escape from the 'world,' when we know
no more of the 'world' than that it is what the religious man must
escape."[23] Thus Oakeshott set out to explore the changing historical
connotations of the term *world*. He argues that *worldliness* has meant
different things in different times in order to show further that *other-
worldliness* has quite practical in-the-world significance, that it has a
history. Other-worldliness is constituted in response to the prevailing idea of worldliness.

For Oakeshott, the religious sensibility must be a way of being in
the world, not a way of escape from it. For the early Christians this
meant rejecting the corruptions of the pagan Roman world, living
in hope of a new age to come that would be purged of those corruptions. In rejecting the "world" they were rejecting not human experience in general but rather aspects of a particular historical era. To
live against those aspects was to reject not the human world but a
particular set of human practices in light of a vision of an alternative set of practices in a "heavenly kingdom" that they expected soon
to appear. As that event was more and more delayed, the emphasis
shifted to living in hope of the age to come; medieval religious practice came to mean living in "comparative freedom from material
interest and a complete abandonment of any save the most elementary pleasures."[24] The emphasis shifted from living for a new time
to living for another place, the heavenly kingdom. This elicited the
distinction between the material world and the spiritual world, a
tension-ridden duality between the natural and the supernatural.
Oakeshott argues that this duality is for us decreasingly convincing.

23. Oakeshott, "Religion and the World," 27–28.
24. Oakeshott, "Religion and the World," 29.

"But this does not imply that there is no world from which the religious man will desire to escape."[25]

Oakeshott thus preserves the idea of the "religious man," but because this idea has a history it is necessary for him to say what being religious can mean for our time. We are to escape from something, but what? Oakeshott considers, critically, the thought of competing "scales of values":

> I suppose when we have rejected the crude dualism of the medieval view, the distinction between the world and religion would seem to turn most naturally upon material and spiritual values. And our belief in money, comfort, pleasure and prosperity, and the peculiar value we set on these things, is taken to distinguish us as worldlings; while a life spent in the service of an ideal is some evidence of religion. But such a view is, I think, scarcely less superficial than that it is designed to replace, for it, also, does but relieve one element in our experience at the cost of another. What really distinguishes the worldly man is, I think, his belief in the reality and permanence of the present order of things.[26]

In addition to rejecting "secularized" modern political idealism, by these remarks Oakeshott points to the fact that we human beings come and go while the world abides, and we seek to perpetuate ourselves in the world. Perpetuation is defined in various ways such as honor, glory, reputation, material prosperity, awards, memorials, descendants—immortality through our works. (Does this explain the obsession with technology?) To live thus is to live for some imagined future outcome or achievement—for what will be, not for what is present to us here and now. This is to "make humanity a Sisyphus."[27] Religion is reduced to either a quaint adornment to make the Sisyphean task less dreary or to nostalgic, antiquarian practices. To live against worldliness—to live religiously—is to live not for external accomplishment but for "the whole value of life,"

25. Oakeshott, "Religion and the World," 29.
26. Oakeshott, "Religion and the World," 30.
27. Oakeshott, "Religion and the World," 32.

which we find only if we attend to the possibilities present in each moment of existence, adopting a personal standard against the external standard.

> Ambition and the world's greed for visible results, in which each stage is a mere approach to the goal, would be superseded by a life which carried in each of its moments its whole meaning and value. . . . The worth of life is measured, then, by its sensibility, not by its external achievement of the reputation behind which it may have been able to hide its lack of actual insight.[28]

For Oakeshott, *salvation* means attaining to a self-understanding that allays anxiety for the future or regret for the past. He reinterprets the meaning of the question, What must I do to be saved? The kingdom of God is at hand here and now. To be religious means to set aside debates about the natural and the supernatural, the material and the spiritual, the past versus the present, science versus religion. Everything depends on self-understanding, which can also mean that the character of religious experience is impossible to define directly because religious experience is constituted in an individual's stance toward all experience, an individual's self-enactment: the attitude one has in everything one does.

Oakeshott asserts that the anxiety to achieve permanence—that which would convey our temporality into immortality—is part of the reason for the misguided conflict between science and religion:

> For science, human life appears as a brief interlude in the history of an insignificant planet, and the importance of human thought and sensibility is proportionate to the space and time it occupies in the physical universe. . . . But to religion the importance of human life is always its felt value, which no "scientific" argument can dictate or destroy. And that such a value could be considered "unreal" beside the "real" value of science is more than a little arbitrary. This "universe" of physics is, after all, the creation of a particular

28. Oakeshott, "Religion and the World," 32–33.

and abstract kind of thinking on the part of an insignificant number of the insignificant inhabitants of this insignificant planet: and the relative *importance* of things is a subject about which science is powerless to enlighten us.[29]

This states a religious stance in Oakeshottian terms. Science is a mode of experience, a particular interpretative framework that wants to make sense in its own terms of the whole of experience. There is nothing to show that the assumptions of this mode either refute the assumptions of other modes (history, poetry, or practical life) or that the others must be subordinated to the scientific mode. We may choose to look at everything through the lens of science, but we will do so knowing that we choose to do so and that we can also refuse to do so. In short, no mode of experience, not even the scientific, captures experience as a whole such that no choice is set before us; no such claim has ever succeeded in bringing debate to a close about what is important in the quest for human self-understanding. To say "We ought to so choose" acknowledges the issue implicitly.

Oakeshott unequivocally asserts that religion belongs to the world of practice. But religion is so bound up in personal self-understanding as to accompany one's sojourn in any of the modes and may perhaps come closer to acknowledging experience as a whole (offering an alternative to philosophy?) than a mode of experience could ever do. Consider the following (rather Kierkegaardian) remarks:

> Religion . . . is simply life itself, life dominated by the belief that its value is in the present, not merely in the past or the future, that if we lose ourselves we lose all. "Very few men, properly speaking, live at present," writes Swift, "but are providing to live another time." Such seems to me an irreligious life, the life of the world. The man of the world is careless of nothing save himself and his life; but to the religious man, life is too short and uncertain to be hoarded, too valuable to be spent on the pleasures of others, of the past or the future, too precious to be thrown away on

29. Oakeshott, "Religion and the World," 32, n. 1.

something he is not convinced is his highest good. In this sense, then, we are all, at moments, religious; and that these moments are not more frequent is due to nothing but our uncertain grasp on life itself, our comparative ignorance of the kind of life which satisfies, not one part of our nature, but the whole, the kind of life for which no retrospective regrets can ever be entertained.[30]

Moreover,

Memento vivere is the sole precept of religion. . . . The religious man, though he may take himself seriously, will not bore others by letting them know that he does so, because it is only in the world's view that a man is better off for being known to be what he is; for religion it is enough to be it.[31]

This is what Oakeshott meant when he said that religion is the consummation of practice, that "religion is, itself, the conduct of life."[32] But this consummation of practice is invisible in the ordinary course of practical affairs. Neither victories nor defeats in the affairs of the world concern the one who leads her life with religious seriousness. Nor is it in propositions, creeds, or rituals that one's experience is of this kind. Theology is a "qualified and limited" form of philosophy.[33] One might even say that, in the logic of Oakeshott's argument, theology offers an alternative to philosophy that philosophy is obliged to refuse. Adherents to propositions, creeds, or rituals can have an acute sense of the inadequacy of these as expressions of the experiential encounter that excites them, or, just as likely, they know too well that they let these practices stand in for their inability to live fully in the present in disregard of worldliness. Religion is the consummation of human conduct, but there is no institutional generalization of it that does not obscure and distort the experience. "Christendom" is a threat to the Christian life.

---

30. Oakeshott, "Religion and the World," 34–35.
31. Oakeshott, "Religion and the World," 37.
32. Oakeshott, *Experience and Its Modes*, 292.
33. Oakeshott, *Experience and Its Modes*, 335, n. 1.

Oakeshott borrows Augustine's insight that even if there is no salvation outside the church (and who knows the boundaries of the church?), to be a member by itself guarantees nothing. Conversely, in Oakeshottian terms, anyone who lives fully in the present moment is "saved." One can live religiously while pursuing scientific inquiry; one can "practice religion" and yet be suffused with worldliness. Augustine's "two cities" are, for Oakeshott, alternative self-understandings within a single world of experience.[34] This orientation of spirit cannot be a "mode" of experience because it surpasses any of the modes in personal significance without rejecting whatever the modes may have to offer with respect to enlarging our grasp of things and without revising the operations that instantiate a modal perspective.

So "religion finds its place in the world of practical experience," and "the most thoroughly and positively practical life is that of the artist or the mystic."[35] Oakeshott made it clear that the practical life "comprises all that we mean by a 'moral' life, a life directed by an idea of the right and the good; it includes all that we mean by beauty; it comprises the religious life; and it comprises a conception of truth and reality."[36] Religious experience designates some ambitions as vulgar, or at least not the whole of practical life. The practical life is constituted in tension between desires for pleasure and lofty aspirations between one's self-image and one's contingent circumstantial temptations.

34. Augustine elaborated in *The City of God* the doctrine of the two cities. There is a single human community, descended from the first parents, Adam and Eve, composed of individuals whose allegiance is either to the temporal things of this world or to the spiritual things of the heavenly kingdom to come, the "earthly city" and the "heavenly city." These "cities" are invisible on Earth, as only God can search the heart of a human being to know to which allegiance, regardless of external appearances, he or she subscribes, and thus to which end they may be destined. The metaphor of the two cities was thought by Oakeshott to represent two differing self-understandings, and he deemphasized Augustine's association of the heavenly city with the institutional church.
35. Oakeshott, *Experience and Its Modes*, 295–96.
36. Oakeshott, *Experience and Its Modes*, 296.

However, because religion in this sense can go with us when we engage in the characteristic activities of any of the modes, it cannot be the practical life merely; it is the practical life with a difference. Is religious experience "in" the practical mode but not "of" it? The "consummation" of practical life is not, in the obvious sense, practical if it is the life of the artist or mystic. Given Oakeshott's later translation of the "voice of poetry" to modal status, perhaps in the end it is not the artist but the mystic who will know this consummation, or perhaps the artist and the mystic are difficult to distinguish from one another. Oakeshott does not say anything explicit about it. However, we find this:

> The gift of a religious faith is that of a reconciliation to the unavoidable dissonances of a human condition, a reconciliation which is neither a denial, nor a substitute for remedial effort, nor a theoretical understanding in which the mystery of their occurrence is abated or even dispelled, but a mode of acceptance, a "graceful" response . . . it is as complete as it may be when it is a release from care and generates an unostentatious, unaccusing serenity in conduct . . . although a faith is an understanding, a theoretical understanding of a faith is not itself a faith.[37]

And,

> Religious faith is the evocation of a sentiment (the love, the glory, or the honour of God, for example, or even a humble *caritas*), to be added to all the others as the motive of all motives in terms of which the fugitive adventures of human conduct, without being released from their mortal and their moral conditions, are graced with an intimation of immortality . . . themselves encounters with eternity.[38]

There is, then, no mode of all modes, but there is a motive of all motives. Oakeshott knew well that the practical mode intrudes itself powerfully and incessantly into the other modes; we observe that

37. Oakeshott, *On Human Conduct*, 81.
38. Oakeshott, *On Human Conduct*, 85.

pursuers of the others—scientists, historians, poets—often fall prey to politicization. Science, history, and philosophy "are wholly independent of the world of practical experience. And when we seek in them the achievement of some practical end, when we approach them from the standpoint of practice, we misconceive their character."[39] Yet we also must admit that most people believe the practical world to be the foundation of all experience: "that it belongs to the character of thought to be for the sake of action, is assured in advance of the concurrence of the majority of mankind."[40]

Politics, which makes conspicuous the coerciveness—the willfulness—of the practical mode, is always with us. How shall we elude this domination? We cannot leave and go to some other universe where politics is absent. "It is impossible to conceive of the modification of experience I have called Practice ever disappearing. It is an arrest in experience, but it is indispensable to life."[41] If the individual's interior religious experience carries one beyond the control of the political, or the control of science, history, or poetry, the issue is the conversion of one's self-understanding to resisting by quiet refusal the obtrusive demands of practical life:

> The general view of the character of practical experience which stands in direct antithesis to the view I have suggested is that which sees in practice the complete and absolute realization of experience. All thought exists for the sake of action; action is the consummation of experience, and we try to understand the universe only in order to learn how to live. . . . To realize the will is itself to realize the mind as a whole.[42]

In the practical mode, there is continual tension between what is and what ought to be. So far, no "what is" has ever ended challenges from further thoughts of what ought to be, and no "ought to be" has been found to be all that it ought to be; there is forever a "not yet," an indissoluble link between what is and what ought to

39. Oakeshott, *Experience and Its Modes*, 297.
40. Oakeshott, *Experience and Its Modes*, 248.
41. Oakeshott, *Experience and Its Modes*, 350.
42. Oakeshott, *Experience and Its Modes*, 317.

be. These are expressions of a continuum of experience of the discrepancy between the present and future imagined and wished-for outcomes. Finality would take us beyond political and moral action, perhaps beyond life itself:

> Practice sees its given world of fact as there, always in order to be changed; and "what ought to be" remains, consequently, always discrepant from "what is here and now." Thus, resolution of this discrepancy which practice undertakes, can never finally be accomplished. . . . A theoretical resolution would be, if it were successful, a final resolution. But, since practical activity undertakes not this general resolution, but the particular resolution of all instances of this discrepancy, it undertakes what, from its nature, can never be brought to a conclusion. . . . For every achievement brings with it a new view of the criterion, which converts this momentary perfection into imperfection. Indeed, we may find that even the "ought not" of one moment is the "ought" of another. Nowhere in experience is there uninterrupted progress or final achievement.[43]

Oakeshott's philosophical exploration, then, delineates modes of experience. Philosophy's exploration cannot attach itself to any mode, and it cannot replace any mode. Popular "ranking" of the modes—such as promoting science to preeminence in our time, or asserting that all relationships are political—fails to notice, or denies, the concrete whole from which these views are abstracted. The glories of science cannot absorb or replace the religious experience; politics will fail repeatedly to provide religious satisfaction; the historian's lust for the past will alienate us from the present. The triumphs of science or of politics may and do challenge received versions of the religious experience, as also will the historian's critical, demythologizing account of the past. Oakeshott thought "history" to be a greater threat to Christianity than "science."[44]

43. Oakeshott, *Experience and Its Modes,* 290–91.
44. Oakeshott, *Experience and Its Modes,* 316.

But for Oakeshott experience exceeds received versions of any kind about anything. All experience is present experience: The historical past is a present understanding of the past; politics is present judgment of the past and hortatory assertions about our future; science is the present understanding of relationships expressed in quantitative terms; poetry is a momentary, passing release into a world of images delightful to contemplate. In all of this, we pursue the intimations of experience, investigating through or around the modes we encounter, with more or less imaginative insight, and we live, more or less attentively, toward the mysterious fullness of experience—that is, we live more or less "religiously."

It remains to note that the world seems to commingle as inseparable all of these modal experiences. We talk both of the politics of science and of the science of politics, of historical guilt and innocence (resisting the study of the past "for its own sake") judging the past by our present convictions, of the "story of history," history's "direction," its "end" or "goal," of "political correctness," of political "change," change putatively "for the better," change toward perfection, or "solving our problems." Is poetry supposed to encourage patriotism or to demythologize war through art? We talk of the "conflict" of science with religion. All of these take their place in the ordinary discourse of the day, and we should not expect them to disappear. From the point of view of philosophic inquiry, as Oakeshott understands it, these are irrelevancies, because they run together the modal perspectives with little regard for their contradictoriness, indicating the reigning passion for the practical/ political mode. He did not think his argument would cause this miscellany to disappear. There is nothing to prevent the world from cultivating its abstractions and muddles. There is little likelihood that self-delusion will often be recognized or acknowledged. Most of the time we live in and for abstractions. The philosopher occasionally breaks through toward concreteness, toward experience as a whole, but, like all humans, cannot live permanently there. For, Oakeshott concludes, "we shall not easily forget the sweet delight which lies in the empty kisses of abstraction."[45]

45. Oakeshott, *Experience and Its Modes,* 356.

The Relation of Philosophy to Conservatism

I

D AVID HUME BEGINS his essay "Of the Original Contract," observing that "no party in the present age, can well support itself, without a philosophical or speculative system of principles, annexed to its political or practical one; we accordingly find, that each of the factions, into which this nation is divided, has reared up a fabric of the former kind, in order to protect and cover the scheme of actions which it pursues."[1] Specifically, Hume tells us, one party traces the basis of government to the Deity, the other to the People in a kind of original contract. Hume does not quarrel with this development, allowing to each party a certain kind of insight. But neither of these views is philosophical. Rather these speculations are, as we would now say, ideological. That is, each party takes its relevant, but partial insight to be sufficient. Neither view exemplifies

Reprinted by permission from Corey Abel, ed., *The Meanings of Michael Oakeshott's Conservatism* (London: Imprint Academic, 2010), 112–25. Title appeared originally as "The Relation of Philosophy to Conservatism in the Thought of Michael Oakeshott."
1. David Hume, *Essays Moral, Political, Literary*, ed. and with a foreword, notes, and glossary by Eugene F. Miller; with an apparatus of variant readings from the 1889 edition by T. H. Green and T. H. Grose (Indianapolis: Liberty Fund, Inc., 1987), 465.

philosophy. In his essay, "Conduct and Ideology in Politics," Oakeshott says this:

> for many of us politics have become an activity in which we
> often believe ourselves to be unable to make decisions until
> we have found the answer to such questions as: What is
> liberty? What is justice? What is Democracy? or Socialism?
> or Liberalism? or Communism? etc. That is to say, we find
> ourselves equipped with a supply of words, most of them
> abstract nouns, and we want to discover their meaning. . . . It
> sometimes happens that even political parties are divided &
> inhibited from action because of a doubt about what one of
> these words means, or a dispute about its meaning. And
> alternatively, we feel well equipped and ready to make
> decisions when we are clear and confident about the mean-
> ings of these words.

In short, our politics have become what we call "ideological politics."[2]

For Hume and Oakeshott, philosophy requires one to consider
these partisan positions and disputes about abstract nouns philosophically, and thus to understand what element of insight we may
find, while recognizing what each leaves out in order to make their
positions or definitions coherent to themselves and, by concealing
ambiguity and abridgement, to give the appearance of authority in
political debate.

The assumption of the sufficiency of a partial insight deprives the
speculations of politicians and intellectuals of philosophical status.
For Hume, to give allegiance to a party is to abandon philosophy.
As a practical matter, the compromise or moderation of these
speculative antagonisms, a compromise between parties or the
acceptance of a loose range of definitional meanings, though they
may be politically efficacious, do not constitute a philosophical understanding. Philosophy is neither about partisanship nor about
compromise. The philosopher recognizes the prevailing political terrain for what it is and must be, but does not intrude to offer policy

2. Michael Oakeshott, "Conduct and Ideology in Politics," in *What Is History?
and Other Essays*, 245.

alternatives. Philosophic reflection might or might not soften partisanship for the sake of stability and the retention of openness to the life of the mind, but what happens will reflect suspension of inquiry and a decision to limit debate.

Philosophy, when considering politics, is not in the business of seeking power but of understanding what is going on. Were the politicians to pursue philosophy they would sacrifice their effectiveness for action, as they are always ready to point out if pressed. The philosopher's critical examination does not seek to overthrow the prevailing order, nor to justify it as if it were in need of a foundation other than that emergent from the choices in contingent circumstances that a set of human beings have made through time and found to work, or not work, for them, in their own terms.

Thus no regime can claim finality in the face of the insuperable temporality and mortality of human things. On the other hand, achieving stability and decency is possible, and the sobriety of the philosopher constrains his desire for more than the human condition permits. Should one call this "conservative"? Needless to say this is not necessarily the meaning of "conservatism" in the contemporary Anglo-American world. In debates this is usually and loosely referred to as political realism, although such realism does not end the debates over what is really the case, and those who call themselves realists regularly offend the others who naturally think they know what is real.

It would be better, perhaps, to call what Hume and Oakeshott present philosophic sobriety. For they recognize, as did Socrates before them, that human claims to know do not amount to much, and that the beginning of wisdom is in knowing that we do not know. It is my contention that Oakeshott follows in Hume's footsteps in his understanding of political philosophy. The real object of Hume's critique of the original contract, however, is not those who, as a practical matter, place their faith in the people and advocate political authority by consent. His sharpest criticism is reserved for those who have elevated the idea of the original contract into a grand philosophical scheme: "They assert," Hume tells us, "not only that government in its earliest infancy arose from consent or rather the voluntary acquiescence of the people; but also, that, even at present, when it has attained full maturity, it rests on no other foundation."[3]

Hume is criticizing the Lockean tradition and the idea that politics has an independently identifiable rational foundation. But he is also noticing the revolutionary character of such thinking. Anticipating Kant, and long before Marx, Hume could see that this type of political philosophy encouraged the proposition that philosophers should change the world in accordance with an abstract idea of how it ought to be. These thinkers, Hume asserts, can find nothing in the observable world corresponding to their abstract ideas. What we do observe are the habits of keeping promises and submitting to laws which emanate from acknowledged authority, all of which is the cumulative result of long periods of trial and error in which those habits were doubtful and intermittent, a difficult achievement to say the least, the end not the beginning of a long, arduous development:

> No compact or agreement, it is evident, was expressly formed for general submission; an idea far beyond the comprehension of savages: Each exertion of authority in the chieftain must have been particular, and called forth by the present exigencies of the case: The sensible utility, resulting from his interposition, made these exertions become daily and more frequent; and their frequency gradually produced an habitual, and, if you please to call it so, a voluntary, and therefore precarious acquiescence, in the people.[4]

The breaking of these civil habits through revolution is perilous. Speaking of the so-called Glorious Revolution of 1689, Hume says:

> Let not the establishment at the Revolution deceive us, or make us so much in love with its philosophical origin to government, as to imagine all others monstrous and irregular. Even that event was far from corresponding to these refined ideas. It was only the succession, and that only in the regal part of the government, which was then changed.[5]

3. Hume, *Essays*, Miller ed., 469.
4. Hume, *Essays*, Miller ed., 468.
5. Hume, *Essays*, Miller ed., 472.

There was no popular consent, but only acquiescence to a change perpetrated by a few hundred individuals. Oakeshott's inaugural address at The London School of Economics in 1951, "Political Education," and his essay from the early 1960s on "Political Discourse," are modern versions of Hume's argument. "Political Discourse" Oakeshott remarks, "has, then, for a very long time been distinguished on account of the variety of special vocabularies of belief in which it is conducted. . . . In this manner they impose conditions upon political deliberation and discourse, and upon the kinds of choice to be made in response to emergent situations."[6] And, he continues, "this craving for demonstrative political argument may make us discontented with ordinary political discourse which, because it is not demonstrative, we may be tempted to regard as a species of unreason."[7] And,

> so far from a political ideology being the quasi-divine parent of political activity, it turns out to be its earthly stepchild. Instead of an independently premeditated scheme of ends to be pursued, it is a system of ideas abstracted from the manner in which people have been accustomed to go about the business of attending to the arrangements of their societies.[8]

Hume does not intend to "exclude the consent of the people from being one just foundation of government where it has place. It is surely the best and most sacred of any. I only pretend," he goes on,

> that it has very seldom had place in any degree, and never almost in its full extent. And that therefore some other foundation of government must also be admitted. . . . Reason, history, and experience shew us, that all political societies have had an origin much less accurate and regular; and were one to choose a period of time, when the people's consent was the least regarded in public transactions, it would be precisely on the establishment of a new government.[9]

6. Michael Oakeshott, *Rationalism in Politics* (1991), 76. Hereafter: *RIP*.
7. Okaeshott, *RIP*, 95.
8. Oakeshott, *RIP*, 51.
9. Hume, *Essays*, Miller ed., 474.

In short, political authority based on consent is an achievement emerging from a long process of accommodation, representing not the origin of political authority but rather the gradual transformation of the relationship of authority from command and obedience to acknowledgment and consent. The revolutionary implication of contract theory lurks in the insistence that existing regimes must be continually re-formed to conform to the shape some imagine they would have if they had originated in a pure contract in which all residual alternative forms of human relationship are also transformed. One need think only of the question of the family today to see this.

Contract theory is thus a sophisticated argument criticizing the past and present in terms of a model for an imagined and desired future, an argument such as Rousseau launched in his "Discourse on the Origins of Inequality." It is philosophizing in order to change, not only, or even principally, to understand and explain. Such a "philosophy" naturally allies itself to party movements attuned to the preferred alterations; and, it is, therefore, a higher form of partisanship, the carrying on of politics by other means, seeking to lend gravity to a party program.

But in criticizing abstraction and thus political radicalism, Hume by no means abandons the radicalism of philosophy. He understands perfectly well that philosophy as such calls into question all conventions and habituations, if only by naming them as conventional and habitual. Philosophy cannot avoid politics because philosophy can have powerful political implications, as is evident in his time. From the Platonic Socrates we learned that radical questioning opens the way to the quest for the best regime altogether, the search for political knowledge transcending mere political opinion. But Hume is content to warn of the disruption philosophy can cause, especially when it is perverted by becoming ideological and partisan, and the quest for the best regime is itself subject to this perversion. Hume's skepticism dictates that neither longing for the heavenly city, nor longing for the end of history, is fulfilled or achieved in the philosophical understanding of politics. When Socrates says at the end of the ninth book of the *Republic* that, having caught sight of the heavenly city, one could order one's life in accordance with the heavenly city, he means to show us that this comes after liberation from the illusion that politics can take us there.

For, Hume argues, "though an appeal to general opinion may justly, in the speculative sciences of metaphysics, natural philosophy, or astronomy, be deemed unfair and inconclusive, yet in all questions with regard to morals, as well as criticism, there is really no other standard, by which any controversy can ever be decided." There can be no moral authority in opinions that run far from the "general practice of mankind." Hume thus draws a "conservative" lesson from his philosophic radicalism in his concluding comment on Plato's *Crito*:

> The only passage I meet with in antiquity, where the obligation of obedience to government is ascribed to a promise, is in PLATO's *Crito*: where SOCRATES refuses to escape from prison, because he had tacitly promised to obey the laws. Thus he builds a *tory* consequence of passive obedience, on a *whig* foundation of the original contract. New discoveries are not to be expected in these matters. If scarce any man, till very lately, ever imagined that government was founded on compact, it is certain, that it cannot, in general, have any such foundation.[10]

What then is political activity? Is it the interminable effort to make our ideals and aspirations cohere with the contingent circumstances in which as historical and mortal beings, saturated with temporality, we live and die? Must we forever live at this intersection in which the actuality of things continually outstrips our comprehension and control? If meaning is to be found, must we look for it elsewhere than in politics? I think this is the lesson from both Hume and Oakeshott.

They are political skeptics: It is only in our latter day political world—suffused by the ideological deformation of philosophy, and which, at the same time, has lost confidence in the ancient pursuit of the divine, eternal things—that they are called conservative. To be conservative in this sense is accused of being itself an ideology.

10. Hume, *Essays*, Miller ed., 487.

To argue this way is ultimately to deny the possibility of philosophy in the classic sense.

Hume and Oakeshott do not live and die by the prevailing sentiments and longings, the political rages, of their time and place. But neither are they reactionaries who long for an imagined past which is, after all, over and done with. Their philosophical reflections are entirely clear and un-deluded as to the dominant political terrain of their times. Philosophically, they think beyond the confines of their time without believing they can leap out of their time into some other. If, as Oakeshott famously argued, the task of politics is to keep the ship afloat, the other tasks of life belong to other modes of living, beyond the comprehension of politics. Politics gains importance because it is intrusive and unavoidable, an intractable feature of human existence; and it is interminable because it must try to make the temporal manageable. Yet because politics is the very emblem of temporality, it cannot extricate itself from temporality's endlessness. Politics must attend to the arrangements of sets of people whom chance and choice have brought together through time. Oakeshott, quoting F. H. Bradley, found politics "a necessary evil." Politics cannot get to the end of its task and terminate itself.

Oakeshott held that practical life, unavoidable and ever-present, is nevertheless not the foundation of other activities such as philosophic reflection, historical study, scientific research, or poetic expression, and the question of religion he left in ambiguity. These are not, for him, peculiar ways to carry on the struggles of practical life by eccentric means; they are revelations of the multidimensional character of human experience in which play counters work, enjoyment moderates ambition, conversation restrains debate, and contemplative delight releases us from the deadliness of doing. Oakeshott of course acknowledged his conservative disposition, but he thought of himself as a philosopher. His interest in policy debates was modest, and he was as capable of criticizing a conservative who mixes politics with philosophy as he was a liberal or a radical. The thinkers he admired were those relative few whom he thought honored the distinction between studying and explaining on the one hand, and asserting and prescribing on the other. For him, philosophy seeks to identify and understand the assumptions

that people make in order to make sense of the world for themselves, and to justify the conclusions they reach. Philosophy, he
said, expresses itself in the indicative mood; to philosophize is to
disengage, not to intervene. To consider politics philosophically is
to describe the necessary character of politics in its endless efforts
to preserve and to change; it is not to prescribe courses of action.

In revealing the character of politics, philosophers have done
what, as philosophers, they can do. They derive from their philosophical understanding no authority to direct politics because, to
act politically, they must, like everyone else, accept uncritically some
presupposition, for purposes of action, thus leaving philosophy
behind; they cannot, as the saying goes, unite theory and practice.
Those who seek this unification may use philosophic ideas to lend
support to their political dispositions, but they are using them in an
unphilosophic way. Oakeshott, in being consistent, does not quite
tell individuals not to do this, but rather tries to identify what they
are doing and to elicit recognition of what they are doing. To make
the point clear: Oakeshott does not think that it is possible to unify
theory and practice. Whatever anyone thinks or claims he is doing,
he is not doing that because it cannot be done.

This is not a conservative argument in the usual sense. That is, it
is not a prudential argument that it would be better for us to be cautious, nor is it an argument that what is older is better than what is
newer. Even if there was an antiquarian or romantic streak in Oakeshott as some allege, there is nothing antiquarian or romantic in
Oakeshott's arguments. He is speaking about what he thinks we can
and cannot do regardless of felt urgency or attractiveness.

Oakeshott is speaking also, as did Hume, of how political parties
are moved by different attitudes and outlooks while all being subject to the limitations of politics. Political activity receives all of these
alternatives and constrains them by its own logic. Radicals will be
radicals; reactionaries will be reactionaries, but what they will not
do is transcend or supersede the interminability of politics, nor the
complications that beset their ideas in action. Of course, they can
cause enormous wreckage in the effort to do what cannot be done,
and in the twentieth century, needless to say, they did so repeatedly.
Nor is there reason to think that this will fail to be repeated in the

twenty-first century, on the contrary, continuations are evident. There can only be better and worse regimes, and there can be a wide range of ways to be better or worse. This will, of course, suggest inquiry into the principles for judging better and worse. Whatever those principles may be, they must acknowledge diverse practical arrangements. Even if there are universal principles, as I think, the local circumstances of regimes cannot be disregarded. Practical judgments of what is possible for local regimes are inevitable and unavoidable.

II

For Oakeshott, the local cannot be replaced by the universal, the abstract cannot control the concrete, even though the idea of the universal is central to thinking about politics in our time. Oakeshott's understanding of the character of politics thus needs further explication. I propose to do this by considering another of Oakeshott's famous remarks: that politics is the "pursuit of intimations." I want to explore this in some detail because to understand it is essential to grasping the relation between his philosophical understanding of politics and what is usually identified as his conservatism.

When Oakeshott said that "this is the best of all possible worlds, and everything in it is a necessary evil," he thereby contradicted the prevailing wisdom in intellectual circles. His view runs athwart much academic opinion—conservative, liberal, and radical alike.

His criticism was directed less at specific beliefs, programs, or actions, and more at what he thought to be a pervasive and mistaken modern understanding of the function of reason in practical life. He thought that virtually all the current political stances, wherever they might be located on the Left/Right spectrum, were infected in some measure by rationalism and ideology. None of them could command the allegiance of the philosopher as Oakeshott understood the philosopher. The central passage from his inaugural address in which he seeks to describe the actuality of political activity is this:

> In politics, then, every enterprise is a consequential enterprise, the pursuit, not of a dream, or of a general principle,

but of an intimation. What we have to do with is something less imposing than logical implications or necessary consequences: but if the intimations of a tradition of behaviour are less dignified or more elusive than these, they are not on that account less important. Of course, there is no piece of mistake-proof apparatus by means of which we can elicit the intimation most worth while pursuing; and not only do we often make gross errors of judgment in this matter, but also the total effect of a desire satisfied is so little to be forecast, that our activity of amendment is often found to lead us where we would not go. Moreover, the whole enterprise is liable at any moment to be perverted by the incursion of an approximation to empiricism in the pursuit of power. These are features which can never be eliminated; they belong to the character of political activity.[11]

Oakeshott intended to put activism, utopianism, policy science, and a certain sort of pietism in their place by demonstrating that their voices in politics promote an illusory understanding of what politics actually is. He did not expect that his critique would silence these voices, nor did he intend to legislate about what voices might express themselves there; to do so would be to expect too much from philosophic understanding, and would betray philosophy by turning it into a political, rather than an explanatory, engagement. In a sense, the philosophic critique is indifferent to the presence or absence of those voices since, once philosophic understanding has been achieved, the philosopher's interest in such goings-on is satisfied. The description of the prevailing political terrain, and the critique of misplaced pretensions within that context, were as far as one could go philosophically. He cast his skeptical eye on his own political predilections as well as those of others.

Oakeshott also thought that modern politics has long been constituted in a dialectic between those who are skeptical of the power of governments to reconstruct and perfect social life, and those with faith in our power to do exactly that. Thus, rationalism will not dis-

11. Oakeshott, *RIP*, 57.

appear, but if its pretensions are prey to disillusionment, they can be restrained from extremism by the continuing presence of the skeptical voice. Nonetheless, his description of political activity as the "pursuit of intimations," which has been attacked as vague traditionalism, mysticism, or romanticism, remains a central summary expression of his thinking. The accusations of vagueness, mysticism, and romanticism are ways of asserting that he lacked, "concreteness in his political philosophy," or that he could not deal with the modern world. Yet to understand what he meant by "the pursuit of intimations," which he thought to be the opposite of these things, is essential to understanding the precise meaning of Oakeshott's position on the character of political activity, and the degree of concreteness Oakeshott achieved. As he said, in response to his critics, the phrase "pursuit of intimations" is intended neither "as a description of the motives of politicians nor of what they believe themselves to be doing, but of what they actually succeed in doing."[12] He intended to make a statement, as he put it, in the indicative mood, not to propose another world.

What, then, did he mean by the "pursuit of intimations"? Let us consider the salient points of the passage cited, and place them in the context of his philosophy of the practical life. Oakeshott used the term "intimations" in contrast to the terms "dreams," "general principles," "logical implications," and "necessary consequence." Dreams and general principles naturally figure constantly in politics. Oakeshott was questioning the adequacy of such terms, philosophically speaking, not their presence. Accurate description notices and accepts their presence.

He knew as well as anyone that dreams of possibilities not yet realized obviously are catalysts of political action. And general principles, such as, for instance, the principles expressed in natural law theories, constitutions, or Declarations of Independence, are central features of political life. He did not think they unambiguously tell us what, in specific cases, to do, and they are appealed to in defense of contradictory interpretations of our rights and duties. Oakeshott thought that natural laws are descriptive of the forms in

---

12. Oakeshott, *RIP*, 67.

which we think about moral duties, but he did not think we could deduce from them legal obligations. Between the expression of moral duty and the statement of legal obligation there must intervene judgment and decision, presumably emanating from an authority acknowledged to be entrusted with this responsibility.

He thought that most of the common terms of political discourse are irreducibly ambiguous in their meaning. We might all agree that *salus populi suprema lex,* but does *salus* mean survival or does it go on to guarantee a certain standard of living? And who exactly do we include in *populi*? Does the term "democracy" imply a procedure for preventing tyranny by limiting the power of governments, or does it mean a plebiscitary legitimation of the unlimited use of that power?

Oakeshott was pointing to the unavoidability in politics of appraisal, judgment, and decision. Political actors continually characterize their states of affairs, and devise what they hope are appropriate responses. If they could deduce logical implications from their situations, they could leap over the familiar, apparently ineluctable, constraints in politics. They would simply know what is to be done instead of having to try a course of action in a condition of uncertainty.

In politics, freedom does not mean being able to devise courses of action unconstrained by previous actions. Yet previous actions do not determine us either, if by that is meant that there is a necessary path, direction, or pattern in our circumstances that cannot but work itself out. The task is to understand better what we already understand: a complex state of affairs susceptible to differing accounts, requiring judgment as to what within it is a resource and what a hindrance, what is desirable and what is undesirable, what is appropriate or not. Wherever the possibilities of conversation or argument are not suppressed, this complexity cannot fail to show itself. We can discover no unarguable path to travel from where we have been to where we imagine we may be going. Yet neither is there an infinite number of paths available to us. There are only those that we can discern emerging from the context we have, and we must decide the relative merits or appropriateness of the alternatives. What is imaginable to us depends on what we are prepared to recognize in the context of what we have already experienced. This actuality coexists with, but is not transformed by, the rhetoric of certainty that also appears. It is part of the reality of politics that we must discriminate among the claims to know according to what seems possible to know.

If we could show that there are logically necessary consequences that follow from our situation, we might in principle transcend the need of argument and persuasion. We would then not be imaginative agents of plausible but uncertain courses of action, but conduits through whom the necessary course of action expresses itself. "Human activity," Oakeshott says,

> with whatever it may be concerned, enjoys a circumscribed range of movement. The limits which define this range are historic, that is to say, they are themselves the product of human activity. Generally speaking, there are no "natural" limits as distinct from historic limits: those which we ascribe to "human nature," for example, are not less historic than those which we immediately recognize as springing from conditions determined by human activity. Even what a man may do with his physical strength is determined by the historic devices and inventions of men, and no community has been without such devices. Being historic, they are not absolute, but on any occasion they are not on that account any the less limits. They may be wide or narrow, they are never absent. The flight of imagination, the poet's power over words and images, the scientist's hypotheses, the philosopher's engagements and disengagements, and the practical man's projects and enterprises are all of them exploitations of what is given or intimated in the condition of the world he inhabits. . . . So it is with our political activity. . . . The politician always has a certain field of vision and a certain range of opportunity; what he is able to contemplate, to desire, or to attempt is subject to the historic limits of his situation. And in order to understand his activity it is necessary first to consider the field within which he moves, the choices that are available to him and the enterprises he is

able to entertain. Indeed, until we have understood this, any other judgment we may make about his activity—judgments of approval or disapproval for example—are liable to lack force and relevance.[13]

The "pursuit of intimations" captures an element in many familiar experiences: imagining possibilities; desiring to try something new; believing that a course of action is necessary or unavoidable; wanting to correct what are believed to be past errors; defending current practices against arguments that they are mistaken or inadequate; reconciling the pressure of the new with affection for the old; extricating oneself from a too constraining situation; trying to settle disputes in the hope of tranquility or orderliness; extrapolating trends from what we understand ourselves to have been doing; responding to what others insist is important; deciding how important an issue is; considering what is appropriate, tasteful, morally acceptable, or simply possible given our resources as we now understand them; translating ideals into something we might actually do; discovering what changes reformers really might undertake; determining what terms like "solidarity," "community," "rights," "social justice," "welfare," or "new world order" mean in terms of policies we might actually adopt. These engagements are all embedded in contexts.

Oakeshott was prone to say, the pursuit of perfection as the crow flies is a delusion. It is all very well for me to say that what I want is to be happy. But eventually I must specify what would make me happy: "I cannot *want* 'happiness,'" Oakeshott once remarked, "what I want is to idle in Avignon or to hear Caruso sing."[14] His point was that the desire to be happy has to turn into something intelligible to do in the practical realm. The abstraction of desire in practical life cannot ultimately escape from the limits imposed by the actually available resources of the practical life. For Oakeshott, then, to examine politics philosophically is to recollect that no direction is logically implicated—there are only intimations. Such recollection may inhibit the politician who equips himself for practical action by

13. Michael Oakeshott, *The Politics of Faith and the Politics of Scepticism*, 116–17. Hereafter: *FS*.
14. Michael Oakeshott, *On Human Conduct*, 53. Hereafter: *OHC*.

forgetting this in discovering a felt necessity. What such a "necessity" is, of course, is the intimation to pursue at that point, but the politician may feel he needs something grander, a cause, or crisis, to grease the skids of persuasion (and he may well be right). What the philosopher risks forgetting is not this, but that for him to transcend the practical life is not to subdue or command it:

> From the standpoint of practical experience there can be no more dangerous disease than the love and pursuit of truth in those who do not understand, or have forgotten, that a man's first business is to live. And life, we have seen, can be conducted only at the expense of an arrest in experience. The practical consciousness knows well enough what is inimical to its existence, and often has the wisdom to avoid it. *Pereat veritas fiat vita.* It is not the clear sighted, not those who are fashioned for thought and the ardours of thought, who can lead the world. Great achievements are accomplished in the mental fog of practical experience. What is farthest from our needs is that kings should be philosophers. The victims of thought, those who are intent upon what is unlimitedly satisfactory in experience, are self-confessed betrayers life, and must pursue their way without the encouragement of the practical consciousness, which is secure in the knowledge that philosophical thought can make no relevant contribution to the coherence of its world of experience.[15]

Oakeshott's skepticism, then, did not exclude accurate description of what goes on in the world. It denied the power to transform the practical life into something else. Oakeshott established that the common acceptance of the primacy of the practical life, and hence of politics was, philosophically speaking, mistaken. It is easy, he admitted, to see why we are receptive to the claims of practicality upon us: We are born into mortality and must, from birth, start to learn how to make our way in the midst of what is both hospitable and inhospitable to our presence. Practical activity requires us to undertake alteration and preservation, and we experience the "necessity

---

15. Michael Oakeshott, *Experience and Its Modes*, 320–21. Hereafter: *EM.*

of which no man can relieve himself."[16] The world, understood practically, is familiar and ever present, it is where we pass our lives. Its necessity does not, however, constitute its comprehensiveness, and its necessity is a "necessary evil": There are strong "prejudices and preconceptions of the larger part of mankind, who find it impossible to entertain the idea that this practical world, within which they are confined as if in a prison, is other than the universe itself."[17] In extricating himself from conventional thinking, Oakeshott sought what he called a philosophy of practical experience, as opposed to a "practical philosophy." He dismissed practical philosophy because it is not an effort to understand politics philosophically, but rather an undertaking to defend a political position by, first, transposing the terms of argument into abstract concepts; and then, secondly, appealing to those concepts as the ground for the practical conclusions one wants to defend. To declare, for example, that all history is the story of class struggle, and then to search for evidence to support this contention with a view to identifying the historically relevant class or classes, is to give up the desire for comprehensive understanding in favor of an abridgement that supports various practical political engagements. That this engagement is wrapped in the trappings of theoretical language, which give the appearance of transcending the limitations of the pursuit of intimations, is either a disguise or a self-deception.

To elaborate a philosophy of practical experience, by contrast, is to try to understand the distinguishing features of practical engagement that will attend every specific practical undertaking whatever. Here, Oakeshott undoubtedly had in mind such achievements as Aristotle's recognition, in the *Nicomachean Ethics,* that a theoretical account of the practical moral life insightfully describes, but offers no relief from, the necessity to act in contingent circumstances, through specific conduct, arrived at by making judgments within a way of life, and not by deductions from abstract principles. There was for Oakeshott, as for Aristotle, no way for a theoretical account of what goes on in practical conduct to eliminate the complex dif-

16. Oakeshott, *EM*, 257.
17. Oakeshott, *EM*, 249.

ficulties of moral decisions. In response to the objection that, by rejecting general principles, he provided no standards for detecting incoherencies or deciding on reforms, Oakeshott replied,

> Do you want to be told that in politics there is, what certainly exists nowhere else, a mistake-proof manner of deciding what should be done? How does a scientist, with the current conditions of physics before him, decide upon a direction of profitable advance? What considerations passed through the minds of medieval builders when they detected the inappropriateness of building in stone as if they were building in wood? How does a critic arrive at the judgment that a picture is incoherent, that the artist's treatment of some passages is inconsistent with his treatment of others?[18]

Practical activity thus has a character of an identifiable sort. The ends pursued there exemplify practical engagement, but do not transform it. A theoretical account is an attempt at saying faithfully, in different words, what is going on. For Oakeshott a philosophical understanding of politics is categorically distinct from theorizing a justification for political ends or goals.

Because practical life is constituted in promoting and preventing change in our existence, it cannot change once and for all. If it could, it would cease to be what it is, and become something altogether different. Claims that we could work through the "necessary evils" of politics to end the necessity of politics, misunderstand what is actually going on. Practical life is driven by the desire to make coherent and satisfactory what is incoherent and unsatisfactory. Oakeshott thought he had accounted for why the practical desire for coherence must remain unfulfilled. In *Experience and Its Modes* he argues along the following lines (to paraphrase):

> In practical life, what seems to offer coherence is what is taken to be true. In practical conduct we always, implicitly or explicitly, consider the degree to which we have achieved coherence. Every human being is, in principle, an agent of

18. Oakeshott, *RIP*, 69.

opinion. Opinions are significant since they are assessments of coherence or incoherence in our lives. The existing state of affairs at every moment exposes possibilities of something "to be" which is "not yet" and each moment of coherence is precarious, an incipient incoherence. There is no point at which it ceases to be possible to think of a "to be" which is "not yet." The "to be" which is "not yet" expresses a possible alteration of "what is" and thus defeats the hope of having already achieved coherence. There are no gaps in consciousness, but always a contiguity—a touching—of what has been, what is, and what we imagine may come to be: "The 'to be' of practice is never a world merely discrepant from 'what is'; it is always and everywhere considered, not merely a 'not yet' or a 'not here,' but in some sense, more coherent than 'what is.'"[19]

Thus the "to be" can become "what ought to be"—we can find value in it. What we take as practical facts are unstable for they are what "is," now, as opposed to what may have been yesterday, and what might be tomorrow. In practical activity, what is the case now could be otherwise, and possibilities for being otherwise are always with us. We look for what is satisfactory, which always involves trying to find what we think coherent. The consequences of specific, practical undertakings cannot suffice. Success, no less than failure, in the gaining of specific ends excites appraisal and assessment, leading on to other "not yets" that we think either ought or ought not to be: "Truth is sought in what is other than what is given."[20]

So long as the future is an essential element in practical appraisal, coherence has to elude us; we are never without unrealized ideas. The completeness we may hope to enjoy is always attended by not yet integrated possibilities. There is no independent body of things we might fix in a conclusive arrangement. Alterability is inexhaustible. Thus, if, as we stated earlier, freedom does not mean liberation from what we have been, it does mean acting toward what we think will make for coherence as a response to what we have been. "Free-

19. Cf. Oakeshott, *EM*, 261 *passim*.
20. Oakeshott, *EM*, 265.

dom," Oakeshott concluded, is to be understood as "an idea which has relevance in the practical world of activity and nowhere else."[21] As Oakeshott saw it, freedom is realized in attaining practical truth in the sense of attaining coherence, of harmonizing the disharmonies of life. To attain what we think true because in it we find coherence involves reconciling conflicting opinions in the practical life. Individuals are agents of the pursuit of coherence, differentiating themselves from each other as they define themselves in the context of each other's presence. But if we think the momentary attainment of coherence is discovering our *telos*, we are mistaken. The restlessness of the human spirit cannot be content; coherence is evanescent. "The practical world," Oakeshott remarks,

> because it is a world of activity and change, is a world of oppositions to be balanced (because they cannot be unified), of contradictions which (because they cannot be resolved) must be coordinated. The practical self and its interests can never give way before the interests of "others," the relationships into which it enters are external to itself; and, since in practical experience the practical self is the very embodiment of reality, its dissolution is a contradiction and inconceivable.[22]

To the extent we find coherence we think ourselves free, unless and until we find the coherence we have attained turning into unlooked for constraint. When this happens, we find ourselves cast once more into necessity:

> If a man thinks to set himself free, in any save a vague and metaphorical sense, by the study of science or of history or by the pursuit of philosophy he is grossly mistaken. The only truth that makes a man free is practical truth, the possession of a coherent world of practical ideas. Indeed, practical truth and freedom seem to me inseparable; wherever the one is, the other will be found also.[23]

21. Oakeshott, *EM*, 267, n. 1.
22. Oakeshott, *EM*, 270.
23. Oakeshott, *EM*, 268.

Practical life undertakes to manage what is never fully under control. Will and desire cannot be purged from a world in which self-awareness and diversity of opinions can at most temporarily be suppressed. There is always more that could be said than has been said, and those who may say it. The stability of coherence is the friendly enemy of the restlessness of freedom. In conjunction, they make for the discordant concord of practical life.

The Philosophical Skeptic
in an Impatient Age

M ICHAEL OAKESHOTT WAS BORN on December 11, 1901, in
Kent, England, and died December 19, 1990, at his cottage in
the village of Acton on the Dorset coast. He distinguished himself
as an undergraduate at Gonville & Caius College, Cambridge, and
then as a fellow of the college and lecturer in history. From the
1920s he remained at Cambridge, except for service in the British
army in World War II, until the late 1940s. Thereafter he spent a brief
period in Oxford before appointment as professor of political science at the London School of Economics and Political Science (LSE)
in 1951. There he taught in and convened the Government Department, introducing the MSc in the History of Political Thought. This
one-year degree program attracted students from many parts of the
world, especially Canada and the United States. Although he officially
retired in 1968, Oakeshott continued to participate in the fall term of
the program, presenting papers in its general seminar until 1980.

Oakeshott was an extraordinary teacher and lecturer, enjoying
exchanges with students that faculty half his age could not match.
In old age he never forgot what it was to be young. He was charmed

Reprinted by permission from Catherine H. Zuckert, ed., *Political Philosophy
in the Twentieth Century* (Cambridge: Cambridge University Press, 2011),
142–53. Title appeared originally as "Michael Oakeshott: The Philosophical
Skeptic in an Impatient Age."

by the exuberance of undergraduates as they were charmed by him. The period from the 1950s to the 1980s was a fertile period for the study of political theory in the Government Department at LSE. Oakeshott had attracted an illustrious group of scholars and teachers: John Charvet, Maurice Cranston, Elie Kedourie, Wolfgang von Leyden, Kenneth Minogue, Robert Orr, and others.

Trained in modern history and an admirer of such greats as Frederick Maitland, Oakeshott was devoted to the study of political thought. In his Cambridge lectures in the 1930s he examined the history of political thought. The distinguished medievalist Brian Tierney and the great Locke scholar Peter Laslett have related to me their vivid recollections as undergraduates of his lectures even after fifty or more years. His notebooks, which go back to the early 1920s, show that he studied the works of Plato and Aristotle with care. A philosopher more than a historian, at times he said he was neither. He ranked thinkers according to the degree to which they escaped preoccupation with merely practical issues of the moment. He was deeply interested in the study of politics but not attracted to political activism. In his celebrated introduction to Hobbes's *Leviathan*,[1] he singled out Plato, Hobbes, and Hegel as exemplary thinkers and wrote of three great moments: Plato exemplified the tradition of "reason and nature," Hobbes that of "will and artifice," and Hegel that of the "rational will." These thinkers examined politics as the intersection of time and eternity—they were interested in understanding the character of politics and the human condition as such while being alert to the pressing contingencies of their time and place.

In essays that he wrote on the nature of philosophy and political philosophy in the 1930s and 1940s, Oakeshott insisted on the open-endedness of thought, referring to philosophy as "radically subver-

---

1. Michael Oakeshott, introduction to *Leviathan*, by Thomas Hobbes, in Oakeshott, ed., Blackwell's Political Texts. I refer to this version because when Oakeshott published a collection of his Hobbes essays in 1975, *Hobbes on Civil Association*, he revised the original introduction substantially. Comparison of the two versions is instructive for those who wish to follow Oakeshott's thinking on Hobbes.

sive" questioning that shuns ideology and political advocacy.[2] By "subversive" he did not mean the attempt to revolutionize regimes or public policy. He meant rather that the aspiration of the philosopher is to grasp experience as a whole without an ulterior motive other than to understand better what one already understands in part. For such an inquirer political allegiances will be weak: Philosophy is not the carrying on of politics by other means. Philosophers may be deeply interested in what is to be learned by examining political life, but ultimately their inquiry carries them beyond politics as they come to realize that interminable incoherencies unavoidably arise in politics. If their vocation is to pursue wisdom or, as Oakeshott put it, to understand better what they already understand in part, then they must accept the implication of that pursuit.

He spells these ideas out in his first major book, *Experience and Its Modes* (1933).[3] This remarkable work, which remains in print to this day, established him as an important and original philosophic voice. In it Oakeshott acknowledges the influence of Hegel's *Phenomenology of Spirit* and F. H. Bradley's *Appearance and Reality.* *Experience and Its Modes* is ostensibly in the tradition of British Hegelianism, but readers will see that it is the work of a most creative mind that has absorbed and digested much, making it his own, and offering thoughts distinctive of the author.

The gist of his argument is this: The distinction between "the world" and our "experience of the world" is untenable. The world and our experience of it are interrelated so tightly that efforts to treat them as separable fail. The world and our interpretation of the world are a single world of our experience. The world is a whole and is a world of thought. We have no access to anything that is not in our thought. We invent various modes for interpreting experience. We try to comprehend experience as a whole through varying, partial interpretations that fasten on some features of experience as if they were sufficient to explain the whole.

---

2. Michael Oakeshott, *Religion, Politics and the Moral Life.*
3. Full bibliographical information for this and other important works by Oakeshott can be found herein, in "Selected Works by Michael Oakeshott."

In 1933 Oakeshott expounded three prominent modes of experience: science, history, and practice. He admitted that there could be many modes and that these three were not exhaustive, but he thought they were both prominent and sufficiently developed for careful analysis. Science makes sense of the world by interpreting all experience in terms of stable, quantitative relationships that are fully transparent (a world understood *sub specie quantitatis*); history makes sense of the world by treating all experience as past experience (a world understood *sub specie praeterito*); and practice—which includes both politics and religion—understands the world as the tension between "what is" and "what ought to be" or *sub specie voluntatis,* a world defined by will and desire.

Each mode attempts to make sense out of experience as a whole from the point of view of its own assumptions or postulates. Each achieves coherence to its own satisfaction only by discounting those elements of experience that would pose difficult, intolerable contradictions. Thus the philosopher's investigation does not "correct" a mode's deficiencies of abstraction by amalgamation with other modes, because doing so will only multiply the contradictions. The aspiration to encounter experience as a whole requires abandoning allegiance to any mode to seek the whole unmodified; every mode in identifiable ways abstracts from the whole. Abstraction is explaining the whole of experience through the partiality of a particular mode. It is not the philosopher's task to "improve" a mode, but rather the philosopher must depart from these abstractions in quest of the "whole unmodified."

The use of one mode to explain the others creates categorical irrelevancies. History may offer a history of science, but it is not an alternative to scientific investigation. Politics tries to draw lessons from history, but uses past events to confirm perspectives or positions we already hold; we invoke historical examples to justify or to undermine current political ambitions. This "practical past" is not the "historian's past." Historians can describe political decisions in the context of the complex of conditions in which they were made, but politicians have to make decisions here and now, pursuing the intimations of their situation and overlooking the inconvenient features of past experience. Studying the past "for its own sake" constrains or even paralyzes practical judgment. Nor can science and politics be integrated.

However, there is much talk about the "politics of science" or the politics of historical research, as we also talk of the "science of politics." Thus Oakeshott eventually arrived at his notion of the "conversation of mankind," which he worked out in the 1950s in a small book, *The Voice of Poetry in the Conversation of Mankind* (1959).[4] If there is no hierarchy of modes, their practitioners nevertheless might talk to each other, even stumbling onto the vocation of the philosopher to seek the whole. Oakeshott thought conversation the most human thing, that which distinguishes us from other creatures. Universities are the "places of learning" where the conversation can be celebrated as an end in itself.

How does this notion affect his concept of political philosophy? For Oakeshott, philosophy is "radically subversive" questioning. Political philosophy is the philosophic investigation of politics, examining the character of political life without political attachments. To use political philosophy to supply intellectual support for political positions or policies is to abandon the philosopher's task for the politician's task, or for ideology. The political philosopher is neither a would-be philosopher-king nor a policy scientist.

That no mode of experience is, philosophically speaking, privileged over any other may seem odd because the practical life is so dominant and intrusive. One is tempted to think that practical life is the foundation from which all the other modes must spring. Oakeshott did not think this. Understandably, intrusiveness is confused with priority. Because there are numerous modes that offer to explain our experience, the choice of a mode is a choice to understand in a certain way. Philosophy itself is not a mode. Rather, philosophy is critical of "arrests in experience" that every mode instantiates. The statements that we "ought" to look at the world scientifically or historically or that we "ought" to take the view that everything is

---

4. Michael Oakeshott, *The Voice of Poetry in the Conversation of Mankind.* This work is reprinted in Michael Oakeshott, *Rationalism in Politics and Other Essays* (1962, 1991).

politics are exhortations prompted by the recognition that one need not exalt one or another of these.

The philosopher in principle chooses none of these alternatives, and thus, qua philosopher, he or she does not examine politics as if it were the key to experience as a whole, even if it is highly revealing of humanity when engaged in to pursue "imagined and wished-for satisfactions" and to resolve the interminable tension between "what is" and "what ought to be."

Yet Oakeshott was mindful of the politics of his time and place. In *The Social and Political Doctrines of Contemporary Europe* (1939)—comprising documents and commentary on liberalism, Catholicism, communism, Fascism, and National Socialism—he called the latter three the "modern authoritarian doctrines":

> To the Liberal and the Catholic mind alike the notion that men can authoritatively plan and impose a way of life upon a society appears to be a piece of pretentious ignorance; it can be entertained only by men who have no respect for human beings and are willing to make them the means to the realization of their own ambitions.[5]

From 1947 to 1960, Oakeshott wrote a series of remarkable essays, many of which he collected and published in 1962 under the title *Rationalism in Politics and Other Essays*. The title essay, "Rationalism in Politics"—together with essays titled "Rational Conduct," "Political Education," "The Political Economy of Freedom," and "On Being Conservative"—constitutes a powerful critique of ideological politics, of the attempt to model the social sciences on the physical sciences, and of the disregard of traditional wisdom and insight in the belief that a kind of Baconian/Cartesian methodology could free us from reliance on our traditions.

Ideological politics asserts an independently premeditated (abstractly idealistic) program for guiding our decision making toward a suppositious perfection or end state. Calling himself a "skeptic who would do better if only he knew how," Oakeshott famously com-

---

5. Michael Oakeshott, *The Social and Political Doctrines of Contemporary Europe*, xxii.

mented that in politics we set sail on a boundless and bottomless sea and its principal task is to keep the ship afloat. By this Oakeshott did not mean that life has no meaning or there is reason to despair, although some of his critics asserted this, one even calling him a "lonely nihilist." Oakeshott saw that meaning may be found elsewhere than in politics—more likely in religion, art, poetry, or philosophy. Oakeshott was avowedly Augustinian in this respect. Ideological politics asserts that political action is the source of meaning rather than a means to provide the background conditions for us to seek our meaning in more promising ways.

Oakeshott was skeptical of the pretensions of politics and spoke of politics as a "necessary evil." He was at the same time reserved in speaking of transcendence even though he had a lifelong interest in religion. He looked for the poetic in the midst of the quotidian experience. Politics—attending to the arrangements of a set of people brought together by choice and chance—is an instrument in maintaining equilibrium but not something in which to put one's faith. He was a skeptical conservative, not a "movement conservative." To him, to be conservative is to look for the possibilities of enjoyment in the present moment. He invoked Augustine, Pascal, Montaigne, Hobbes, and Hume. He was not an enthusiast for Burke or Russell Kirk, nor was he anything like a neoconservative. In early essays from the 1920s, Oakeshott wrote explicitly about the religious character as living in the present.[6] He later wrote explicitly about the tension between the "politics of skepticism" and the "politics of faith" ("faith" here meaning political faith of the ideological/utopian sort) in his posthumously published *The Politics of Faith and the Politics of Scepticism* (1996; probably written circa 1950–52).

In the idealist philosophical tradition from which he began, Oakeshott dismissed dualistic versions of experience, specifically the duality of worldliness and other-worldliness. He spoke rather of different motives of self-understanding in a single world of experience. To reject worldliness is to reject the current confusions and preoccupations that distract one from the effort to penetrate the mystery of life without imagining that mystery can be explained

6. See Oakeshott, *Religion, Politics and the Moral Life*.

away. To be religious meant to him to live so far as possible without anxiety about past actions or future uncertainties. To be distracted by what has been or by what we imagine may come to pass is to lose the religious understanding of life, and it also promotes susceptibility both to ideology and to using the powers of government to "pursue perfection as the crow flies." Oakeshott saw that longing for an orderly world is likely, through excess and concentrated power, to turn ideologies into recipes for graveyards. He said that the philosopher might have a heavenly home but is in no hurry to get there. This assertion may be taken in two ways: First, there is no point in "hurrying" because there is no plan, program, map, or shortcut to speed one on the way; second, the enjoyment and careful exploration of the present possibilities are ruined if one is preoccupied with the sense that one ought always to be somewhere else than where one is.

Among Oakeshott's favorite biblical stories was the Tower of Babel. He wrote two essays with this title. The first, written in the 1940s, appeared in *Rationalism in Politics*; the second appeared in *On History and Other Essays* (1983). In both, Oakeshott shows that this tale provides a permanent insight into our incessant proclivity to storm the heavenly kingdom and occupy it. The disaster that follows is eventually forgotten in new attempts to succeed where all before us have failed. Modern rationalism and the preoccupation with technology that goes with it are our versions of this primordial experience.

Yet Oakeshott was more than a mere skeptic. His positive political theory appears in *On Human Conduct* (1975), his magnum opus. Oakeshott described *On Human Conduct* as a set of three essays. Readers will see that the three essays, in fact, constitute a tightly structured, systematic effort to summarize Oakeshott's political philosophy. The first essay is "On the Theoretical Understanding of Human Conduct," the second is "On the Civil Condition," and the third is "On the Character of a Modern European State." This structure corresponds to the structure of Hobbes's political philosophy, the political philosopher on whom Oakeshott published more than on any other. The first essay explores what it means to be human; the second, how human beings of the sort he describes interact in the civil condition; and he concludes with a historical essay on the achievement of the modern European state as the structure most suited to human beings who understand themselves as individuals trying to come to terms with each other under modern conditions.

What is a human being? Oakeshott addressed this question most systematically in *On Human Conduct*, but he considered this question also in his essays on liberal education (most of which are collected in *The Voice of Liberal Learning* [1989]). For Oakeshott, human beings are individual agents learning to become something in terms of their self-understanding. We are, he said, "in ourselves what we are for ourselves." "Conduct" is not "behavior," where behavior is understood as exhibitions and emissions determined by and emanating from underlying processes that allow us no choice. We must seek to understand ourselves and the world we inhabit, and we remain active in this endeavor from birth to death, responding to the world in terms of how we understand ourselves and the circumstances in which we must operate.

Oakeshott was a radical individualist. Every human being is an essay in self-understanding; every human being thinks and interprets and responds to the world. Freedom, Oakeshott thought, is "intelligent response." We are not autonomous, because we are constrained by a preexisting world into which we are inserted, a world of goings-on that emerged and developed long before us and will likely go on long after us. We cannot live without this background inheritance—whether we like or do not like it—because we have to learn everything, and we need to start somewhere. Yet what we acquire from this inheritance does not determine how we appropriate it and respond to it. Every human action is an "intelligent response," in which we are neither autonomous nor predetermined. Of course, Oakeshott does not mean that every human action is sensible or successful, but that every action for good or ill is the response of a being reasoning about a situation, pursuing imagined and wished-for outcomes, avoiding what is thought to be undesirable or dangerous. All human beings, no matter how bizarre their actions, are agents in this sense.

Oakeshott understands the civil condition in terms of such beings. He replaces the familiar term "civil society" with the term "civil association." Oakeshott's Hobbes (and his Hume) qualified his Hegel: Individuals associate but do not compose a "society," which, for Oakeshott, is an abstraction obscuring the fact that individuals do not cease to be individuals even when they wish to escape the ordeal of consciousness. A human being is *homo inter homines*, a self among other selves, inescapably a "for itself." "Civil association" acknowledges individuality and points to the question of what formal structures may be appropriate to a set of human beings associating with each other in this way. The structure includes the rule of law and the exercise of authority by those authorized and recognized among the associates.

In the third essay, on the origins of the modern European state, Oakeshott argues that political authority based on consent is a European achievement emerging from a long process of trial, error, and accommodation, a history representing the gradual transformation of the authority relationship from command and obedience to acknowledgment and consent. The theory of the social contract is a summary statement of what in the seventeenth and eighteenth centuries it was believed Europeans had already achieved in the transition from the medieval to the modern world, including the identification of individuality and involving a new concept of authority and of the state as the organizing principle in modern politics. If in antiquity the central object of investigation was the polis, the central object in modern times is the state. The theory of the social contract, which offers an explanation of the modern European state, comes at the end of a long historical development that it did not initiate.

However, a revolutionary implication in contract theory is lurking in the demand that existing regimes must be continually reformed to con-form to the shape some imagine they would have if they had originated in a pure contract in which all residual alternative forms of human relationship are also transformed. One need only think of John Rawls's work to see this implication. Contract theory is thus a sophisticated argument criticizing both the past and the present in terms of a model for an imagined and wished-for future. It is philosophizing to change, not only to explain or describe, the prevailing order. Like Hume, Oakeshott is a political skeptic about a world suffused by the ideological deformation of philosophy and is, in this sense, a skeptical conservative. Oakeshott offers not a prudential argument that it is better for us to be cautious, nor is it an argument that what is older is better than what is newer. There may have been a romantic streak in Oakeshott—there certainly was an attraction to the poetic—but there is nothing romantic in his arguments. Against the universalism of our time, Oakeshott did not think the universal could replace the local, or the abstract the concrete.

Politics is important to us because it is intrusive and unavoidable, an intractable feature of human existence. It is interminable because it must try to make the temporal manageable. Politics is the very emblem of temporality unable to extricate itself from temporality's endlessness. The reconciliation of "what is" with "what ought to be" will forever elude us. Oakeshott's critique focused not so much on specific beliefs, programs, or actions as on what he thought to be a pervasive and mistaken modern understanding of the function of reason in practical life: to imagine perfection and to gather the power necessary to put it into practice. To him this understanding contradicts the character of civil association.

A civil association is a set of people bound together by a recognized authority and rule of law. However, being "an authority" is not being "in authority." Officeholders who are "in authority" govern not by claims to special knowledge or insight but because they have been acknowledged to have a right to exercise the office of authority through which they establish law for all and adjudicate disputes impartially. They have authority because they are recognized to have it.

In the modern state, the holders of an office of authority are authorized by those whom they govern to make rules to which those associated within the bounds of a given territory are expected to subscribe. They are expected to subscribe because the laws emanate from those whom they have entrusted with the task to make them. Both the makers of law and the subscribers to the law can understand the basic purpose of law; reasons can be given for the particular laws that are made. This does not preclude argument about the merits of the laws, but such argument occurs within a structure acknowledging that they are authoritative.

The authority is exercised in respect of individuals who are civilly associated. Such rules as may proceed from that authority are not intended to transform or override individuality or to define for individuals who they are "for themselves." A large proportion of their activities will consist in private, voluntary transactions facilitated by the rule of law. Typically, in civil association there will be incessant arguments over the scope of the government's powers.

There is an alternative image of the modern state that sees it as a joint enterprise to achieve a common goal within a "community" transcending civil association, in which the governors are understood to be managing a productive enterprise and citizens are seen as role players in a cooperative effort to achieve a common final end: In this view the state does not preside over an association but rather a corporation, or what might be called the administrative/regulatory bureaucratic state. Oakeshott thought that these alternatives, civil association and the managerial enterprise association, constituted a continuing dialectic in modern European—and North American—history, explaining a good deal about why modern politics carries on as it does. Modern politics has long been an argument between those who are skeptical of the power of governments to reconstruct and perfect social life and those with faith in our power to do exactly that. In our time the rationalist voice of the politics of faith seems dominant. Yet Oakeshott hoped that, even if modern rationalism is not in retreat, its pretensions, which will always be prey to disillusion, might be restrained by the continuing presence of the skeptical voice. In terms of his own understanding of political philosophy, he could not, qua political philosopher, simply prescribe one of the alternatives, but he could show reasons for thinking carefully. Philosophically speaking, he had to remain skeptical even of his skepticism. There is no doubt, however, as to what direction his own inclinations tend. As he said in "Political Education" (1951), his inaugural address at the University of London,

Political philosophy cannot be expected to increase our ability to be successful in political activity. It will not help us to distinguish between good and bad political projects; it has no power to guide or to direct us in the enterprise of pursuing the intimations of our tradition. But the patient analysis of the general ideas which have come to be connected with political activity—ideas such as nature, artifice, reason, will, law, authority, obligation, etc.—in so far as it succeeds in removing some of the crookedness from our thinking and leads to a more economical use of concepts, is an activity neither to be overrated nor despised. But it must be understood as an explanatory, not a practical, activity, and if we pursue it, we may only hope to be less often cheated by ambiguous statement and irrelevant argument.[7]

Many students of political philosophy will argue that this constrained role is too limiting. It may be useful to remember, however, that the modesty of his refusal to lionize political activity is reminiscent of the Socratic admonition that the beginning of wisdom lies in "not knowing" what everyone around one claims to know. It is also a means to avoid opposing one "rationalism" with another.

On Human Conduct (1975) not only summarizes his political philosophy but is also Oakeshott's philosophic valedictory, in which he expresses the serenity of one who, inspired by Socrates and Montaigne, is learning how to die:

Philosophic reflection is recognized here as the adventure of one who seeks to understand in other terms what he already understands and in which the understanding sought (itself unavoidably conditional) is a disclosure of the conditions of the understanding enjoyed and not a substitute for it. Its most appropriate expression is an essay where the character of the utterance (a traveller's tale) matches the character of the engagement, an intellectual adventure which has a course to follow but no destination. A philosophical essay leaves much to the reader, often saying too little for fear of saying too much; its attention is concentrated, but it does not stay to cross all the ts of the argument; its mood is cautious

7. Michael Oakeshott, "Political Education," in *Rationalism in Politics* (1991), 132. This was Oakeshott's inaugural address as professor at the London School of Economics in 1951.

without being defensive; it is personal but never merely "subjective"; it does not dissemble the conditionality of the conclusions it throws up and although it may enlighten it does not instruct. It is, in short, a well-considered intellectual adventure recollected in tranquility.[8]

One of Oakeshott's favorite stories was of the Chinese wheelwright who was unable, at age seventy, to turn over his craft to his son because his son could not get the hang of it. Generalizing from his son's failure to learn more than the abstract rules of the craft, the wheelwright remarked to his duke, who was reading the works of the sages, that books are the "lees and scum of bygone men." "All that was worth handing on," the wheelwright said, "died with them; the rest they put into their books."[9] I suppose Oakeshott was also thinking of the Platonic Socrates who refused to write philosophy down. We recall, however, that Plato devised a method of writing it down without writing it down. I think Oakeshott's intent was along those lines: In the lees and scum there may linger something of the essence that is a blessing in disguise. In his preference for the essay, he locates himself in a line of British authors (not to mention Montaigne and Pascal) extending from Bacon to Hume to Macaulay to John Stuart Mill. His voice is his own, distinguishing himself as a most worthy conversational entrant in the great conversation of humankind in which they, and he, continue to speak to us.

8. Michael Oakeshott, *On Human Conduct*, vii.
9. Oakeshott's account of this story from Chuang Tzu is found in the title essay of *Rationalism in Politics* (1991), 14.

Politics as the Pursuit of Intimations
On the Central Theme
of Oakeshott's Political Philosophy

MICHAEL OAKESHOTT TAUGHT THE HISTORY of political thought at Cambridge from the 1920s to the late 1940s, spent a brief period in Oxford, and then assumed the chair of political science at The London School of Economics in 1951, where his inaugural lecture, "Political Education," caused an immediate storm of controversy. The point of his lecture was that to be educated about politics first requires an accurate idea of what sort of activity politics actually is. His argument was that, in recent times, rationalist and ideological versions of politics had come to dominate thinking about politics while failing to make good on claims to surmount the limitations of what politics can accomplish. In his essay, "Rationalism in Politics," the course of examining the Baconian and Cartesian origins of modern rationalism, he summarized his point this way:

> [The Rationalist] does not recognize change unless it is a self-consciously induced change, and consequently he falls easily into the error of identifying the customary and the traditional with the changeless. This is, of course, no question either of retaining or improving such a tradition, for

Reprinted with permission from *Lo Stato*, no. 3 (2014): 39–52.

both these involve an attitude of submission. It must be destroyed. And to fill its place the Rationalist puts something of his own making—an ideology, the formalized abridgement of the supposed substratum of rational truth contained in the tradition.[1]

This was Oakeshott's response to what he found increasingly many academic students of politics and some politicians to be doing. He thought the claims emanating from such rationalism illusory. The illusion, moreover, is not merely an interim failure to have found the effective form of policy science or ideological program, but is a misunderstanding of what is ever actually possible in politics. Politics, Oakeshott thought, has certain inevitable characteristics which will forever defeat the efforts of theoreticians to, as he put it, "pursue perfection as the crow flies."

He ended his lecture by quoting F. H. Bradley's remark that "this is the best of all possible worlds, and everything in it is a necessary evil." Politics, of course, could not be exempted from this judgment. It is an activity the necessity of which in no way promises anything more than its interminability. He thereby contradicted the prevailing wisdom in intellectual circles. His view runs athwart much academic opinion—conservative, liberal, and radical alike—to this day. Although he is usually described as a conservative, he thought of himself as a philosophical skeptic, engaged in trying to understand the world, but lacking the knowledge to direct it. He confessed to a conservative disposition from which followed a skeptical attitude toward schemes to enlarge the scope of governmental activity, but no specific program. The political rationalism he opposed justifies the aggregation of power in governments in the belief that this would provide the means to realize the capacity to reconstruct social life toward the achievement of an ideal condition.

His criticism was directed less at specific beliefs, programs, or actions, and more at what he thought to be a pervasive and mistaken modern understanding of the function of reason in practical life. He

1. Michael Oakeshott, "Rationalism in Politics," in *Rationalism in Politics* (1991), 8–9 (hereafter *RP*).

thought that virtually all current political stances, wherever they might be located on the left-right spectrum, were infected in some measure by rationalism and ideology. None of them could command the allegiance of the philosopher as Oakeshott understood the philosopher. The central passage from his inaugural in which he seeks to describe the actuality of political activity is this lecture:

> In politics, then, every enterprise is a consequential enter-
> prise, the pursuit, not of a dream, or of a general principle,
> but of an intimation. What we have to do with is something
> less imposing than logical implications or necessary conse-
> quences: but if the intimations of a tradition of behaviour
> are less dignified or more elusive than these, they are not on
> that account less important.
>
> Of course, there is no piece of mistake-proof apparatus by
> means of which we can elicit the intimation most worth
> while pursuing; and not only do we often make gross errors
> of judgment in this matter, but also the total effect of a desire
> satisfied is so little to be forecast, that our activity of amend-
> ment is often found to lead us where we would not go. More,
> the whole enterprise is liable at any moment to be perverted
> by the incursion of an approximation to empiricism in the
> pursuit of power.
>
> These are features which can never be eliminated; they
> belong to the character of political activity. But it may be
> believed that our mistakes of understanding will be less
> frequent and less disastrous if we escape the illusion that
> politics is ever anything more than the pursuit of intimations;
> a conversation, not an argument. . . . In political activity, then,
> men sail a boundless and bottomless sea; there is neither
> harbor for shelter nor floor for anchorage, neither starting-place
> nor appointed destination. The enterprise is to keep afloat on an
> even keel; the sea is both friend and enemy; and the seaman-
> ship consists in using the resources of a traditional manner of
> behavior in order to make a friend of every hostile occasion.[2]

2. Oakeshott, *RP*, 57–58, 60.

Oakeshott intended to put activism, utopianism, policy science, and a certain sort of pietism in their place by demonstrating that their voices in politics promote an illusory understanding of what politics actually is. He did not expect that his critique would silence these voices, nor did he intend to legislate about what voices might express themselves there; to do so would be to expect too much from philosophic understanding, and would betray philosophy by turning it into a political, rather than an explanatory, engagement. In a sense, the philosophic critique is indifferent to the presence or absence of those voices since, once philosophic understanding has been achieved, the philosopher's interest in such goings on is satisfied. The description of the prevailing political terrain, and the critique of misplaced pretensions within that context, were as far as one could go philosophically. He cast his skeptical eye on his own political predilections as well as those of others.

Oakeshott also thought that modern politics has long been constituted in a dialectic between those who are skeptical of the power of governments to reconstruct and perfect social life, and those with faith in our power to do exactly that. Thus, rationalism will not disappear, but if its pretensions are prey to disillusionment, they can be restrained from extremism by the continuing presence of the skeptical voice.

Oakeshott subsequently wrote a great deal more about politics, and a great deal more has been written about Oakeshott's political philosophy. Nonetheless, his description of political activity as the "pursuit of intimations," which has been attacked as vague traditionalism, mysticism, or romanticism, remains a central summary expression of his thinking. The accusations of vagueness, mysticism, and romanticism, are ways of asserting that he lacked concreteness in his political philosophy, or that he could not deal with the modern world. Yet to understand what he meant by "the pursuit of intimations," which he thought to be the opposite of these things, is essential to understanding the precise meaning of Oakeshott's position on the character of political activity, and the degree of concreteness Oakeshott achieved. As he said, in response to his critics, the phrase "pursuit of intimations" is intended neither "as a description of the motives of politicians nor of what they believe themselves to be doing, but of what they actually succeed in doing."[3] He intended to make a statement, as he put it, in the indicative mood, not to propose what political actors should or should not do.

Oakeshott wanted to describe the character of politics so as to show its limits without intruding into the activity as if he were a special kind of political practitioner. This was the application of the philosophic method Oakeshott employed in regard to every activity he wanted to understand. For Oakeshott, to show the limits of any mode of activity was also to establish its character as a self-moved activity, not dependent on or reducible to something else, and needing to be understood in terms of what it disclosed to observation. Is this important? Oakeshott accepted that no one need philosophize in this way. He did suggest that a modest benefit might be derived by dampening the excesses of misguided expectation, while he also insisted that this benefit should not be overrated. The motive of many of his critics has always been to insist on the practical payoff for political philosophy, and he steadfastly always refused, because he did not know how to provide, this satisfaction.

What, then, did he mean by the "pursuit of intimations"? Let us consider the salient points of the passage cited, and place them in the context of his philosophy of the practical life. Oakeshott used the term "intimations" in contrast to the terms "dreams," "general principles," "logical implications," and "necessary consequences." Dreams naturally figure constantly in politics. Oakeshott was questioning the explanatory adequacy of such terms, philosophically speaking, not their presence. Accurate description notices and accepts their presence.

He knew as well as anyone that dreams of possibilities not yet realized obviously are catalysts of political action. And general principles, such as, for instance, the principles expressed in natural law theories, constitutions, or Declarations of Independence, are central features of political life. He did not think they unambiguously tell us what, in specific cases, to do, and they are appealed to in defense of contradictory interpretations of our rights and duties. Oakeshott thought that natural laws are descriptive of the forms in

3. Oakeshott, *RP*, 67.

which we think about moral duties, but he did not think we could deduce from them legal obligations. Between the expression of moral duty and the statement of legal obligation there must intervene judgment and decision, presumably emanating from an authority acknowledged to be entrusted with this responsibility.

He thought that most of the common terms of political discourse are irreducibly ambiguous in their meaning. We might all agree that *salus populi suprema lex,* but does *salus* mean survival or does it go on to guarantee a certain standard of living? And who exactly do we include in *populi*? Does the term "democracy" imply a procedure for preventing tyranny by limiting the power of governments, or does it mean a plebiscitary legitimation of the unlimited use of that power?

Oakeshott was pointing to the unavoidability in politics of appraisal, judgment, and decision. Political actors continually characterize their states of affairs, and devise what they hope are appropriate responses. If they could deduce logical implications from their situations, they could leap over the familiar, apparently ineluctable, constraints in politics. They would simply know what is to be done instead of having to try a course of action in a condition of uncertainty.

In politics, freedom does not mean being able to devise courses of action unconstrained by previous actions. Yet previous actions do not determine us either if by that is meant that there is a necessary path, direction, or pattern in our circumstance that cannot but work itself out. The task is to understand better what we already understand: a complex state of affairs susceptible to differing accounts, requiring judgement as to what within it is a resource and what a hindrance, what is desirable and what is undesirable, what is appropriate or not. Wherever the possibilities of conversation or argument are not suppressed, this complexity cannot fail to show itself. We can discover no unarguable path to travel from where we have been to where we imagine we may be going. Yet neither is there an infinite number of paths available to us. There are only those that we can discern emerging from the context we have, and we must decide the relative merits or appropriateness of the alternatives. What is imaginable to us depends on what we are prepared to recognize in the context of what we have already experienced. This actuality coexists with, but is not transformed by, the rhetorics of certainty that also appears. It is part of the reality of politics that we must discriminate among the claims to know according to what seems possible to know.

If we could show that there are logically necessary consequences to flow from our situation, we might in principle transcend the need of argument and persuasion. We would then not be imaginative agents of plausible but uncertain courses of action, but conduits through whom the necessary course of action expresses itself. "Human activity," Oakeshott says,

> with whatever it may be concerned, enjoys a circumscribed range of movement. The limits which define this range are historic, that is to say, they are themselves the product of human activity. Generally speaking, there are no "natural" limits as distinct from historic limits: those which we ascribe to "human nature," for example, are not less historic than those which we immediately recognize as springing from conditions determined by human activity. Even what a man may do with his physical strength is determined by the historic devices and inventions of men, and no community has been without such devices. Being historic, they are not absolute, but on any occasion they are not on that account any the less limits. They may be wide or narrow, they are never absent. The flight of imagination, the poet's power over words and images, the scientist's hypotheses, the philosopher's engagements and disengagements, and the practical man's projects and enterprises are all of them exploitations of what is given or intimated in the condition of the world he inhabits. . . . So it is with our political activity. . . . The politician has always a certain field of vision and a certain range of opportunity; what he is able to contemplate, to desire, or to attempt is subject to the historic limits of this situation. And in order to understand his activity it is necessary first to consider the field within which he moves, the choices that are available to him, and the enterprises he is able to entertain. Indeed, until we have understood this, any other judgement we may make about his activity—judgements of

approval or disapproval, for example—are liable to lack force and relevance.[4]

When lawyers in court, for instance, argue for a certain level of damages to be awarded to clients, they do not merely assert that lower damages would be a gross injustice. They connect the ideas of justice and injustice to the damages they request by means of a middle term which states what damages have been in other cases alleged to be similar to the present one. Such argument seeks to avoid the appearance of arbitrariness: it presses for an award which establishes continuity with past instances or perhaps tries to make explicit an alleged pattern of increasing awards from past cases which should be realized explicitly in the present case. That there is such a pattern is established by the court's finding it plausible, not by its inevitability.

When followers of baseball debate such questions as whether the spitball should be legal, they appeal to the "true spirit" or the "proper form" of the game to decide the question. For one half of major league baseball, the designated hitter presently is in the spirit and form of the game. For the other half, it is not. Yet if the true spirit of the game were independently available to consult, the question of the proper form of the game would be indisputable. Different individuals enjoying equal knowledge and experience of the game reach differing conclusions. The dispute shows us that the true spirit and form of the game will be discovered by what we decide, or fail to decide, the true spirit and form of the game are going to be. Efforts at persuasion will insist on the necessity of a particular conclusion which is, as we can see, not logically necessary at all. What is alleged to be the necessity here is actually a claim, made with greater or less intensity, to identify the preponderance of direction in the game as we have known it so far. Against this, arguments may be made that the direction has had bad results and must be reversed or altered in some other way.

The pursuit of intimations, for Oakeshott, captures an element in many familiar experiences: imagining possibilities, desiring to try something new, believing that a course of action is necessary or un-

---

4. Michael Oakeshott, *The Politics of Faith & the Politics of Scepticism*, 116–17.

avoidable, wanting to correct what are believed to be past errors, defending current practices against arguments that they are mistaken or inadequate, reconciling the pressure of the new with affection for the old, extricating oneself from a too constraining situation, trying to settle disputes in the hope of tranquility or orderliness, extrapolating trends from what we understand ourselves to have been doing, responding to what others insist is important, deciding how important an issue is, considering what is appropriate, or simply possible, given our resources as we now understand them, translating ideals into something we might actually do, discovering what changes reformers really might undertake, determining what terms like "solidarity," "community," "rights," "social justice," "welfare," or "new world order," mean in terms of policies we might actually adopt. These engagements are all embedded in contexts. As Oakeshott was prone to say, the pursuit of perfection as the crow flies is a delusion. It is all very well for me to say that what I want is to be happy. But eventually I must specify what would make me happy. "I do not want to be happy," Oakeshott once remarked, "what I want is to idle in Avignon or hear Caruso sing." His point was that the desire to be happy has to turn into something intelligible to do in the practical realm. The abstraction of desire in practical life cannot ultimately escape from the limits imposed by the actually available resources of the practical life.

People have always known that to get along in life one has to learn to be tolerant of the peculiarities of others and to hope that the others can learn to get along with yours. We begin to go astray, Oakeshott thought, when we develop an abstract doctrine of "toleration," the consequence of which is that, no matter how diligently we strive to get along and be tolerant, the abstract idea of toleration encourages a sense of failure to have achieved toleration as such. But if there is no toleration as such, we shall never attain pure toleration. What we shall find are the customs, procedures, rules of thumb, and moral pressures which shape our conduct. The pursuit of philosophic understanding might help to dampen the temptation of abstraction, but it could not tell us what to do.

For Oakeshott, then, to examine politics philosophically is to recollect that no direction is logically implicated—there are only intimations. Such recollection may inhibit the politician who equips himself for practical action by forgetting this in discovering a felt necessity: the intimation to pursue at that point. What the philosopher risks forgetting is not this, but that for him to transcend the practical life is not to subdue or command it:

> From the standpoint of practical experience there can be no more dangerous disease than the love and pursuit of truth in those who do not understand, or have forgotten, that a man's first business is to live. And life, we have seen, can be conducted only at the expense of an arrest in experience. The practical consciousness knows well enough what is inimical to its existence, and often has the wisdom to avoid it. *Pereat veritas, fiat vita*. It is not the clearsighted, not those who are fashioned for thought and the ardours of thought, who can lead the world. Great achievements are accomplished in the mental fog of practical experience. What is farthest from our needs is that kings should be philosophers. The victims of thought, those who are intent upon what is unlimitedly satisfactory in experience, are self-confessed betrayers of life, and must pursue their way without the encouragement of the practical consciousness, which is secure in the knowledge that philosophical thought can make no relevant contribution to the coherence of its world of experience.[5]

Oakeshott's skepticism, then, did not exclude accurate description of what goes on in the world. It denied the power to transform the practical life into something else.

≡ ≡

Let us turn now to *Experience and Its Modes* (1933), Oakeshott's first major work and first major effort to theorize the distinguishing characteristics of the practical life. Here he laid out the basis upon which he then expounded the character of politics as a pervasive form of practical life. The practical life can be seen as a tension between freedom and coherence, freedom taken as the restlessness of

5. Michael Oakeshott, *Experience and Its Modes*, 320–21 (hereafter *EM*).

the human spirit in quest of coherence; coherence taken as the relief from that restlessness in full satisfaction. The pursuit of intimations, in this context, can be understood as the imaginative responses of human beings in attempting to reconcile freedom and coherence.

Oakeshott proposed that the whole of experience, which we cannot directly grasp, appears to us divided into modes of experience or ways of trying to express the whole of experience from specific, but limited, perspectives. Each of these modes achieves what, in its terms, is a satisfactory grasp of experience in excluding what is to be seen in the perspective of the other modes. He said,

> As I understand it, experience is capable, not of division but of modal diversity. A mode of experience is an organization of the real world in terms of specific considerabilities. Each mode has a coherence of its own; each is a different intellectual possibility; each, so to speak, is a game with rules peculiar to itself; each is abstract with its own principles of abstraction; each necessarily diverges from all others; and, consequently, none may be understood to have a logical relationship with any other. Thus, what may be true in "history" is neither true nor false in "science" or in "practice," but merely irrelevant. And while the real world is entailed (indeed, asserted) in each of these modes, it is not to be understood as, in any sense, composed of them.[6]

For Oakeshott, none of the modes of experience is, philosophically speaking, privileged. The practical life is one of these modes—no less a particular, limited way of trying to characterize the whole of experience. The fact that the practical life is intrusive and inescapable does not alter the situation. It is in this sense, and not in any ordinary moral sense, that, for Oakeshott, politics is a "necessary evil." It is neither the foundation of other modes of experience nor simply experience as a whole, and other modes take their distinctive character in differentiation rather than in derivation from the practical.

To understand experience historically (*sub specie praeterito*), for example, meant to Oakeshott to understand all experience as past, as

---

6. Michael Oakeshott, preface to unpublished Spanish edition of *EM*.

the historian *qua* historian might understand it. The historian *qua* historian examines all experience as past, as what is not suceptible to his practical will and desire but only to his contemplation of it. To understand experience scientifically (*sub specie quantitates*) is to discover patterns of relationships expressed quantitatively in abstraction from ordinary encounters with nature; it is to see the world as independent of ourselves, our wishes and fears. To know in either of these ways was specifically not to know things practically (*sub specie voluntatis*), just as to know the world practically, that is, from the standpoint of will and desire, prevention and change, use and misuse, precludes seeing the world historically or scientifically.

The mutual presence of the modes convicts all of them of falling short of comprehensive understanding or the coherence of full satisfaction. Later, Oakeshott discussed also the mode of poetic experience, the composing of images which need not point beyond themselves, eliciting momentary delight in the contemplation of their beauty, having nothing to do with practicality. The point is not that no one ever has a practical motive for doing science, investigating the past, or writing poetry; but what makes an expression specifically scientific, historical, or poetic is not determined by the presence or absence of practical intent on the part of the agents of those achievements.

Philosophy, however, is not a mode. The philosopher, as Oakeshott saw him, is seeking the whole of experience without modification. Thus, the philosopher examines the diverse modes that have, for whatever reasons, come to be, establishing their presence to such a degree that the reflective person cannot fail to notice their claims and, eventually, their limitations. The philosopher's curiosity excites a wish to understand each mode, but dissatisfaction intrudes with the failure of each mode to reveal the whole of experience unmodified. The desire for the whole remains unfulfilled. The philosopher cannot add anything to transform them into something else or into each other. It followed for Oakeshott that he should speak relatively little about the quest for the whole unmodified since such talk does not bring the whole of experience into our grasp. Thus philosophers cannot resolve the predicament into which they have stumbled even if they come to love the experience of it.

Oakeshott established, then, that the common acceptance of the primacy of the practical life, and hence of politics, was, philosophically speaking, mistaken. It is easy, he admitted, to see why we are receptive to the claims of practicality upon us: We are born into mortality and must, from birth, start to learn how to make our way in the midst of what is both hospitable and inhospitable to our presence. Practical activity requires us to undertake alteration and preservation, and we experience the "necessity of which no man can relieve himself."[7] The world, understood practically, is familiar and ever present, it is where we pass our lives. Its necessity does not, however, constitute its comprehensiveness, and its necessity is a "necessary evil": There are strong

> prejudices and preconceptions of the larger part of mankind, who find it impossible to entertain the idea that this practical world, within which they are confined as if in a prison, is other than the universe itself.[8]

In extricating himself from conventional thinking, Oakeshott sought what he called a "philosophy of practical experience," as opposed to "practical philosophy." He dimissed practical philosophy because it is not an effort to understand politics philosophically, but rather an undertaking to defend a political position by, first, transposing the terms of argument into abstract concepts; and then, secondly, appealing to those concepts as the ground for the practical conclusions one wants to defend. To declare, for example, that all history is the story of class struggle, and then to search for evidence to support this contention with a view to identifying the historically relevant class or classes, is to give up the desire for comprehensive understanding in favor of an abridgement that supports various practical political engagements. That this engagement is wrapped in the trappings of theoretical language, which give the appearance of transcending the limitations of the pursuit of intimations, is either a disguise or a self-deception.

To elaborate a philosophy of practical experience, by contrast, is to try to understand the distinguishing features of practical engagement

7. Oakeshott, *EM*, 256.
8. Oakeshott, *EM*, 249.

that will attend every specific practical undertaking whatever. Here, Oakeshott undoubtedly had in mind such achievements as Aristotle's recognition, in the *Nicomachean Ethics,* that a theoretical account of the practical moral life insightfully describes, but offers no relief from, the necessity to act in contingent circumstances, through specific conduct, arrived at by making judgments within a way of life, and not by deductions from abstract principles. There was for Oakeshott, as for Aristotle, no way for a theoretical account of what goes on in practical conduct to eliminate the complex difficulties of moral decisions. In response to the objection that, by rejecting general principles, Oakeshott provided no standards for detecting incoherencies or deciding on reforms, he replied:

> Do you want to be told that in politics there is, what certainly exists nowhere else, a mistake-proof manner of deciding what should be done? How does a scientist, with the current condition of physics before him, decide upon a direction of profitable advance? What considerations passed through the minds of medieval builders when they detected the inappropriateness of building in stone as if they were building in wood? How does a critic arrive at the judgement that a picture is incoherent, that the artist's treatment of some passages is inconsistent with his treatment of others?[9]

This remark shows that, for Oakeshott, conduct within any mode of experience involves something like the pursuit of intimations. Implicit is a general critique of the claims of reason to certainty, and hence a skeptical response to rationalism in general. There is much to be gained by reasoning historically, or scientifically, or poetically, but what is not gained is an archimedean standpoint. A philosophy of science is not itself scientific investigation; a philosophy of history is not the achievement of historical study; a literary theory is not poetry. A theoretical account of the practical life cannot substitute for the connoisseurship of a practiced eye and a sense of appropriateness; it determines neither the wisdom

9. Oakeshott, *RP,* 69.

nor the folly of the ends pursued in practical life, and has nothing to do with determining success or failure as those occur in the flow of practical activity.

Practical activity thus has a character of an identifiable sort. The ends pursued there exemplify practical engagement, but do not transform it. A theoretical account is an attempt at saying faithfully, in different words, what is going on. For Oakeshott a philosophical understanding of politics is categorically distinct from theorizing a justification for political ends or goals.

Because practical life is constituted in promoting and preventing change in our existence, it cannot change once and for all. If it could, it would cease to be what it is, and become something altogether different. Claims that we could work through the "necessary evils" of politics to end the necessity of politics, misunderstand what is actually going on. Practical life is driven by the desire to make coherent and satisfactory what is incoherent and unsatisfactory. Oakeshott thought he had accounted for why the practical desire for coherence must remain unfulfilled. In *Experience and Its Modes* he argues along the following lines:

In practical life, what seems to offer coherence is what is taken to be true. In practical conduct we always, implicitly or explicitly, consider the degree to which we have achieved coherence. Every human being is, in principle, an agent of opinion. Opinions are significant since they are assessments of coherence or incoherence in our lives. The existing state of affairs at every moment exposes possibilities of something "to be" which is "not yet," and each moment of coherence is precarious, an incipient incoherence. There is no point at which it ceases to be possible to think of a "to be" which is "not yet." The "to be" which is "not yet" expresses a possible alteration of "what is" and thus defeats the hope of having already achieved coherence. There are no gaps in consciousness, but always a contiguity—a touching—of what has been, what is, and what we imagine may come to be:

The "to be" of practice is never a world merely discrepant from "what is"; it is always and everywhere considered, not merely a "not yet" or a "not here," but in some sense, more coherent than "what is."[10]

Thus the "to be" can become "what ought to be." We can find value in it. What we take as practical facts are unstable for they are what is now, as opposed to what may have been yesterday, and what might be tomorrow. In practical activity, what is the case now could be otherwise, and possibilities for being otherwise are always with us. We look for what is satisfactory which always involves trying to find what we think coherent. The consequences of specific, practical undertakings cannot suffice. Success, no less than failure, in the gaining of specific ends excites appraisal and assessment, leading on to other "not yets" that we think either ought or ought not to be. "Truth is sought in what is 'other' than what is given."[11]

So long as the future is an essential element in practical appraisal, coherence has to elude us; we are never without unrealized ideas. The completeness we may hope to enjoy is always attended by not yet integrated possibilities. There is no independent body of things we might fix in a conclusive arrangement. Alterability is inexhaustible.

Thus, if, as we stated earlier, freedom does not mean liberation from what we have been, it does mean acting toward what we think will make for coherence as a response to what we have been. "Freedom," Oakeshott concluded, is to be understood as "an idea which has relevance in the practical world of activity and nowhere else."[12] As Oakeshott saw it, freedom is realized in attaining practical truth in the sense of attaining coherence, of harmonizing the disharmonies of life. To attain what we think true because in it we find coherence involves reconciling conflicting opinions in the practical life. Individuals are agents of the pursuit of coherence, differentiating themselves from each other as they define themselves in the context of each other's presence. But if we think the momentary attainment of coherence is discovering our "telos," we are mistaken.

10. Oakeshott, *EM*, 261.
11. Oakeshott, *EM*, 265.
12. Oakeshott, *EM*, 267 fn.

The restlessness of the human spirit cannot be content; coherence is evanescent. The "practical world," Oakeshott remarks,

> because it is a world of activity and change, is a world of oppositions to be balanced (because they cannot be unified), of contradictions which (because they cannot be resolved) must be co-ordinated. The practical self and its interests can never give way before the interests of "others"; the relationships into which it enters are external to itself; and, since in practical experience the practical self is the very embodiment of reality, its dissolution is a contradiction and inconceivable.[13]

To the extent we find coherence we think ourselves free, unless and until we find the coherence we have attained turning into unlooked for constraint. When this happens, we find ourselves cast once more into necessity:

> If a man thinks to set himself free, in any save a vague and metaphorical sense, by the study of science or of history or by the pursuit of philosophy he is grossly mistaken. The only truth that makes a man free is practical truth, the possession of a coherent world of practical ideas. Indeed, practical truth and freedom seem to me inseparable; wherever the one is, the other will be found also.[14]

Practical life undertakes to manage what is never fully under control. Will and desire cannot be purged from a world in which self-awareness and diversity of opinions can at most temporarily be suppressed. There is always more that could be said than has been said, and those who may say it. The stability of coherence is the friendly enemy of the restlessness of freedom. In conjunction, they make for the discordant concord of practical life.

13. Oakeshott, *EM*, 270.
14. Oakeshott, *EM*, 268.

Radical Temporality and the
Modern Moral Imagination

M Y INTENTION IS TO REFLECT on two themes that run through the whole of Oakeshott's thought: first, the radical temporality of the human condition and, second, the character of modernity's response to radical temporality. The first is, for Oakeshott, universal in experience to all times and places; the second is peculiar to a development in the modern West that, Oakeshott suggests, began to come into sight about five centuries ago and persists into the present and that manifests our particular experience of, and response as he understands it to, the universal condition of radical temporality. The second theme emerges as Oakeshott's exploration of the distinctively modern response to the universal condition. My approach here prepares the way to expound a "philosophy of politics," which Oakeshott has described as "an explanation or view of political life and activity from the standpoint of the totality of experience."[1]

My reflections are based on considering the whole of his work, published and unpublished, but among those writings especially important are the following: *Experience and Its Modes* (1933); "The

Reprinted by permission from Paul Franco and Leslie Marsh, eds., *A Companion to Michael Oakeshott* (University Park: Penn State University Press, 2012), 120–33. Title appeared originally as "Radical Temporality and the Modern Moral Imagination: Two Themes in the Thought of Michael Oakeshott."
1. Michael Oakeshott, *Religion, Politics, and the Moral Life*, 126.

Concept of a Philosophical Jurisprudence" (1938); *The Politics of Faith and the Politics of Scepticism* (1950–52); the essays in *Rationalism in Politics* (1962); his various writings on Hobbes (especially the original 1946 introduction to the Blackwell edition of *Leviathan*); *On Human Conduct* (1975); and the essays in *Religion, Politics, and the Moral Life* (1993). In short, I am attempting, following his lead, to put into other words what I already understand Oakeshott to be saying. I begin with radical temporality.

On Radical Temporality and Human Conduct

In our day the word *change* is much used, often more or less arbitrarily associated with progress and improvement, even though, in itself, the word can equally carry the connotation of loss or decline. In current parlance little thought of any depth is given to the significance of this word or to its prominence in contemporary discourse. No doubt this is because its usage is largely associated with various public policy proposals laden with ideological implications, far removed from philosophical reflection.

Inherent to human existence, change is a defining feature of practical life and, dramatically, of politics. Oakeshott understands the human being to be "for itself," trying to make more coherent what seems incoherent, trying to cure dissatisfaction in quest of what is imagined will bring satisfaction.[2] We are free beings, according to Oakeshott, because we must determine for ourselves what we understand ourselves to be. This is the ordeal of consciousness; we are incomplete beings searching for completion. This is the human condition.

In short, the practical life is constituted in efforts to alter our existence as we currently understand it or to ward off alterations that threaten what we at present take to be satisfactory. Initiating change or defending against change are both alterations and, as they are ever present, have no point of termination. We may talk of programs or plans for change, but we do not require programs or plans for us to be immersed in the experience of change, which proceeds regardless

2. Michael Oakeshott, *The Voice of Liberal Learning* (1989), 19.

of programs or plans. The conduct of life is inseparable from the experience of change, and every attempt to get beyond the felt necessity of change is an effort to get beyond the life that we have been given.

Since this radical temporality is a universal condition of human existence, all human actions belong to the realm of change, including actions that aim to bring changes to conclusive closure. We talk of what is practical or impractical, but these terms are themselves immersed in the medium of change about which we are trying to get our bearings. What is practical or impractical is a matter that can never be finally settled, because human conduct can never be finally settled except perhaps in death. "Practice is activity, the activity inseparable from the conduct of life and from the necessity of which no living man can relieve himself."[3] "Change we can believe in" is an argument within this endlessness, as is the proposition to be "suspicious of all change." We need hardly profess belief in change, although much rhetorical energy is spent in such professions; indeed, we have no choice but to accept it. Believing that this or that particular change is the change to end all changes requires suspension of disbelief of a certain kind.

There is a discrepancy between the way things seem to be and what we would like to be the case. If we want to preserve a state of affairs we must characterize what it is we wish to save. To characterize it is already on the road to an abstraction that is not identical to the state of affairs we started out to save. We save, so to speak, a version of that state of affairs. There will thus always be a residual something that is not saved, and an incipient dissatisfaction with what we believe we have saved, leading to further adjustments to "get it right" this time, and the next time that is sure to follow. This is a world that may justly be called mortal: everything in it is coming to an end in the course of a beginning of something else. It is, as Hobbes would say, a restless search for power after power unto death. But, in the meantime, at each moment there is an experience of mortality, as endings and beginnings intrude on each other in a ceaseless

---

3. Michael Oakeshott, *Experience and Its Modes*, 257.

flow of actions, with little deaths prompted by our will to make the world more coherent than for us it is.

It is natural that we should have ideas about how change has proceeded up to this point and ideas about where change seems to be taking us. But where change seems to be going is a matter of intimations extrapolated from what we already know in experience. There is no break between past and future, although it is common for us to impose conceptual breaks on the flow of our experience. We do have plans, programs, and theories, which we construct out of this flow, and they do have effects on how we interpret the past and also on how we will go forward, but they cannot be developed independently of the contingent conditions in which we pursue them or, as we like to say, "put them into practice." The point is, they were never outside of practice, whatever that could possibly mean.

Nevertheless, there is a tendency to imagine ideal worlds that are taken to exist independently and that we wish to bring into the currently unsatisfactory world to transform it. This too is natural to us and is implied in our desire to transcend the ordeal of change, and as well because we quite understandably want to assuage the pains of conscious existence. Such ideal worlds may be helpful in clarifying our self-understanding and purposes to ourselves, but the reality in which we are immersed, and which we experience as transcending the momentary and evanescent, is never captured by the images of it that we make for ourselves, even if we fall in love with those images, as we frequently do.

The appeal of the "to be" that is "not yet" depends on forgetting or downplaying the mortal flow within which the "to be" must be born and to which it forever owes a debt. Human action generates the thought of two realms of experience, but the two are one world conceived in different aspects. The mediation of them through action can reach only some degree of satisfaction because the two already inhabit one realm from the outset, and every mediation is within the one world of experience. Were this not so, it is hard to see what mediation, as an act of human willing, could possibly mean. And certainly no mediation to end all mediation is available to us. It is rather as if we must both acknowledge the character of our existence and yet deny it at the same time. We are moved in recognizing that what is the case now may not be the case tomorrow and was not the case yesterday, and yet we are also moved by the thought that we can bring this situation under our control. We engage to do what cannot be done, but this very condition drives us on to try to do it.

There are those who hope to make a virtue out of this necessity by appealing to the consequences of alternative courses of action, for example, the pragmatists and the utilitarians. But here too the consequences are integral to the flow of experience. What we take to be the consequences will be what we abstract from the mortal flow of endings and beginnings to designate as relevant outcomes by which to judge success or failure. We may initiate actions but we do not control the unfolding that follows from those actions. In short, the appeal to "what works" cannot resolve the endlessness of practical life. We know in any case that whether something works is itself a matter of argument. We should admit that we cannot know in advance the success of the ideas we put forth, for they are dependent on what is "not yet" and thus their validation remains to be seen. Even substantial agreements on outcomes, when we get them, are unstable and subject to revision, although some come to seem to us inevitable and irrevocable. We will forever be hostage to developments of which we cannot, at present, know, albeit we must proceed as if we knew what we need to know. One might call this the "delayed eschaton" of modern progressivism. Moreover, the appeal of this lies in the implicit thought that a time will come when there will be no further consequences of concern to us—the time when consequences, which were always driving forces before, are no longer consequential, and thus no longer mutating criteria of what we take to be true. Against this faith the endlessness of practical life reasserts itself, and we still do not know what a fully satisfactory world might be.

The attempted escape from the endlessness of practical life is only the promise of ultimate rescue at some distant point when what we think we want now will come to pass in such a way that we will be glad to have it. As Hegel reminds us, however, much human effort is spent in undoing the results of our past successes. In this situation we have the experience of freedom but seek a condition beyond freedom. The unavoidable question of what our freedom is for dramatizes the predicament we are considering. The ordeal of freedom is that we must deal with the question of purpose, direction, or redemption. We participate in defining what purpose, direction, or redemption means, even as we want these to have independent validity in themselves. We understand ourselves to be deciding for ourselves how we ought to be, but how do we deal with the absence of a voice to proclaim, "Well done thou good and faithful servant"?

How we ought to be is embedded in what we have been and imagine ourselves to be coming to be. Does this "ought to be" belong to one as an individual? That is, do we individuals merely place value on matters that interest us or that we find desirable? Is the "ought to be" emergent in a social matrix shaping what we take to be our individuality? We suffer tension between self-assertion and self-forgetting, between separation and adjustment, and if we engage to mediate this tension by seeking the life we wish to live, this too is the inescapable onwardness of our existence. Mutability and thus mortality bespeak "the central fact of practical existence; death is the central fact of life. I do not, of course, mean merely human mortality, the fact that we must one day cease to be; I mean the far more devastating mortality of every element of practical existence, the mortality of pleasures and pains, desires, achievements, emotions and affections. Mortality is the presiding character in practical experience. . . . Practice is never the mere assertion of the present; it is essentially action, the alteration of 'what is' so as to make it agree with 'what ought to be.'"[4]

As Montaigne would tell us, the unacknowledged goal of life is death. That is, we move forward through time both by necessity and by design. We go on to new things as if we want to speed toward death, when we are actually trying to run away from it. In this sense every day is equally natural and equally on the path of time. To be anxious for the future is usually to be anxious for a future other than the one we will with certainty experience. Habits help to dampen these anxieties, bringing an unstudied propensity toward balance against lurching from one thing to another. But judgment and assertion cannot be circumvented, nor can we avoid revision of judgments

4. Oakeshott, *Experience and Its Modes*, 273–74.

and assertions. Habits, however, allow the eye of judgment a little rest. Custom mediates these tensions. To depart from habit and custom involves the belief, as in modern rationalism, that we can get to the end of the road more efficiently, without hesitations and qualms. By "divers paths" we come to the same end.

If we say that certain ideas are necessary, or that "their time has come," and thereby appeal to finality, we do not thereby extricate ourselves from the endlessness of practical life. Goals to be sought because they "ought to be" are already intimated in the current state of affairs. But because these are intimations and not necessary implications, there are dissenting voices and alternative views. Attempts to silence the dissents only confirm their practical reality. Indeed, the dissenting voice may be, and often is, within ourselves. If the goals were necessary implications of the current state of affairs, perhaps they would unfold more naturally and easily. All of these are productions of the human mind, which show the open-endedness of the human imagination. Behind the rational plan lurks Fortuna. If we thought that discussion is more important than winning or losing, we would perhaps make peace with our mutability. But we seldom do this. Politics is unforgiving in this respect, prompting us to overcome the limitations we cannot avoid.

We must, then, live in radical temporality, but we do not have to live for it. We can come to terms with it by acknowledging it and learning to expect no more of it than it gives. "To philosophize is to learn how to die." But traditional philosophy is drawn to a transcendent dimension of which we would say not that "it ought to be" but that "it is" and does not require to be "put into practice." The temporal/mortal existence gives rise to the thought of its negation or its completion in the eternal/immortal. But unless we experience this through living fully in the present moment we will at best have a momentary sense of release from our ineluctable time-boundedness. The philosopher is the "victim of thought"[5] dwelling in the tension between the quest for the whole and the spectacle of irrationality, prejudice, and contingency:

5. Oakeshott, *Experience and Its Modes*, 3.

We hope one day for what we fear the next. What gave us
pleasure yesterday causes only pain to-day. We desire what
does not bring us satisfaction. We love what we hate, and
hate what we love. Neither our desires nor our hopes nor any
other mood in practical experience can be persuaded to
compose a consistent whole; the random, unguided element
is on the surface for all to see. . . . Our particular attempts to
convert "what is here and now" into "what ought to be" are
governed by no general rules. Nobody not forced to do so by
some moral or spiritual tyranny—tyranny of education or
command—conducts his life according to a set of absolute
principles, unmodified by the common-sense, intuition, or
insight which interprets such principles. . . . We shall find
nowhere a completely integrated world of practical
experience.[6]

The philosopher—the victim of thought—in attempting to live in
but not for the world of radical temporality discovers the unforgiving nature of practical life, offended as it is by the reminder that it
cannot fulfill itself, that its part is to pursue what it must ultimately
fail to procure. We know it as the combination of romantic quest
with calculating struggle for power.

The presupposition of practical experience is that "what is
here and now" and "what ought to be" are discrepant. And
practice is not the reconciliation of these worlds as worlds,
but the reconciliation of particular instances of this discrepancy. To reconcile these worlds generally and absolutely
would involve the abolition of discrepancy, the denial of what
is presupposed throughout. . . . Permanent dissatisfaction . . .
is inherent in practical experience. . . . The modification or
change of reality is a meaningless conception. . . . Practice
purports to throw reality into the future, into something
new and to be made, only to discover that this is also a
contradiction of the character of experience. . . . Change is
the concept or category under which reality is known in the

6. Oakeshott, *Experience and Its Modes*, 300.

world of practical existence. What is not transient is, for that reason, not real for practical experience.[7]

And "the principle of transience lies . . . beyond the reach of practical activity itself. . . . Consequently, the world achieved in practical experience does not differ from the given world. . . . Practical truth is not ultimate truth."[8] To be dead to the world of practice, of change, as Socrates says, is the beginning of philosophy. And, as Oakeshott says, "freedom from extraneous purpose and irrelevant interest is the sign of all seriously undertaken thought."[9]

The Modern Moral Imagination Responds to Radical Temporality

By "moral imagination" I mean, along lines suggested by Charles Taylor, "the ways people imagine their social existence, how they fit together with others, how things go on between them and their fellows, the expectations that are normally met, and the deeper normative notions and images that underlie these expectations . . . shared by large groups of people . . . that makes possible common practices and a widely shared sense of legitimacy."[10] Or as Oakeshott says, "Again, all moral judgment whatever may take the form of a reference of a situation to a rule of action, good always appearing as 'what is my duty,' but this is no reason for rejecting the view that, in the last analysis, moral judgment is the reference of a situation to an end, or the view that moral judgment is a judgment with regard to the coherence of life involved in living and acting in a particular way."[11]

More specifically, I focus here on the modern moral imagination as it informs modern thinking on human relations. I want to start by considering Hobbes (on whom Oakeshott wrote more systemati-

---

7. Oakeshott, *Experience and Its Modes*, 346.
8. Oakeshott, *Experience and Its Modes*, 308.
9. Oakeshott, *Experience and Its Modes*, 311.
10. Charles Taylor, *Modern Social Imaginaries* (Durham: Duke University Press, 2003), 23.
11. Oakeshott, *Religion, Politics, and the Moral Life*, 136.

cally than on any other political philosopher) and in particular the following observation in Hobbes's introduction to *Leviathan*:

> But there is another saying not of late understood, by which [human beings] might learn truly to read one another, if they would take the pains; and that is *nosce teipsum, read thy self* . . . to teach us that for the similitude of the thoughts and passions of one man to the thoughts and passions of another, whosoever looketh into himself and considereth what he doth, when he does *think, opine, reason, hope,* &c, and upon what grounds, he shall thereby read and know, what are the thoughts and passions of all other men upon the like occasions. . . . He that is to govern a whole nation must read in himself, not this or that particular man, but mankind, which though it be hard to do, harder than to learn any language or science, yet when I shall have set down my own reading orderly and perspicuously, the pains left another will be only to consider if he also find not the same in himself.[12]

This sets a direction for the modern moral imagination down to the present day. Let us notice all that Hobbes is saying to us: (1) the thoughts and passions are basically similar from one person to the next; (2) by introspection into one's own inner self one can imagine the basic pattern of reasoning and passion common to human beings and thus can infer how others are likely to respond in similar circumstances; (3) at the level of governing a nation this knowledge is essential because the task of governing extends far beyond our close personal relations—indeed, governing requires a certain kind of impersonal or depersonalized relationship to all subjects of a commonwealth; (4) at the same time, since there is no fundamental difference in these patterns between rulers and subjects, there is basic similarity in capacity for insight among all human beings; (5) what distinguishes one human being from another is the relative ability to grasp the basic structure of human conduct accurately by bracketing one's idiosyncrasies, foibles, and particular goals;

12. Thomas Hobbes, *Leviathan*, ed. Michael Oakeshott (Oxford: Blackwell, 1946), 5–6.

and (6) the office one holds does not distinguish one's basic humanity from that of others. Hobbes claims that in *Leviathan* he has worked out in detail what this basic human similitude is, and the test of his argument is for the reader to consider whether he has expounded the fundamental character of human relations "scientifically," that is, in detachment from merely personal preferences and goals.

Hobbes is, in other words, elaborating the prototype of the modern moral imagination that emphasizes not mere self-interestedness—the aspect of Hobbes's thought most commonly noticed—but also the capacity to enter into the views of others by inference from the universal basic structure of thought and emotion. We thus eventually arrive at enlightened or rational self-interest: the conscious and disciplined pursuit of our interests by which we take account of our inevitable implication in the unavoidable presence of others similarly self-interested and capable of disciplining their pursuits in the same way.

Reflection on our experience leads us to conclude that our desire to set ourselves apart from, or above, others will be frustrated if we do not learn to behave in a "moral way." The moral way is the disciplined way of self-restraint of enlightened self-interest, which individuals acquire through reflection on the lessons of experience. We can acquire the practice of self-regulation. We find it possible to imagine the inner life of others according to the basic similarity of one person to another in the common human condition. It is in learning how to discipline our self-interestedness that we demonstrate "moral imagination." We recognize something about ourselves in others. As Oakeshott says, following Hobbes, "moral activity may be said to be the observation of a balance of accommodation between the demands of desiring selves each recognized by the others to be an end and not a mere slave of somebody else's desires."[13]

Hobbes sets the stage for further development of the modern moral imagination. Subsequently, John Locke, Adam Smith, and David Hume, for instance, emphasize the instinct of sympathy, the capacity for pity at the sight of others' pain. The moral imagination

13. Michael Oakeshott, *Rationalism in Politics and Other Essays* (1991), 502.

allows us to identify ourselves with others even though each of us must be a "for itself," always remaining individuals who are "for ourselves."[14] The combination of self-interestedness with sympathy defines the modern moral imagination. Out of it we imagine and can systematically describe a spontaneous civil association of innumerable voluntary transactions governed by a procedural rule of law that, as it turns out, permits the growth of wealth and the projection of an ideal of infinitely expanding prosperity. Consider also Immanuel Kant's project to achieve perpetual peace through the expansion of the commercial-republican order to all the world. The movement from Hobbes to Kant and beyond brings to sight two great moral aspirations of modernity: perpetual peace and ever-expanding prosperity.

What appears to many readers to be Hobbes's pessimism about the human condition is nearly the opposite of the truth. Hobbes thought he had outlined the basic science of human conduct that, to the extent we learn it, makes it possible for us to transform human relations along the lines further developed in the movement from Locke to Smith and Hume to Kant, to John Stuart Mill, and beyond. These later writers work out the basis for confidence that the spontaneous order enabled by enlightened self-interest is not reliant for its stability on massive coercive power in central governments. Rather, it promises a more enduring stability than that maintainable by coercion, and it expresses the faith of classic modern liberal thought. These are fundamental assumptions of modernity. What does an Oakeshottian philosophical appraisal of these assumptions reveal? Let us consider Kant's expression of these assumptions as a means to this appraisal.

Kant's essay—"An Old Question Raised Again: Is the Human Race Constantly Progressing?"—advocates a "predictive history," a philosophy of the future, a kind of prophetic history. This is possible only if we commit ourselves in advance to goals that certify the dignity and enlightenment of humanity. That is, we must adopt ideals for the future worthy in themselves and then act toward the future under their inspiration. Given the sorry record of human history

14. Oakeshott, *Voice of Liberal Learning*, 19.

how can we believe in, or summon the energy to work for, these ideals? Kant's answer is that nothing less is worthy of a being who wishes to achieve true dignity and happiness. Here the modern moral imagination projects a moral transformation in the human condition. We must imagine our perfection and then gather the resources to pursue that imagined perfection. We must strive for what Kant calls "moralized politics" as opposed to "political morality."

Kant means by "political morality" the expedient calculation of self-interest we associate with Machiavelli. By "moralized politics" Kant means transforming enlightened self-interest to include the goal of a perfected human condition. This goal builds into enlightened self-interest the motive of transforming self-interest, no matter how rationally it may be pursued, into that higher virtue to which enlightened self-interest in the past seemed to be a barrier. This is to say that human beings have the capacity to construct their own vision of perfection and then find ways to make the vision a visible reality in human relations. We incorporate the ideal end-state into our self-interest. The science of conduct in Hobbes is to be perfected in the moral idealism of Kant.

Kant fully understands that the plausibility of the path to perfection is hindered by the record of past history. But if human beings are genuinely free in the sense that they make their ideals for themselves, they can thereby inspire themselves to strive unceasingly to make the ideals actual. We must become the cause of our own advance to completed enlightenment. To do this we must achieve a cosmopolitan point of view in which we regard humanity as a whole and not only in local identity. This is to extend Hobbes's original insight for the possibility of a permanently stable commonwealth— the internal cosmopolitanism of the citizens or subjects of the state—to the possibility of a universal commonwealth composed of republics who see the similitude of the thoughts and desires of one another.

The emergence of this ideal in Kant's time, which he thought was incarnated in the great revolutions of the seventeenth and eighteenth centuries, is for him the sign of progress because the new ideals of peace and prosperity are coming to be accepted as self-evident to modern people. Their validity does not lie initially in their plausibility but in their intrinsic appeal to beings who seek dignity and affirmation in their own terms. There is a latent moral disposition in the human race that at this moment in history is coming triumphally to sight. Perpetual peace will replace perpetual conflict. Living in hope for the heavenly kingdom will be transposed into a project to use self-interest to transform ourselves into an existence beyond self-interest. This is the apex of the modern moral imagination. Kant sees himself at a revelatory moment in which the moral disposition of the human race begins to reveal itself fully, to be formulated as a project for the future that, he thinks, cannot disappear. Contingent events cannot derail the moral direction, history cannot sweep away the ideal:

> The human race has always been in progress toward the better and will continue to be so henceforth. To him who does not consider what happens in just some one nation but who has regard to the whole scope of all the peoples on earth who will gradually come to participate in progress, this reveals the prospect of an immeasurable time—provided at least that there does not, by some chance, occur a second epoch of natural evolution which will push aside the human race for other creatures.

As the sense of duty to what ought to happen expands, it "will also extend to nations in their external relations toward one another up to the realization of the cosmopolitan society," increasingly resistant to the "mockery of the politician who would willingly take the hope of man as the dreaming of a distraught mind." And offensive war, "which constantly retards this advancement," will be renounced altogether.[15]

If the modern moral imagination is preoccupied with the ideals of peace and prosperity, bolstered by free market economy and

---

15. Immanuel Kant, "An Old Question Raised Again: Is the Human Race Constantly Progressing?," in *Kant on History*, ed. Lewis White Beck (New York: Macmillan/Library of Liberal Arts, 1963), 147–48, 151.

the confidence science and technology impart, that imagination is nevertheless attended by a haunting question: is it possible that we could advance materially and decline spiritually? From the first appearance of the modern moral imagination there has been an accompanying, dissenting theme. "Modernity" constitutes itself in the dialectic of what Oakeshott calls the "politics of faith" with the "politics of skepticism." This is the internal dialectic of the modern moral imagination.

The politics of skepticism is the modern renewal of the residual legacy of the classic/Christian heritage of Western civilization, which, in refusing to subscribe to Kant's (and those following him such as Marx) predictive history of the future, remembers and contemplates both the past record of the corruption induced by the acquisition of power and also Hobbes's admonition that "covenants without the sword are but words." As Oakeshott puts it,

> In the politics of faith, the activity of governing is understood to be in the service of the perfection of mankind. . . . Human perfection is sought precisely because it is not present . . . [and] is to be achieved by human effort, and confidence in the evanescence of imperfection springs here from the faith in human power and not from trust in divine providence. . . . Man is redeemable in history . . . [and] the chief agent of the improvement, which is to culminate in perfection, is government.[16]

Moreover,

> One of the characteristic assumptions, then, of the politics of faith is that human power is sufficient, or may become sufficient, to procure salvation. A second assumption is that the word "perfection" (and its synonyms) denotes a single, comprehensive condition of human circumstances. . . . Consequently, this style of politics requires a double confidence: the conviction that the necessary power is available or can be generated, and the conviction that, even if we do not

16. Michael Oakeshott, *The Politics of Faith and the Politics of Scepticism*, 23–24.

know exactly what constitutes perfection, at least we know the road that leads to it.[17]

By contrast, the politics of skepticism expresses "prudent diffidence" in recognizing politics as a "necessary evil" and "expects human conflict . . . seeing no way of abolishing it without abolishing much else at the same time . . . to be sparing of the quantity of power invested in government."[18]

Modernity constitutes itself both in rejecting the classic/Christian heritage and in acknowledging that heritage only insofar as it is made the preamble to our present and yet also in its failure to rid itself of this heritage that irritatingly reminds us that the ideal picture of our future opposes the actual structure of reality as we have always experienced it. In the terms of this chapter, the modern imagination's response to radical temporality is haunted by the fear that its response is inadequate and hostage to the actual future that may befall us. Modernity knows itself to be responding to a powerful critique that it cannot embrace but that it cannot shake off and forget either. Like all eschatological speculations it suffers indefinite postponement.

One can go on to suggest that the modern moral imagination exemplifies a profound dialectical tension between the philosophy of the future and the classic/Christian inheritance. What we call the "postmodern" bespeaks a condition of declining confidence in the claims of enlightenment embodied in philosophies of the future. This uncertainty is accompanied by aggressive bewilderment about alternative ways of imagining ourselves. The loss of confidence in utopian politics understandably issues in the feeling that we have lost the meaning of life because we have put so much faith in politics as the locus of meaning. The modern departure from the Platonic/Aristotelian/biblical understanding—that politics is an instrument in the service of that which transcends the mundane—makes us resistant to a return or leaves us with the sense that there is no path of return. Nor can we cure this disease by projecting yet new and

---

17. Oakeshott, *Politics of Faith and the Politics of Scepticism*, 26.
18. Oakeshott, *The Politics of Faith and the Politics of Scepticism*, 33.

different imagined futures, insofar as the enlightenment project has lost its innocence in its own crisis of faith.

Among his responses to this, Oakeshott offers openness to the "voice of poetry in the conversation of mankind." The voice of poetry is an alternative to, but not a substitute or replacement for, the scientific/technological/progressive voice. The voice of poetry is also not a political voice. For Oakeshott the poetic voice is a different way—within the modern context—of imagining our world. He does not intend it as an alternative to the historical reality in which we must think and act, but as the way to find experiences of delight that captivate us but do not urge us to look beyond this world to an alternative world. It is to seek the poetic in the interstices of the quotidian. Poetic images in our contemplation of them

> provoke neither speculation nor inquiry about the occasion or conditions of their appearing but only delight in their having appeared. They have no antecedents or consequents; they are not recognized as causes or conditions or signs of some other image to follow, or as the products or effects of one that went before; they are not instances of a kind, nor are they means to an end; they are neither "useful" nor "useless." . . . Moreover, the image in contemplation is neither pleasurable nor painful; and it does not attract to itself either moral approval or disapproval. Pleasure and pain, approval and disapproval are characteristics of images of desire and aversion, but the partner of desire and aversion is incapable of being the partner of contemplation.[19]

We note that this establishes Oakeshott's dialectical, or perhaps one should say his conversational, response to the preoccupation with historical existence in favor of an experience where the anxieties of seeking perfection and perpetuating imperfection do not intrude. It falls short of the pull of the eternal, but it does not necessarily exclude it since that, for Oakeshott, is a matter for individuals to consider. He offers the poetic voice as a gentle way to acknowledge the terrors of the radical temporality of the human

---

19. Oakeshott, *Rationalism in Politics*, 510.

condition, at least in offering release for a time from the interminable modern project to perfect ourselves in the realm of perpetual peace and infinite prosperity. The project is interminable, because there can be no guarantee against falling back into war (which may seem obvious in a way) nor insulation from the failure of material wealth to assuage spiritual longing (for which empirical evidence abounds). Oakeshott allows for a glimpse of the transcendent in the transitory release into the contemplative experience of the poetic voice. He is stoic, but he points to a more comprehensive moral imagination that, while it need not abandon modern accomplishments, would recognize their subordinate and inevitably incomplete character. It is his Socratic turn, disclosing his philosophical imagination by questioning the assumptions of the modern moral imagination in the universal context of the radical temporality that is the human condition.

Oakeshott's Pilgrimage Past J. S. Mill

STUDENTS OF MICHAEL OAKESHOTT's thought will remember that his 1951 inaugural lecture at the London School of Economics, "Political Education," was the occasion of much critical comment, not least on his use of the phrase "pursuit of intimations" to describe the conduct of politics. He replied to his critics with an appendix to the 1962 publication of the lecture in *Rationalism in Politics and Other Essays.* In that appendix, he included a brief remark about John Stuart Mill that, to my knowledge, is rarely if ever commented on. As was often the case in his writings, Oakeshott allowed this somewhat cryptic remark to stand for itself. In the appendix, Oakeshott quotes from Mill's *Autobiography,* elaborating a reference in the body of the lecture to Mill's *Considerations on Representative Government.* I have long been curious about this—I wrote my doctoral thesis on Mill under the influence of Oakeshott's thought in the midst of the controversies spawned by Gertrude Himmelfarb and Maurice Cowling alleging that Mill was less a liberal than his reputation had long suggested. I want to explain as I see it what Oakeshott meant.

Here is Oakeshott's comment from that appendix:

Reprinted with permission from Intercollegiate Studies Institute from *Modern Age*, vol. 57, no. 2 (Spring 2015): 36–44.

J. S. Mill (*Autobiography*, OUP, 136–37, 144–45), when he abandoned reference to general principle either as a reliable guide in political activity or as a satisfactory explanatory device, put in its place a "theory of human progress" and what he called a "philosophy of history." The view I have expressed in this essay may be taken to represent a further stage in this intellectual pilgrimage, a stage reached when neither "principle" (on account of what it turns out to be: a mere index of concrete behaviour) nor any general theory about the character and direction of social change seems to supply an adequate reference for explanation or for practical conduct.[1]

What was Oakeshott's intellectual pilgrimage? To understand better what Oakeshott meant, I want to consider some features of Mill's thought compared to Oakeshott's, especially Oakeshott's use of the term "pursuit of intimations" as an explanatory description of politics. Here are his words: he says of the phrase the "pursuit of intimations" that "it is neither intended as a description of the motives of politicians nor of what they believe themselves to be doing, but of what they actually succeed in doing."[2] And Oakeshott goes on to say that, if this is an accurate description, it should have some "bearing upon how we study politics."[3] This is consistent with his argument that the study of politics is categorically different from the practice of politics, a distinction Mill had made between the art of politics and the science of politics in his "Logic of the Moral Sciences," and that was later elaborated upon by Max Weber. Oakeshott concludes,

> If this understanding of political activity were true, certain
> forms of argument (e.g. arguments designed to determine
> the correspondence of a political proposal with Natural Law

1. Michael Oakeshott, *Rationalism in Politics* (1991), 69. The J. S. Mill reference is from Mill, *Autobiography*, in Collected Works of John Stuart Mill, vol. 1 (Indianapolis: Liberty Fund, Inc., 2006), 166–69, 177–79.
2. Oakeshott, *Rationalism in Politics* (1991), 67.
3. Oakeshott, *Rationalism in Politics*, 67.

or with abstract "justice") must be considered either irrelevant or as clumsy formulations of other and relevant inquiries, and must be understood to have merely rhetorical or persuasive value.[4]

Oakeshott argues that the precepts of natural law are background considerations in the formation of laws and policies, but they do not dictate exactly what contingent circumstances require in acknowledging them in practice. For that, judgment is required and cannot be avoided.

To study politics in the way proper to a university study, Oakeshott also thought, requires us to maintain this distinction. University study is not the carrying on of politics by other means. Like Weber, Oakeshott distinguishes the lecture hall from the political stage. The teacher qua teacher is not to engage in persuasive speech. Oakeshott means not merely that teachers ought not to do this, but that as teachers, in the precise sense, persuasive speech is irrelevant to the pedagogical task. "Political Education" was thus an essay instantiating his approach to the study of politics, and the phrase "pursuit of intimations" tries to express adequately what this approach to the study of politics reveals. This also fits with what Oakeshott understands to be the aim of the philosophical study of politics, or, more generally, the study of the practical mode in human experience, as he set forth in *Experience and Its Modes* (1933). As he would later say in *On Human Conduct* (1975), Oakeshott wanted to understand better what he already understood in part. To understand is to describe what one observes going on in a particular area of human activity. Philosophy, he says, achieves its proper expression in the indicative mode. This understanding also informs Oakeshott's idea of academic education on politics. Thus he also says that the proper texts for such study are historical and philosophical, where the standard for the texts is how closely historians or philosophers adhere, in the texts they offer, to their tasks in the precise sense. The philosopher observes what is going on in detachment from it. The activity of the historian qua historian is to study

4. Oakeshott, *Rationalism in Politics*, 67.

the past "for its own sake," not to pronounce moral lessons or defend political arguments.

⟹   ⟸

As a student of both history and philosophy, Oakeshott finds that politics operates as he describes it. The strong form of his argument is not that politicians "ought not" to act merely according to abstract principles but that they cannot so act regardless of what they claim or believe themselves to be doing. Even in revolutionary moments, the actors on the political stage will inevitably fall back on practices, customs, and ideas they claim to have superseded. Of course, turmoil and mayhem may follow given the capacity of political actors to misunderstand what they can do—witness the French and Russian revolutions—but the revolutionaries no less than any others are feeling their way forward on an uncertain path the end of which is not in sight, and which is likely to be quite different from anything they imagine in advance. They are pursuing intimations of the situation that befalls them. They may extrapolate theoretical formulations from their experiences, but the experiences come first, constraining their theoretical formulations of experience.

In this respect Oakeshott has absorbed an ancient, Aristotelian lesson: action always requires appraisal and judgment; there are better and worse, more and less fortunate, judgments, but there is no formula to guarantee success; there is never a conclusion that will not be subject to argument, reconsideration, and revision; politics is interminable, an ineluctable aspect of the human condition. There is no Ideal Form from which to derive guidance or to replace judgment and decision making. Modern political idealism that imagines an end to politics, say in perpetual peace, uses politics in the hope of transcending politics, but, as we have repeatedly seen, fails to achieve the hoped-for result. This, as we know from *Experience and Its Modes*, Oakeshott identifies as the incoherency of the practical life that both defines the sort of activity it is and limits its possibilities. And in other essays, Oakeshott expresses his Augustinian skepticism about endless Babel-like construction projects to immanentize the heavenly kingdom, and he explores political skepticism in *The Politics of Faith and the Politics of Scepticism.*

However, Oakeshott's remarks on Mill in "Political Education" do not invoke Aristotle or Augustine. Instead he admits some inspiration from Mill, who was no Augustinian and only distantly Aristotelian. Let us consider further what Mill said in his *Autobiography*. I mention in passing Mill's description of his father's abandonment of traditional Christianity and his own education devoid of religion. J. S. Mill eventually advocated the religion of humanity, a humanistic moral commitment to progress in the human condition, grounded in no inherited dogmas. He learned from his father the firm conviction that moderation is the crucial practical virtue. Mill describes his father as a Stoic, and his father's morals as Epicurean/Utilitarian, "taking as the exclusive test of right and wrong, the tendency of actions to produce pleasure or pain."[5] Like the Epicurean, James Mill advocated curtailing indulgences, was suspicious of passionate emotions, and sought to avoid misery by refusing pleasures that bring suffering and disillusionment in the long run.

Mill's position with the East India Company gave him the opportunity to learn "by personal observation the necessary conditions of the practical conduct of public affairs."[6] In his capacity as a speculative writer, Mill could contemplate visions of order without obstruction, but in practice he had to justify everything to those who saw the world differently:

> I became practically conversant with the difficulties of moving bodies of men, the necessities of compromise, the art of sacrificing the non-essential to preserve the essential. . . . I have found, through life, these acquisitions to be of the greatest possible importance for personal happiness, and they are also a very necessary condition for enabling anyone, either as theorist or as practical man, to effect the greatest amount of good compatible with his opportunities.[7]

5. Mill, *Autobiography*, 49.
6. Mill, *Autobiography*, 87.
7. Mill, *Autobiography*, 87.

Both as a theorist and as a practical man, Mill wanted to achieve the greatest good. Mill retained his political idealism and guide to the future, which in his thinking had an integrity independent of the necessary compromises through which to promote that good as much as and whenever possible. Oakeshott rejects Mill's residual dualism—its implicit Platonism as Nietzsche would insist—in favor of the view that the ideal itself changes with the changing circumstances, even if the vocabulary employed persists so as to suggest a continuity that is superficial or illusory.

To pursue intimations, then, would mean not merely compromising with others but actually altering our understanding of what we are pursuing even as we pursue it. Ideals and contingent circumstances are inseparable. Politics is what happens at the intersection of these. By contrast, in *On Liberty* the ultimate justification of absolute freedom of thought and discussion is the convergence on truth in what Mill called the spontaneously improving society. Of course, Mill also prefers Socrates to the fool. Opinions will vary from better to worse, wise to foolish, and Mill's regime would facilitate sorting this out. Mill believes that absolute freedom of thought and discussion will eventually reveal the best opinions, that there is a method for uniting power and wisdom that precludes direct dictation by the wisest while, in the long run, satisfying their aspirations. Everyone, he believes, will come finally to see what the best among us had already seen long since.

From Oakeshott's perspective, this is Mill's last-gasp effort to preserve some fixity in a world of radical temporality, or to find a substitute for the old natural law and revelation, and to avoid the skepticism for which Oakeshott is well known and for which he is frequently criticized. When Oakeshott says that we have set sail on a boundless and bottomless sea without anchorage or safe harbor, at best keeping the ship afloat, he is taking the step that Mill would not take but that Oakeshott took to be implied in Mill's thought. A philosophy of history, in this case, is a narrative of how the good will necessarily prevail ultimately. It cannot be explicated in terms of abstract principles if it is fully to respect the temporal-historical character of human conduct, but in the absence of abstract principles, it is also impossible to assess the alleged progress of the human condition.

If Oakeshott had retained his religion, he would have been a strict Augustinian because the doctrine of the two cities allows both for the radical temporality of the human condition and for faith in a transcendent salvation. Occasionally, when Oakeshott talked theology, he would invoke Augustine's view that we live in the interim between the Incarnation and the Second Coming, more or less free on our own recognizance to do the best we can. But Oakeshott was himself enough of a Hegelian to think that one's historical time and place dictated the terms in which to express oneself. There are not two cities but only one world of experience within which imaginative characterizations of the human predicament may be formulated: Augustine's was a work of imaginative genius to be appreciated in that sense.

Oakeshott understood that modern religiosity had come to be associated with the idea of immanent historical improvement or progress, and he saw no way to go back to an earlier understanding. If the age of dualism is over, then one might find solace in the evanescent delights of poetry or music (Mill's reliance on poetry to bring him out of depression also symbolizes this) but no release from the hard realization, evocatively described by Montaigne, that the flow of experience undermines every effort to frame it in permanent meaning. Ours is an age suspicious of permanency. In vulgar terms it is the age in which the many shout, in hope and fear, that change is good. Yet Mill was convinced that, even though feeling is indispensable, analysis trumps feeling.[8]

≡ ≡

We come then to the turning point in Mill's thought that Oakeshott quotes in the appendix to "Political Education." Considering what Mill said in the full context of the *Autobiography*, we learn that he admired the historical narratives of the Saint-Simonians and the Comteans, and, while he never adopted their views entirely, he was intrigued by the threefold scheme of historical development

8. Mill, *Autobiography*, 147.

and the distinction of historical periods as "organic" and "critical." Mill adopted the latter distinction as the movement from organic ancient polytheism to critical Greek philosophy to organic Christianity to the modern critical era spawned by the Reformation. He thought the critical era emergent in the Reformation was still powerful in his time but was threatened by the rise of the tyranny of opinion, the tyranny of the majority, by conformism, and the uncertain future of democratization. Mill wanted to perpetuate the critical era or to forestall as far as possible a new organic period. Much of his political thought is explained by this.

From the French literature, Mill said,

> I derived, among other ideas which the general turning
> upside down of the opinions of the European thinkers had
> brought uppermost, these in particular: That the human
> mind had a certain order of possible progress, in which some
> things must precede others, an order which governments
> and public instructors can modify to some, but not an
> unlimited extent: That all questions of political institutions
> are relative, not absolute, and that different stages of human
> progress not only *will* have, but *ought* to have, different
> institutions: . . . That any general theory or philosophy of
> politics supposes a previous theory of human progress, and
> that this is the same thing with a philosophy of history.[9]

Mill then reaffirms the eighteenth-century Enlightenment thinkers even while absorbing the perspective of the nineteenth-century thinkers. Mill seeks to preserve the aspirations of the Enlightenment but with heightened sensitivity to the evolutionary complexities of political life in historical existence. This is not far from Hegel's assessment of the French Revolution in its achievements and its failures. Mill did not think this precluded continued progress in the long run. Mill sees the obstacles but remained committed to progress.

Mill was a methodological Stoic and a constrained utopian. He saw the constraints that inevitably attend political action, though he

9. Mill, *Autobiography*, 169–71.

resisted what he called fatalism. From Oakeshott's perspective, moderation is too weak a qualifier to the utopian aspiration to save it from radical critique. Mill, like many less sophisticated than he, was caught between two worlds. Characteristically, he saw value in both. With Oakeshott, however, philosophy is uncompromising and thus alien to the political world. Oakeshott takes as his task to explicate the assumptions each of the parties makes in order to clarify why they see the world as they do. His analysis places him outside the alternatives as a nonpracticing observer. Oakeshott's philosopher disarms himself and is of little use to either side. He seeks to understand, but not to change, the world.

Mill's *Considerations on Representative Government* further illustrates that from which Oakeshott took his leave. Speaking of forms of government, Mill says,

> Like all things, therefore, which are made by men, they may be either well or ill made; judgment and skill may have been exercised in their production, or the reverse of these. And again, if a people have omitted, or from outward pressure have not had it in their power, to give themselves a constitution by the tentative process of applying a corrective to each evil as it arose, or as the sufferers gained strength to resist it, this retardation of political progress is no doubt a great disadvantage to them, but it does not prove that what has been found good for others would not have been good also for them, and will not be so still when they think fit to adopt it.[10]

Oakeshott, in describing politics as attending to the arrangements of a set of people brought together by chance or choice, could be paraphrasing a part of Mill's thinking. The pursuit of intimations involves correcting perceived evils as they come to sight. But Oakeshott's point is that the "evils" themselves are defined variously from different perspectives. Oakeshott thinks that there would be no end to arguments over the identity of evils needing correction, nor over

10. J. S. Mill, *Considerations on Representative Government*, ed. R. B. McCallum (Oxford: Blackwell, 1946), 111.

what the correctives should be. A "tradition of behaviour," Oakeshott says, "is not susceptible of the distinction between essence and accident. Knowledge of it is unavoidably knowledge of its detail: to know only the gist is to know nothing. What has to be learned is not an abstract idea, or a set of tricks, not even a ritual, but a concrete, coherent manner of living in all its intricateness."[11] "In politics, then, every enterprise is a consequential enterprise, the pursuit, not of a dream, or of a general principle, but of an intimation."[12] And,

> The most insidious current misunderstandings of political activity—the misunderstanding in which institutions and procedures appear as pieces of machinery designed to achieve a purpose settled in advance, instead of as manners of behaviour which are meaningless when separated from their context; the misunderstanding, for example, in which Mill convinced himself that something called "Representative Government" was a "form" of politics which could be regarded as proper to any society which reached a certain level of what he called "civilization"; in short, the misunderstanding in which we regard our arrangements and institutions as something more significant than the footprints of thinkers and statesmen who knew which way to turn their feet without knowing anything about a final destination.[13]

Political rhetoric may justify correctives as contributing to progress, but for Oakeshott philosophic understanding stands back from such pronouncements. When he discusses women's right to vote, for example, Oakeshott explains it as the elimination of the absurdity in which women were treated increasingly as citizens in every other respect except this. He does not assert that this significant change in our arrangements is progress, even though most say that it is.[14]

Generally speaking, those who pursue political philosophy feel an affinity with Mill more than with Oakeshott at this point. It is not

11. Oakeshott, *Rationalism in Politics*, 62.
12. Oakeshott, *Rationalism in Politics*, 57.
13. Oakeshott, *Rationalism in Politics*, 63–64.
14. Oakeshott, *Rationalism in Politics*, 57.

that Oakeshott stands in the way of change; on the contrary, he accepts change as natural to humanity; the real objection is that he does not glorify change, or indeed particular changes, and that he is skeptical about proposals for change. The pursuit of intimations is a description that avoids endorsements.

Of course, Oakeshott had strong views on some political questions, and there are discernible tensions at times in his writings between his philosophic understanding and those views—the inevitable consequence of living while seeking, philosophically speaking, to die. For him, thought about experience separates itself from the vitality of experience. Philosophers, he says, are the "victims of thought." Mill himself asserts, in his *Autobiography*, that analysis is the enemy of feeling. Weber says that choosing a method of knowing is choosing a way of life; science is, after all, a vocation, as is politics. To choose one path is to leave another behind. Oakeshott accepts this. But Mill pursues both analysis and feeling. He could describe political conduct consonant with Oakeshott's description but with the proviso that there is, however distant, a goal for history. Like Weber after him (but Weber, with Nietzsche, was profoundly more skeptical than Mill), Mill hopes that analysis could be employed to assist the formation of rational political opinions without dictating them. He seeks fruitful alliance between the art and the science of policy. There is an analogy in this to Marx's project to align theory and practice, superseding the division of labor between intellectuals and workers. Mill's virtue is to recognize the danger of that revolutionary impatience that abolishes debate and argument, imposing an arbitrary unity, and that dismisses procedural limitations on the exercise of power.

But even so, Mill subscribes to progressive improvement and perfectibility. In *Representative Government*, Mill says,

> The capability of any given people for fulfilling the conditions of a given form of government cannot be pronounced on by any sweeping rule. Knowledge of the particular people, and general practical judgment and sagacity, must be the guides. There is also another consideration not to be lost sight of. A people may be unprepared for good institutions;

but to kindle a desire for them is a necessary part of the preparation. To recommend and advocate a particular institution or form of government, and set its advantages in the strongest light, is one of the modes, often the only mode within reach, of educating the mind of the nation not only for accepting or claiming, but also for working, the institution.[15]

In a society enjoying absolute freedom of thought and discussion there is, nevertheless, an intellectual elite that understands better what the society as a whole implicitly understands. To exercise intellectual responsibility is to make the implicit explicit:

They who can succeed in creating a general persuasion that a certain form of government, or social fact of any kind, deserves to be preferred, have made nearly the most important step which can possibly be taken towards ranging the powers of society on its side. . . . It is what men think that determines how they act; and though the persuasions and convictions of average men are in a much greater degree determined by their personal position than by reason, no little power is exercised over them by the persuasions and convictions of those whose personal position is different, and by the united authority of the instructed . . . the maxim, that the government of a country is what the social forces in existence compel it to be, is true only in the sense in which it favours, instead of discouraging, the attempt to exercise, among all forms of government practicable in the existing condition of society, a rational choice.[16]

In discussing "Order" and "Progress," Mill defines "Order as the preservation of all kinds and amounts of good which already exist, and Progress as consisting in the increase of them."[17] Mill values Order for providing stability and preserving what good had already been attained. But Order is the staging area for subsequent advance.

15. Mill, *Representative Government*, 115.
16. Mill, *Representative Government*, 117–18.
17. Mill, *Representative Government*, 121.

Both Order and Progress are good, but Order is subordinate to Progress in that Order keeps open the way to the next stage of improvement.

The movement from organic to critical periods is progressive and cumulative in principle. While it remains possible to fall back, Mill believed that we had reached a moment in civilizational history wherein we could grasp the dynamics of historical development sufficiently to guide the way into a future of continual and spontaneous improvement. The danger is that we will relax and be content with what we have so far achieved. Human beings, left to their own devices, tend to slack off. Christianity was once a catalyst for aspiring to a new level of moral achievement, but it is now exhausted.

≡ ≡

What will encourage advancement in our era? It is the belief in progress or the religion of humanity, the commitment to taking charge of our destiny and keeping open the way of Progress, employing Order as an instrument in the service of Progress. It is the responsibility of the intellectual community to evangelize the religion of humanity:

> It would be more philosophically correct to leave out of the definition the word Order, and to say that the best government is that which is most conducive to Progress. For Progress includes Order, but Order does not include Progress. Progress is a greater degree of that of which Order is a less. Order, in any other sense, stands only for a part of the pre-requisites of good government, not for its idea and essence. . . . Order, thus considered, is not an additional end to be reconciled with Progress, but a part and means of Progress itself.[18]

Compare these remarks to Oakeshott's description—composed around the same time as "Political Education"—of the "politics of faith" and the "politics of skepticism." Oakeshott describes these as poles achieving identity in tension with each other, in their polarity

18. Mill, *Representative Government*, 123–24.

ordering a charged political field. Note the difference in his choice of terms from Mill's "Order" and "Progress." The politics of faith and the politics of skepticism began to appear more or less simultaneously at the beginning of modern European history about five centuries ago. In their dialectical opposition—for example, whether the power of governments should be aggregated or dispersed—they spawn a long-developing manner of argument forming the background conditions in which the particular struggles of modern European politics are interpreted and play themselves out.

The politics of faith claims to be progressive and seeks to dominate in much the way Mill describes and approves. But for the political skeptic, this is a faith in things unseen and unseeable. The politics of skepticism resists the politics of faith: it does not seek to put an alternative political faith in play but recognizes politics as a necessary evil, something we cannot do without but that is commonly overrated both as to its claims for the future and its claims of accomplishment in the present. Oakeshott, in describing the claims of progress and improvement, accepts their continual presence as claims but does not endorse them. They are indigenous to modern political life, but there is no foundation for their claims apart from a strong commitment to them among the intellectual elite. The claims of progress provoke dialectical opposition from political skeptics and portend disillusion among those who invest themselves in such claims.

Thus Oakeshott, in speaking of the pursuit of intimations, summarizes both his thinking about the appropriate approach to political education or the study of politics, as well as his conclusion about what politics is and can or cannot be, and what politics, upon reflection, shows about the human condition in the modern world.

Historicism and Political Philosophy
Reflections on Oakeshott, Collingwood, Gadamer, and Strauss

The voice of practical activity may be the commonest to be heard, but it is partnered by others whose utterance is in a different idiom . . . "history" also has acquired, or has begun to acquire, an authentic voice and idiom of its own.
—*Michael Oakeshott*, "The Voice of Poetry in the Conversation of Mankind"

History is a predicament for man who must live in it. In order to act in history, he must seek to rise above it. He needs perspectives in terms of which to understand his situation, and timeless truths and values in terms of which to act in it. Yet the perspectives which he finds often merely reflect his age; and what he accepts as timelessly true and valid is apt to be merely the opinion that is in fashion. Thus while man must always try to rise above his historical situation he succeeds at best only precariously.
—*Emil Fackenheim*, Metaphysics and Historicity

Reprinted with permission from Noel O'Sullivan, ed., *The Place of Michael Oakeshott in Contemporary Western and Non-Western Thought* (London: Imprint Academic, 2017), 73–89.

Preface

What follows reflects on the issue of historicism and the status of political philosophy as illustrated in the thought of Michael Oakeshott, R. G. Collingwood, Hans-Georg Gadamer, and Leo Strauss. All four take seriously that we live in an age of heightened historical consciousness, and they all reflect on the status of past thought in the present. Modern historical research makes us aware that the more detailed historical knowledge we gain of the past, the more the past can seem distant and strange. Accumulating historical knowledge questions the prospect of an agreed upon historical narrative, and casts doubt on access to perennial questions and timeless truths. In the introduction to Hegel's *Philosophy of History*, one already encounters a typology of different approaches to understanding the past, coupled with Hegel's attempt to find meaning in history through a philosophic narrative of history's rational progress toward its end, seeking to mediate the tension between the quest for meaning in history and the historian's detailed account of history. Since Hegel's time the question of the relationship of historical and philosophical thought has become unavoidable, especially when we turn to the question of political philosophy which inevitably involves both. This question was raised in the twentieth century in a particularly trenchant way by these four thinkers who struggled to make sense of the philosophical relevance of history and the historical relevance of philosophy in the face of the political catastrophe that engulfed European civilization. In addressing such matters, the four thinkers discussed here offer varied responses ranging from Collingwood's embrace of historicism to Strauss's critique of historicism. Oakeshott and Gadamer occupy a middle ground seeking to mediate this opposition in ways discussed below.

Oakeshott on Political Philosophy

In his original Introduction (1946) to Hobbes's *Leviathan*, Oakeshott remarks that "Every masterpiece of political philosophy springs from a new vision of the predicament; each is the glimpse of a deliverance

or the suggestion of a remedy."[1] And he identifies three great traditions of philosophic reflection on politics. The first involves the
"master conceptions of Reason and Nature," associated pre-
eminently with Plato's *Republic*, of which tradition he says:

> It is coeval with our civilization; it has an unbroken history
> into the modern world; and it has survived by a matchless
> power of adaptability all the changes of the European
> consciousness.[2]

Oakeshott also identifies the tradition of "will and artifice" with
Hobbes and the tradition of "rational will" with Hegel. He does not
treat them as superseding the Platonic tradition in a linear progression. They are persisting ways of thinking about politics which are
available to us through changing historical circumstances: "I cannot detect a history of political thought which reveals a gradual ac-
cumulation of political wisdom and understanding . . . anything
which could properly correspond to the expression *the* history of
political thought."[3] Implicit is a vital conversation among the great
voices of political philosophy. Here, for example, is his summary of
the achievement of Saint Thomas Aquinas:

> [His is] the enterprise of *explaining* political activity and the
> activity of governing. It is a subtle union of Christian theol-
> ogy and the Aristotelian philosophy of "nature," in which
> these two components were brought together, and made to
> modify one another and generate an explanation, not only
> remarkably new in the thirteenth century, but one that has
> had a profound influence upon all subsequent explanatory
> enterprises in this field.[4]

And having described the various dimensions of Aristotle's analysis of polis-life in which Aristotle "finds a place for *politike* on the

1. Michael Oakeshott, introduction to *Leviathan*, xi.
2. Oakeshott, introduction to *Leviathan*, xii.
3. Michael Oakeshott, *Lectures in the History of Political Thought*, 32; italics in
original.
4. Oakeshott, *Lectures in the History of Political Thought*, 358; italics in
original.

map of human activity," Oakeshott remarks that there is a "mode of activity in which human beings employ an aptitude which Aristotle understands to be the supreme aptitude of their 'nature,' an aptitude even more fundamental than that of a life governed by rational choice of what to do and not to do . . . another aptitude which he calls 'theoretical reason' . . . the ability to understand and explain what they are doing . . . human beings are not only *praktikos*, but also *theoretikos*. . . . This Aristotelian map, with a few amendments scribbled on it by later thinkers, was the context of all European political thought for 2,000 years."[5] In short, human beings know that they are historically situated and thus are drawn to wonder about the greater context of their situatedness. This would not be possible if their situatedness entirely determined and confined their thinking. The historical perspective is a particular response to situatedness which is universal to human existence; in principle, historicism cannot foreclose philosophic argument about its own premises.

Political philosophy for Oakeshott, then, while it may acknowledge both, is confined neither to the historian's past (the mere history of thought which is neither *praktikos* nor *theoretikos*), nor to serving the practical life which exploits the past in its concern for present and future political purposes. Oakeshott identifies "masterpieces" which rise above their contexts to become permanent contributions to our thinking. Philosophers of politics, situated in their own time and place, under the philosophic impulse look beyond, even to "eternity." "There has been," Oakeshott remarks, "no fully considered politics that has not looked for its reflection in eternity. The history of political philosophy is, then, the context of the masterpiece."[6] Moreover, a philosophy of politics is "an explanation or view of political life and activity from the standpoint of the totality of experience."[7] This meant for Oakeshott to embrace a conversational exchange where the initial context of time and place does not confine the masterpiece of political thought. Speaking of

---

5. Oakeshott, *Lectures in the History of Political Thought*, 128–29.
6. Oakeshott, introduction to *Leviathan*, xi.
7. Michael Oakeshott, "The Concept of a Philosophy of Politics," in *Religion, Politics and the Moral Life*, 126–27.

Hobbes's *Leviathan*, he says, "in reading the *Leviathan* I seem to find, not only a book the significance of which lies in the seventeenth century, not only a book which offers an explanation of the origin and character of political life constructed to meet particular circumstances, but to find also something which, because it can relevantly be separated from time and place and for other reasons, I should call a philosophy of politics."[8]

Oakeshott on the Nature and Limits of the Historical Mode of Experience

The historical point of view is not an inevitable acquisition imposing itself upon us as the practical task of survival does; it is not an obvious view of the past; it is an acquisition motivated by our critical faculty in developing methods that are to be learned in learning to become not just a receptor but a critical analyst of the past. The historical point of view does not replace the practical life, but nor is the practical life the key to understanding the historical point of view. These are "categorially distinct modes of understanding."[9] Nonetheless, they are prone to tension: the historian's present "is perhaps the most sophisticated of all presents, difficult to achieve and difficult to sustain . . . historical understanding is especially prone to relapse into some other engagement."[10]

In the historical mode of explanation events cannot be understood apart from the particular manner in which the historian considers them. "The historian's business is not to discover, recapture, or even to interpret; it is to create and construct . . . discovery without judgment is impossible; and a course of events independent of experience, untouched by thought and judgment, is a contradiction."[11] Historical "facts" are conclusions historians may eventually reach, not the raw material from which the historian begins. To achieve this

---

8. Oakeshott, "The Concept of a Philosophy of Politics," 119.
9. Michael Oakeshott, "Present, Past and Future," in *On History and Other Essays* (1999).
10. Oakeshott, "Present, Past and Future," 31.
11. Michael Oakeshott, *Experience and Its Modes*, 93–94.

requires training in the historian's task in order to master the presuppositions of historical inquiry.

What are these presuppositions? First, experience is understood
as past. Separating from the practical/political past is the most significant development of the historical consciousness: "In practical
experience, the past is designed to justify, to make valid practical beliefs about the present and the future, about the world in general . . .
the language is that of history, while its thought is that of practice."[12]
By contrast the historical past "is the past for its own sake." The historian's is a "dead past."[13]

On the other hand, the persistence of the Platonic, the Aristotelian, the Thomistic, the Hobbesian, and the Hegelian voices shows
that, in responding to them, we are not merely locating them in the
flow of events. They speak to us through all the contingent changes
of temporal existence. Oakeshott does not foreclose a dialogue with
past thinkers and thus distinguishes political philosophy both from
the past "for its own sake," and also from political ideology.

What the historian accounts for is not what "really happened," but
rather for "what the evidence obliges us to believe" happened.[14] "The
present in historical understanding, then, is itself a past . . . a past
which itself survived and is present. It is composed of actual utterances and artefacts which have survived, which are understood as
survivals, and are now present exactly as they were uttered or made
except for any damage they may have suffered on the way."[15] "There
are not two worlds—the world of past happenings and the world of
our present knowledge of those past events—there is only one world,
and it is a world of present experience" full of survivals which are
evidence. "The past in history is, then, always an inference; it is the
product of judgment and consequently always belongs to the historian's present world of experience. All he has is his present world of
ideas, and the historical past is a constituent of that world or nothing

---

12. Oakeshott, *Experience and Its Modes*, 105.
13. Oakeshott, *Experience and Its Modes*, 106.
14. Oakeshott, *Experience and Its Modes*, 107.
15. Oakeshott, "Present, Past and Future," 32–33.

at all."[16] In contrast, to engage with the masterpieces of political thought is to consider arguments about what is true about politics independent of what political actors may claim to be doing, and in terms that speak beyond mere time and place. Oakeshott does not think that the study of history for its own sake will elicit practical wisdom or philosophic argument. We see also why, for Oakeshott, this is an abstract account of the whole of experience since the whole of experience is never solely past experience. To assess the argument of a masterpiece as merely reflective of the time and place of its author may be the task of the historian *qua* historian, but it cannot be the sole task of human understanding: "whenever history invades any other world of experience, the result is always the disintegration of experience."[17] Oakeshott did not adopt historicism. He saw that, in the great thinkers, while there are of course historical elements, there is also a capacity to express something surmounting those elements, inviting our response: "Wherever there is genuinely philosophical reflection something is being said, such that if true, things will be as they permanently are—that is, as they are *not* in the world of practical politics."[18]

Collingwood on Re-enacting Past Thought

Is historical understanding for Collingwood basic? Oakeshott thought so. In his review of *The Idea of History*, Oakeshott says, "it must be observed that, almost imperceptibly, Collingwood's philosophy of history turned into a philosophy in which all knowledge is assimilated to historical knowledge, and consequently into a radically sceptical philosophy."[19] To explore this further, consider Collingwood's *Essay on Metaphysics*.[20]

16. Oakeshott, *Experience and Its Modes*, 109.
17. Oakeshott, *Experience and Its Modes*, 156.
18. Michael Oakeshott, "Political Philosophy," in *Religion, Politics and the Moral Life*, 155.
19. Michael Oakeshott, review of *The Idea of History* by R. G. Collingwood, in *English Historical Review*, 1947.
20. R. G. Collingwood, *An Essay on Metaphysics* (Oxford: Clarendon Press, 1940).

In that essay, Collingwood asserts that metaphysical questions are historical questions: "Metaphysics has always been an historical science; but metaphysicians have not always been fully aware of that fact."[21] Metaphysics identifies "absolute presuppositions," assumptions a thinker or set of thinkers take to be indispensable. Metaphysical analysis identifies what for a given thinker or group those absolute presuppositions are. This is not a matter of whether they are "true" or "false," but a matter of identifying what grounds for disciplined inquiries their practitioners take to be indispensable to do their work.

The historian studies the context in which questions arise to which answers, grounded on metaphysical assumptions, are given. These absolute presuppositions can be identified and described. Collingwood dismisses the idea that we could judge among absolute presuppositions in terms of which are "true" or not because the "efficacy of a supposition does not depend on its being true, nor even on its being thought true, but only on its being supposed."[22]

How, on Collingwood's terms, could there be a conversational relationship with or among these thinkers? He argued that, once identified, absolute presuppositions are shown to be grounded in particular historical contexts; they are not universal or eternal. It is a mistake, he argues, to think that "the characteristics of a certain historical milieu" are "characteristics of mankind at large."[23] This conclusion is Collingwood's absolute presupposition: "The problems of metaphysics are historical problems; its methods are historical methods. We must have no more nonsense about its being meritorious to inhabit a fog. A metaphysician is a man who has to get at facts. . . . We live in the twentieth century; there is no excuse for us if we do not know what the methods of history are."[24]

If absolute presuppositions are to be treated as historical facts, philosophers must become historians, accounting for what have at different times been taken to be absolute presuppositions. One can gain a history of presuppositions, but metaphysics reveals no transcendent

---

21. Collingwood, *Essay on Metaphysics*, 58.
22. Collingwood, *Essay on Metaphysics*, 52.
23. Collingwood, *Essay on Metaphysics*, 57.
24. Collingwood, *Essay on Metaphysics*, 62–63.

questions: comparative study will show that "there are no 'eternal' or 'crucial' or 'central' problems in metaphysics."[25] In short, metaphysicians properly understood are intellectual historians.

Thus, when Collingwood proposes that we can re-enact past thought in the present, he means only that we can describe the absolute presuppositions as evidence of past circumstances in the stream of historical becoming. We may be able to understand absolute presuppositions, and some might even convince themselves to believe in such presuppositions though living in a different historical context from the original; but we cannot forget that we are choosing without an independent standard of judgement. In "A Philosophy of Progress," he said: "Whether you think the course of events is an upward or downward course depends not on *it* but on *you*."[26] And, "we have developed social and political institutions that suit *our* psychological structure."[27]

Collingwood had also said that "the historian must re-enact the past in his own mind."[28] The strong meaning of the re-enactment of past thought is that the historian re-enacts "in his own mind the experience" as it occurred to those he studies.[29] What does the word "experience" mean in this context? The historian must re-think "for himself the thought of his author, and nothing short of that will make him the historian of that author's philosophy."[30] This seems to mean that one must try to understand an ancient thinker as he understood himself. But this does not mean one identifies with that thinker or reaffirms his thought. Rather, one describes the thinker's response to his historical situation, while one's own historical situation distances one from the thinker whose thought one is re-enacting. In re-enacting the thought, one is responding to the recorded expression of an experience, but one is not thereby

25. Collingwood, *Essay on Metaphysics*, 72.
26. R. G. Collingwood, "A Philosophy of Progress" (1929), in *Essays in the Philosophy of History*, ed. William Debbins (Austin: University of Texas Press, 1965), 109; italics in original.
27. Collingwood, "A Philosophy of Progress" 119; italics in original.
28. Collingwood, *The Idea of History*, 282.
29. Collingwood, *The Idea of History*, 282–83.
30. Collingwood, *The Idea of History*, 283.

re-enacting (or undergoing) the experience which gave rise to the expressed thought. The "Allegory of the Cave" is an image intended to express an encounter with transcendent reality. But does Collingwood re-enact the encounter itself? To identify Plato's "absolute presupposition" does not mean Collingwood experiences an encounter with transcendent reality; it only means he is describing an experience Plato claimed to have had and recorded.

Collingwood distinguishes the thought he is re-enacting from the situation of those whose thought he is re-enacting; but their situation included the experience of transcendence. Collingwood asserted that there can be no "science of being," distancing himself from classical expressions of transcendence which classical thinkers understood to go beyond science in responding to the mystery of existence, not as final explanations of that experience. If we take their situation to include attempts to find adequate expression of their encounter with transcendent truth, Collingwood is not re-enacting past thought even if he is reporting its recorded expressions accurately. In short, the meaning of experiencing past thought in his usage is equivocal. Collingwood says that if we are to bridge the gap of time we must bridge it "at both ends."[31] To rethink past thoughts, one "must be the right man to study that object." The "historian's mind must be such as to offer home for that revival."[32] But metaphysicians, *qua* intellectual historians, have already distanced themselves from the past thought's significance for the one who expressed it. I may see that a past thought is really a past thought present to me now, but is the experience which gave rise to the thought present to me? Collingwood does not provide a convincing answer to this question. This led Strauss, as we shall see shortly, to doubt that Collingwood was really rethinking past thought, and Oakeshott to conclude that Collingwood ended in scepticism.

Historicism and Political Philosophy: Strauss and Gadamer

Living in our age of heightened historical consciousness has imposed the question whether traditional philosophy, and hence traditional

---

31. Collingwood, *The Idea of History*, 304.
32. Collingwood, *The Idea of History*, 304.

political philosophy—examining permanent questions, seeking timeless truth or permanent standards of right and wrong—are shown to be impossible. Here I introduce the argument between Leo Strauss and Hans-Georg Gadamer alongside Oakeshott and Collingwood on the presentness of past thought, noting Strauss's critique of Collingwood, and Gadamer's critical engagement with Strauss in *Truth and Method.*

Strauss is well known for his critique of historicism. He insisted that the task of the modern reader of ancient texts is to understand authors as they understood themselves before one could seek to understand better than they did. For Strauss, this meant, among other questions, whether the inquiry into the best regime for human beings is meaningful or an illusion. Such an inquiry involves taking seriously the classic view that the search for truth beyond one's situation is not fruitless. In "Natural Right and the Historical Approach," Strauss says,

> The modern opponents of natural right reject precisely this idea. According to them, all human thought is historical and hence unable ever to grasp anything eternal. Whereas, according to the ancients, philosophizing means to leave the cave, according to our contemporaries all philosophizing essentially belongs to a "historical world," "culture," "civilization," "Weltanschauung," that is, to what Plato had called the cave. We shall call this view "historicism."[33]

From this perspective, we can only approach old texts from within the spirit of our own age and hence reinterpret them in ways that make sense to us from our perspective. Strauss did not accept that all thinking is conditioned by present and future concerns of practical life. Denial of transcendent reality means that the metaphysical claim of ancient writers to encounter such reality cannot be taken seriously. We have, so it is said, become wiser than the ancients and thus we can understand better than they understood.

---

33. L. Strauss, "Natural Right and the Historical Approach," in *An Introduction to Political Philosophy, Ten Essays by Leo Strauss,* ed. Hilail Gildin (Detroit: Wayne State University Press, 1989), 102.

Here is Collingwood's assertion of that: "Was it really true that different philosophies were, even in the loosest sense of that word, eternal? I soon discovered that it was not true; it was merely a vulgar error, consequent on a kind of historical myopia which, deceived by superficial resemblances, failed to detect profound differences."[34] It seems to me that he confuses the experience of the eternal with varying efforts to describe in words that experience.

Gadamer's response to Strauss sheds further light on the issues discussed above. He recognizes that we live in a global age wherein we experience the pressures of different ways of life on each other, questioning that there is a single historical narrative, grounded in the Western experience, which reveals a unique standard. The question of understanding past thought in our own tradition is paralleled by the question of understanding other civilizational experiences. It seems to me that Strauss's argument for natural right, albeit facing this further complexity, is relevant in calling for an investigation of universality without presupposing in advance an answer one way or the other.

In *Truth and Method*, Gadamer takes up Strauss's critique of historicism in the section on "Hermeneutics and Historicism," where he enters a dialogue with Strauss, both on the ground of historicism and on the question of how we understand the thought of past thinkers. The premise of *Truth and Method* is that, despite the importance we now attribute to the methods of modern science, methods cannot capture truth in its fullness: Gadamer is "concerned to seek that experience of truth that transcends the sphere of the control of scientific method. . . . Hence the human sciences are joined with modes of experience which lie outside science: with the experience of philosophy, of art, and of history itself. These are all modes of experience in which a truth is communicated that cannot be verified by the methodological means proper to science."[35] Gadamer adds,

34. R. G. Collingwood, *An Autobiography* (Oxford: Oxford University Press, 1939), 60–61.
35. H.-G. Gadamer, *Truth and Method* (New York: Crossroad Publishing, 1985; English translation, 1975), xii.

The philosophical endeavor of our day differs from the classical tradition of philosophy in that it is not a direct and unbroken continuation of it. In spite of all its connections with its historical origin, philosophy today is well aware of the historical distance between it and its classical models . . . the emergence of historical consciousness over the last few centuries is a much more radical development. Since then, the continuity of the Western philosophical tradition has been effective only in a fragmentary way. We have lost that naïve innocence with which traditional concepts were made to support one's own thinking.[36]

But we have not lost the "natural inclination" to philosophy:

It is evident that what we call philosophy is not science in the same way as the so-called positive sciences are. It is not the case that philosophy has a positive datum alongside the standard research areas of the other sciences to be investigated by it alone, for philosophy has to do with the whole. . . . As the whole, it is an idea that transcends every finite possibility of knowledge, and so it is nothing we could know in a scientific way.[37]

The similarity of this to Oakeshott's statement of philosophy is obvious though Gadamer does not mention him. But Gadamer does say that the way Collingwood presents the idea of rethinking past thoughts involves him in tension between past thoughts and the "psychological particularity" of a past thinker who had the thoughts being rethought. Collingwood seeks access to the thought freed from the contingent conditions (including the encounter with the divine that many ancient thinkers report) in which the thought appeared. In order to achieve this, Gadamer thinks that Collingwood relied on the "spirit of the age" (what Collingwood called "constellations of presuppositions") in which the thought occurred in order

36. Gadamer, *Truth and Method*, xiv–xv.
37. H.-G. Gadamer, "On the Philosophic Element in the Sciences and the Scientific Character of Philosophy," in *Reason in the Age of Science* (English translation, Cambridge: MIT Press, 1981), 1.

to depersonalize the thought which is being rethought, a task for the intellectual historian. Can a thought detached from its original context be a rethinking of the past thought (re-enacting the experience which gives rise to the thought) or is it a rethinking that inevitably is a reinterpreting of thought (as an "absolute presupposition" but not as an encounter with transcendence)? In reenacting past thought are we not reinterpreting what the original thought meant to the one thinking it in accord with a modern criterion? This is the logic of Collingwood's position: the re-enactment of past thought as here understood precludes encounter with permanent truths or questions.

Strauss was a radical critic of this historical point of view. Gadamer sympathetically approaches Strauss's view in terms of Strauss's commitment to reopening the famous quarrel of the ancients and the moderns which, for modern thinkers, is taken to have ended with a decisive victory for the moderns and their view that the insights of the ancients have been superseded, or that philosophy has been revealed to be historical, which is to say that philosophy as such has been superseded, since we have radically altered the meaning of the term "philosophy." For such moderns, the fundamental questions now cannot be what they were in antiquity. Strauss's aim is to "set against the modern historical self-confidence the clear rightness of classical philosophy. . . . Such an elementary human concern as the distinction between right and wrong assumes that man is able to raise himself above his historical conditionedness."[38] Strauss put it this way in commenting on Collingwood's *The Idea of History*:

> The largest part of his book is devoted to a history of historical knowledge. That history is on the whole conventional. In studying earlier thinkers, Collingwood never considered the possibility that the point of view from which the present day reader approaches them, or the questions which he addresses to them, might be in need of a fundamental change. He set out to praise or blame the earlier thinkers according to whether they helped or hindered the emergence of scientific history. He did not attempt to look at scientific history, for

38. Gadamer, *Truth and Method*, 482–83.

once, from the point of view of earlier thinkers. . . . Collingwood writes the history of history in almost the same way in
which the eighteenth century historians, whom he censored
so severely, are said to have written history in general. The
latter condemned the thought of the past as deficient in full
reasonableness; Collingwood condemned it as deficient in
the true sense of history. . . . Collingwood therefore rejected
the thought of the past in the decisive respect. Hence he
could not take that thought seriously, for to take a thought
seriously means to regard it as possible that the thought in
question is true. He therefore lacked the incentive for re-
enacting the thought of the past; he did not re-enact the
thought of the past. . . . For, if to understand the thought
of the past necessarily means to understand it differently
from the way the thinkers of the past understood it, one will
never be able to compare the thought of the present with the
thought of the past: one would merely compare one's own
thought with the reflection of one's own thought in ancient
materials or with a hybrid begotten by the intercourse of
one's own thought with earlier thought.[39]

Granted that human beings are historically situated, it remains to
be shown that one cannot think outside, or rise above, the constraints of the dominant views of one's time. Collingwood denies
access to timeless truths. Strauss calls for openness to the possibility of timeless truths. The questioning of historicism requires such
openness, otherwise the resolution of the argument (on both sides)
is assumed from the start: "that there are N types of absolute presuppositions, as Collingwood called them, none of which can be said
to be rationally superior to any other . . . means the abandonment
of the very idea of the truth as rational philosophy has always understood it . . . the choice of any of these presuppositions is ground-
less and leads us again into the abyss of freedom."[40]

39. L. Strauss, "Review of *The Idea of History* by R. G. Collingwood," in *Review of Metaphysics* (1952), 566, 574, 575, 578–79.
40. L. Strauss, "An Introduction to Heideggerian Existentialism," in *The Rebirth of Classical Political Rationalism, and Introduction to the Thought of*

For Collingwood, there is a conspectus of presuppositions that have been asserted. Classical philosophy, as the "science of being," he rejects on historicist assumptions. But historicism is itself subject to criticism since the advent of historicism (for Collingwood, the advent of our intellectual maturity) was a matter of argument, and classical arguments against it remain known to us (as of course Collingwood knows even as he dismisses them). This is what Gadamer called our fragmentary connection to the classics; the now alien ancient orientation hauntingly reminds us of limits to what we can settle once and for all. One response is to conceal these issues in the name of "progress."

The question is not only whether we are precisely describing Plato's thought; rather, it is a matter of whether we take seriously the fundamental questions posed by Plato and other classical thinkers as questions for us as well. It is not a matter of "going back" to the classics; rather, it is a matter of discovering in our own situation the presence of fundamental questions whose continual presence has been covered over by the dominance of the historical point of view. Strauss thought that the crisis of meaning in our time has alerted us to the possibility of the continuing presence of those questions against the "spirit of the age," where "spirit of the age" is a device, an assertion, inhibiting the questioning of historicism. Strauss is thus criticizing the claim of intellectual progress for refusing to acknowledge the questioning of its assumptions.

Collingwood thought we had for centuries in our "immaturity" thought unhistorically, and he questioned whether one who does think that way is to be taken seriously. Collingwood could only take such thought seriously as an artefact of a bygone historical situation, but not seriously in its own terms. Logically, the absolute presuppositions of historicism cannot command the future any more than previous absolute presuppositions could. This led Strauss to the view that Collingwood necessarily must judge in terms of his own assumptions. We must ask the question whether we necessarily understand past thought better than it understood itself given the

Leo Strauss, ed. Thomas Pangle (Chicago: Chicago University Press, 1989), 34.

advance claimed for our historical perspective. Not to question the historicist insight is to neglect an essential element in responding to past thought as it presented itself. In posing such questions Strauss identifies the dogmatism of historicism which denies the dialogue or what Gadamer refers to as the quarrel of the ancients with the moderns. Gadamer agrees with Strauss in part:

> What he [Strauss] criticises is that the "historical" under-
> standing of traditional thought claims to be able to under-
> stand the thought of the past better than it understood itself.
> Whoever thinks like this excludes from the outset the possi-
> bility that the thoughts that are handed down to us could
> simply be true. This is the practically universal dogmatism of
> this way of thought. . . . The application of the superior per-
> spective of the present to the whole of the past does not appear
> to me at all to be the true nature of historical thinking, but
> characterises the obstinate positivity of a naïve historicism.[41]

But Gadamer also questions Strauss:

> But when Strauss argues that in order to understand better it
> is necessary first to understand an author as he understood
> himself, he under-estimates, I think, the difficulties of
> understanding, because he ignores what might be called the
> dialectic of the statement.[42]

Gadamer thinks that, given that we must live in an ever-changing "present," it is not possible for there to be a final, superior view of past thought. Hence the claim of superior understanding is always subject to counter claims. Claims to understand better tempt us and arise because we see the works of the past in changing historical contexts. We have to establish the pertinence of an ancient work in our historical context—to see the ancient expression of an experi-ence in terms of an equivalence in our experience. The desire to un-derstand a past author as he understood himself is not mistaken, but we must see this task as dialectical, as a response to past thought,

41. Gadamer, *Truth and Method*, 484.
42. Gadamer, *Truth and Method*, 484.

not mere repetition of it: "I would define hermeneutics as the skill to let things speak which come to us in a fixed, petrified form, that of the text."[43] In this respect, Gadamer seeks a middle ground between the classical and the historical, and proposes something resembling what Oakeshott meant by "the conversation of mankind." Finding relevance in a new historical context is not just thinking the same thought even if it preserves the significance of that thought. "The interpreter of what is written, like the interpreter of divine or human utterance, has the task of overcoming and removing the strangeness and making its assimilation possible."[44] Gadamer likens this to the task of the translator who must make a foreign language accessible to us while preserving the thought thus expressed. Interpretation in this sense is not the overcoming or supersession of past thought.

In discussing Plato, Gadamer points out the dialectical character of the dialogues which has stimulated many extraordinary interpretations of Plato's thought, not least those of Strauss himself. Plato understood this in addressing the problem of writing down philosophy. The dialogues are a way of writing down which eludes the fixity of writing down. Gadamer says, "Everything that is set down in writing is to some extent foreign and strange, and hence it poses the same task of understanding as what is spoken in a foreign language."[45] It is clear that for Gadamer there is a fundamental starting point in the Socratic/Platonic experience which is valid for us: "I believe there is continuity, for example, in the sense that the famous Socratic inquiry into the good, his claim that no one in society had the expertise to give a satisfactory answer to this question, remains significant for our times, for we face the danger of becoming too dependent on experts."[46]

Plato, in other words, was aware of the issue of interpretation and the unavoidable necessity for argument about how to understand

43. H.-G. Gadamer, "Interview: Writing and the Living Voice," in *Hans-Georg Gadamer on Education, Poetry and History, Applied Hermeneutics* (New York: State University of New York Press, 1992), 65.
44. Gadamer, *Truth and Method*, 487.
45. Gadamer, *Truth and Method*, 487.
46. Gadamer, "Interview," 67.

what has been thought and said, which does not preclude entering into past thought. For Gadamer, "the Platonic dialogue is a model of writing that embraces many meanings and inner relationships." Does an author know exactly what he means to say in every sentence he utters or writes down? Part of the Platonic argument against writing down philosophy was to preserve the exchange through which interlocutors could attempt to clarify to each other what they really wanted to say. The fixity of written words constrains such exchange. In other words, we can resist historicism without denying the necessity of interpreting past thought in light of current circumstances. In rejecting "naïve historicism," Gadamer does not simply endorse Strauss's position. Rather, he engages to mediate the quarrel of the ancients and the moderns. His thinking eludes easy categorization.

So far as I know, Strauss never claimed to have reached final, definitive understanding of past thinkers even though he argued vigorously for his readings of them, and for the importance of their questions. The search for wisdom in these matters requires a combination of tenacious argument and of reserve, even if one has strong inclinations in one direction or another, about claiming to have acquired final knowledge. We recall Heidegger's remark that for all our mental effort we are still not thinking.

We encounter these issues on at least two different levels: one is the conviction that political philosophy in the classical sense is now impossible and therefore we must reinterpret political philosophy as the history of political thought, that is as responses to contingent and limiting historical conditions—analysis as intellectual history; the other considers political philosophy as engagement in current politics, providing intellectual support either for or against such practical political goals as currently capture the interests of politicians by adjudicating among past authors as to whether they advance or hinder present and future practical goals. This intellectual impasse demands thinking further. The authors considered here are catalysts for reinvigorating the philosophical conversation in order, as Oakeshott said, to listen to the conversation in which human beings forever seek to understand themselves.

Taking Natural Law Seriously
within the Liberal Tradition

I. Taking Rights Seriously

No one is startled by the thought of taking rights seriously in our political tradition. Yet controversies over what it may mean to do so, or over the question of our sincerity in the effort, abound.

Ours is also a tradition honoring the rule of law. There is a connection between the rule of law and taking rights seriously. Thus, to take rights seriously ultimately leads us to jurisprudential considerations, or to the controversies of the legal philosophers. Law must be protected from falling into the hands of the calculators of utility. The latter is prone to erode procedure and formality, to circumvent the fixities of the law, in order to procure a desired substantive condition of civil society whose benefits will transform retrospectively, it is claimed, the initial appearance of expedient partiality. But can the rule of law be saved in the rule of expediency whatever may be thought of the substantive condition that actually emerges? And then what of rights? Can rights be taken seriously if acknowledging them is contingent on the compatibility of claims with the substantive outcomes dictated by policy? Can utility be ef-

Reprinted by permission of Springer Nature Customer Service Center GmbH from Eric S. Kos, ed., *Michael Oakeshott on Authority, Governance and the State* (Cham, Switzerland: Palgrave Macmillan, 2019), 89–110.

fectively opposed by the dominant legal positivism in contemporary jurisprudence:

> Legal positivism rejects the idea that legal rights can pre-exist any form of legislation; it rejects the idea, that is, that individuals or groups can have rights in adjudication other than the rights explicitly provided in the collection of explicit rules that compose the whole of a community's law. Economic utilitarianism rejects the idea that political rights can pre-exist legal rights; that is, that citizens can justifiably protest a legislative decision on any ground except that the decision does not in fact serve the general welfare.[1]

The preference today for views of this sort rests on the rejection of classical natural law theories in favor of "empirical metaphysics." Dworkin himself intends to remain within the general framework of the dominant utilitarian-positivist outlook defending an idea of rights which is itself "parasitic on the dominant idea of utilitarianism, which is the idea of a collective goal of the community as a whole."[2] Dworkin believes that individual claims may be overridden if collective claims should prevail, but rights should be taken seriously.

According to Dworkin, even in hard cases it is the judge's duty not to invent new rights but to discover which of the parties to a dispute has a right to win. The hard case is any in which there is no obvious rule or custom, no consensus among competent experts, and hence no demonstrable conclusion in the matter. Nevertheless, Dworkin says there may be a truth in the matter and it must be pursued.[3]

The practical objection regularly made to this idea is the general fear of permitting judges to interpret law creatively: "adjudication should be as unoriginal as possible."[4] Dworkin skirts this by arguing that the judge can discover a right in the hard case, not invent

1. Ronald Dworkin, *Taking Rights Seriously* (Cambridge, Mass.: Harvard University Press, 1977), xi.
2. Dworkin, *Taking Rights Seriously*, xi.
3. Dworkin, *Taking Rights Seriously*, 81.
4. Dworkin, *Taking Rights Seriously*, 84.

one.[5] He wishes to persuade us to separate "discovery" from "originality." He denies that the appearance of originality proves that a right has been invented but not discovered. Dworkin argues that the abstract distinction between discovery and originality is, in actual social life, always in a process of mediation through judicial agency.[6] The discovery of a right in a hard case is not, then, an intuition. One might better call it an informed interpretation, which may be evaluated for its acceptability as a successful mediation between the general character of prevailing law and the disposition of the case. It has a force of "truth" despite the fact that prior to its expression by the judge it could not be known to be true. Without the agency of the judge, the truth remains hidden. Yet one can estimate whether to evaluate the decision as effectively a discovery or whether it is ineligible to be accepted that way.

Among other things, we should consider whether a decision is generally consistent with other decisions in the same area, and whether it is non-arbitrary in not serving some parties at the expense of other similar ones. But it would seem that the aim of all this is to defend a conception of the judicial function as simultaneously serving to defend rights and allowing rights to evolve as a contribution to some putative increase in general, communal welfare. The ultimate mediation, then, would be between the maintenance of those already acknowledged rights which protect subjective freedom and the "newly discovered" rights which enhance objective freedom (to use Hegelian terms) or (to use Deweyite terms) to mediate between "formal" and "effective" liberty. Dworkin refers to mediating "policy" and "principle," or transposing "political right" into "legal right." It is not a distortion, therefore, to suggest that, in Dworkin's outlook, there could and should be a continuous effort at engineering social change through judicial activity, and that this can be carried out so as to transcend, in principle, political partisanship. If so, it would be possible to show how rights could be defended by interpreting them so as to promote certain goals. Conversely, the promotion of certain goals would be necessary to the defense of rights. The

5. Dworkin, *Taking Rights Seriously*, 280.
6. Dworkin, *Taking Rights Seriously*, 87.

political would pass over into the trans-political. Lack of universal agreement would not disprove the adequacy of the judicial decision.

According to Dworkin, a political right is the claim to an opportunity that is justified (rational) insofar as the realization of such opportunity would enhance the possible realization of a larger pattern congenial to the individual who makes the claim.[7] Is this anything more than a defense of interest group pluralism and a relativity of group ends? Only, it would seem, if the interest served would contribute to the enhancement of the collective welfare goal of a given community. Thus relativist pluralism would at most be a procedural premise for the purposes of eliciting all those expressions of interest that would permit comprehensive articulation of communal well-being. The satisfaction of some group claims as opposed to others would cease to be arbitrary when such preferences contribute to a further development toward the communal goal. But since the features of the communal goal are multifaceted there will be trade-offs between competing component elements of the general welfare.[8]

On the other hand, there can be absolute rights, presumably they are trans-political from the start, which are virtually always eligible to stand against policies even if the policies would enhance the general welfare in some way (e.g., free speech). It would appear that Dworkin has provided in his own vocabulary a combination of ideas drawn from J. S. Mill and John Rawls: From Mill, he has taken the notion of articulation of all views toward the end of progressive improvement or perfection of social life in the most comprehensive and eventually non-controversial manner; from Rawls he has taken the priority of liberty in relation to a principle of distribution ruling out unnecessary inequalities, pointing to an order in which every participant understands and can accept his social position as the best possible. The temperamental strain common to all three, and to a certain mode of liberal thinking in general, is the desire to transform the partisan into the non-partisan, the political into the

---

7. Dworkin, *Taking Rights Seriously*, 91.
8. Dworkin, *Taking Rights Seriously*, 91–92.

consensual, without resort to significant coercion: an historically evolving social covenant without the sword.

An ideal judge will facilitate the general social enhancement by constructing an adequate theoretical understanding of how to apply the generally accepted constituting rules of a society.[9] In so doing, the judge articulates policy designed to maintain and to fill out the intention of the law. The law is always open to contested interpretations. The law cannot be self-enacting or self-interpreting. However, "decisions about legal rights depend upon judgments of political theory that might be made differently by different judges or by the public at large" and this may be so even if the decision was in some sense a "principled" decision (sincerely arrived at in an effort to do right according to a political theory taken by the judge to be correct). In short, the judge is liable to a charge of subjective decision-making.

According to Dworkin, a judge must "rely upon the substance of his own judgment at some point, in order to make any judgment at all." Hence, the real issue is the judge's decision between opposing and submitting to some prevailing authoritative opinion as to how decisions in given areas of law should come out. The decision to submit to prevailing "wisdom" is itself a personal judgment.[10]

But it would appear that this argument gains its principal strength from a prior assumption that the law is to be understood as embedded in a process of social evolution which neutralizes the preference for unoriginality over originality or "discovery." That is, Dworkin does not presume that it is the rule of law as such which is to be protected. He assumes, rather, that the process of mediating between principle and policy, or translating political claims into legal entitlements is what is to be protected. Sometimes no doubt unoriginality is fitting, but in a general sense it is what is progressive that must be served. Dworkin would appear, therefore, to be intent upon transforming the commitment to the rule of law into a commitment to social engineering. Implicitly, Dworkin's defense of a residual element of inevitable personal choice in the judge's decision-making is

---

9. Dworkin, *Taking Rights Seriously*, 105ff.
10. Dworkin, *Taking Rights Seriously*, 123–24.

intended to legitimize judicial autonomy, limited primarily by the soundness of the judge's political theory and by prudential considerations of the pace of social evolution that could be hoped for. In short, the ideal judge is self-determining with regard to the definition of his judicial duty.

The ideal judge's "theory identifies a particular conception of community morality as decisive of legal issues; that conception holds that community morality is the political morality presupposed by the laws and institutions of the community. He must, of course, rely on his own judgment as to what the principles of that morality are."[11] In controversial matters, the ideal judge will "become like any reflective member of the community willing to debate."[12]

There is, however, a difference between the ideal judge and any willing debater:

> It does not follow from the fact that the man in the street
> disapproves of abortion, or supports legislation making it
> criminal, that he has considered whether the concept of
> dignity presupposed by the Constitution, consistently applied,
> supports his political position. That is a sophisticated ques-
> tion requiring some dialectical skill . . . it is not to be taken for
> granted that his political preferences, expressed casually or in
> the ballot, have been subjected to that form of examination.[13]

The ideal judge will bring genuine moral insight to bear, effectively relating principles to policies. Ordinary judges may, of course, be fallible or decide out of unreflected prejudice. Mistakes may be made. But who could know when that will happen and what group other than judges will have "better facilities of moral argument"?[14]

Taking rights seriously means here incorporating political claims into law under the auspices of a process of judicial decision-making that aims at uniting the normative and the conceptual. The union is accomplished by relating an "adequate" description of social

11. Dworkin, *Taking Rights Seriously*, 126.
12. Dworkin, *Taking Rights Seriously*, 128.
13. Dworkin, *Taking Rights Seriously*, 129.
14. Dworkin, *Taking Rights Seriously*, 130.

arrangements in a positivist sense to a "discovered" right as between contending forces in the described social arrangement. The judge is ideally only the vanguard of social change, assuring "proper" direction, a privileged participant in an endless debate over the desired end-state of social order.

II. Taking the Rule of Law Seriously

While it is not uncommon to defend the idea of the rule of law, even as an intrinsic good, it is clear that taking the rule of law seriously conflicts with the intent to take rights seriously in the manner described above. With Dworkin, taking rights seriously ultimately sets up an autonomous standard, political in nature, on the basis of which one is to judge the validity of the commitment to the rule of law. Dworkin's commitment to the rule of law is instrumental in nature. Indeed, it must be so if the principal task is to take rights seriously. The most uncompromising defense of the rule of law on non-instrumental grounds is to be found in the writings of Michael Oakeshott.

According to Oakeshott, the interaction of individuals in civil society falls into two modes: The first is an

> intermittent transactional association of reciprocity in
> which agents, responding to their understood situations,
> seek the satisfactions of their wants in the responses of one
> another. . . . It is a relationship of bargainers and from it
> emerge whatever substantive satisfactions are from time to
> time enjoyed.[15]

In this mode, agents are transactionally related in an "enterprise association" agreeing upon a purpose to pursue.

There is another primary mode of association in defense of which Oakeshott challenges those theorists who "find it impossible to imagine association except in terms of a common purpose."[16] The attempt to identify the civil association with common purpose

---

15. Michael Oakeshott, *On Human Conduct*, 112–13.
16. Oakeshott, *On Human Conduct*, 118.

carries the "difficulty of specifying a common purpose in terms of which to distinguish civil association from all other enterprise relationship."[17] The substantive purposes of enterprises are easy enough to identify but what is the substantive purpose of civil society?

Oakeshott approaches this question by describing a mode of relationship "in terms of the conditions of a practice."[18] The "two most important practices in terms of which agents are durably related to one another in conduct are a common tongue and a language of moral converse."[19] However,

> a moral practice is not a prudential art concerned with the success of the enterprises of agents; it is not instrumental to the achievement of any substantive purpose or to the satisfaction of any substantive want. . . . It is concerned with the act, not the event.[20]

A practice does not

> prescribe choices to be made or satisfactions to be sought; instead, it intimates considerations to be subscribed to in making choices, in performing actions, and in pursuing purposes. . . . It postulates "free" agents and it is powerless to deprive them of their freedom.[21]

> Thus, conduct *inter homines* may properly be said to be "social" only in virtue of the manners in which "free" agents are actually associated; that is, in respect of their being associated in a multiplicity of practices of various dimensions and complexities, degrees of independence, and differences of status. This multiplicity of association does not itself compose a "society," much less anything that may properly be called a "community"; but a moral practice, as the *ars artium* of agency, is agents related to one another in terms of

17. Oakeshott, *On Human Conduct*, 119.
18. Oakeshott, *On Human Conduct*, 119–21.
19. Oakeshott, *On Human Conduct*, 59.
20. Oakeshott, *On Human Conduct*, 60–61.
21. Oakeshott, *On Human Conduct*, 79.

conditional proprieties which are expressly or tacitly recognized in the conditions of all other special prudential relationships and manners of being associated in conduct.[22]

The "civil" association cannot be the implementation of theorems or propositions. It cannot be the consequence of a program or a plan. A practice reduced to these things would find itself abstracted from the contingency pervasive in human existence. By insisting that human beings as agents *subscribe* to practices, Oakeshott points to the understanding of a human being as the interpreting mediator between the features of a practice and particular occasions wherein the exercise of the practice is called forth. It is not possible to *obey* a practice or a rule. Practices and rules are not commands but modes of proceeding that have emerged in the flow of experience:

> In short, we may suppose there to be available to an agent a store of well-attested propositions purporting to be general principles of conduct, and by no means worthless. Nevertheless, what is certain is that the understanding exercised by the agent in conduct cannot be an ad hoc mobilization of his knowledge of these theorems of moral and prudential lore enlisted to tell him what to do, because they are incapable of any such utterance. These theorems cannot themselves be performed, and acting cannot be "implementing" or "applying" them to contingent situations because they are unable to specify actions. What the agent needs to know . . . is how to *illustrate* them.[23]

The chosen actions of agents illustrate practices and rules rather than implement them because in no sense are the chosen actions of individuals "correct" displays of human conduct. One will not know how to conduct oneself by knowing this or that particular human action. One conducts oneself by finding a fitting illustration of a practice for a given, contingent situation. Each human being is the exhibition of "a sequential relationship of intelligent individual

22. Oakeshott, *On Human Conduct*, 88.
23. Oakeshott, *On Human Conduct*, 90.

occurrences where what comes after is recognized to be conditional on what went before" without a "mediator between occurrences which is not itself an occurrence, e.g., a 'law' or a 'function.'"[24] "Progress" is an extrinsic interpretation of change.

Practices qualify what human beings do but do not determine what they do. Relationships between individuals that arise from subscription to practices without the specification of a joint enterprise suggest the proper meaning of "civil" association. Citizenship in a civil association is constituted in the "acknowledgement of the authority of *respublica*," but "recognizing the authority of *respublica* is not finding its conditions to be desirable or believing that others better informed than oneself have approved of them."[25]

Acknowledgment, in this case, is not synonymous with approval of the conditions acknowledged, nor a judgment of utility or advantage, nor is it the result of a calculation that one cannot escape acknowledgment. Critics of this argument are wont to say that there must always be some background of cultural ties to make this acknowledgment possible.

Such critics are correct insofar as all real associations of actual individuals are sustained through a mixture of learned motivations. Oakeshott presents an "ideal" of civil association. What is to be gained from doing this?

The answer depends on the significance of an "ideal character." For Oakeshott, it is the delineation of a pattern intimated within a conglomeration of actual goings-on. Here what is at stake is the theorization of a relationship among individuals that does not compromise their self-identification. It is the elaboration of an inquiry, inaugurated as much by Hobbes as by anyone, into the possibility of imagining an orderly relation between selves who inevitably measure the world according to their own measure.

> This ideal character is among the instruments which may be used in seeking to understand complex, ambiguous, historic human associations . . . it is ideal not in the sense of being a

24. Oakeshott, *On Human Conduct*, 104.
25. Oakeshott, *On Human Conduct*, 149.

wished-for perfect condition of things but in being abstracted from the contingencies and ambiguities of actual goings-on in the world.[26]

The ideal character is simply a consistent interpretation of the logical requirements of order for an association of human beings who cannot help but understand themselves as individuals. The ideal condition is a "civitas" composed of "cives" who accept "respublica" as a postulate of the civil condition.[27] If subscription to authority were necessarily predicated on the reception of benefits, it would be open to doubt whether individuals, seeking benefits sharply at odds with each other, could successfully associate. Obviously, there are such associations. That they are workable, even persistent, suggests at least implicit recognition of "respublica" as a "system of moral (not instrumental) rules, specifying its own jurisdiction, and recognized solely as rules . . . binding to consideration independently of their origin or likely or actual outcome in use and of approval of what they prescribe."[28]

> The only understanding of *respublica* capable of evoking the acceptance of all *cives* without exception, and thus eligible to be recognized as the terms of civil association, is *respublica* understood in respect of its authority.[29]

To consider human beings in terms of their conduct is to see them as

> reflective intelligences whose actions and utterances are choices to do or to say *this* rather than *that* in relation to imagined and wished-for outcomes. And the relationships between them to be investigated are recognized to be themselves expressions of intelligence which may be enjoyed only by their having been learned and understood and in virtue of an acknowledgement of the authority of their

26. Oakeshott, *On Human Conduct*, 109.
27. Oakeshott, *On Human Conduct*, 150.
28. Oakeshott, *On Human Conduct*, 153–54.
29. Oakeshott, *On Human Conduct*, 153–54.

conditions or of a recognition of their utility. . . . It is a
science of intelligent procedures, not processes.[30]

To emphasize procedure rather than process, intelligent response
rather than caused behavior is the basis of Oakeshott's understanding of citizenship and the association of citizens: They are associated in the recognition of a rule of law, but they are not bound by
necessary interests, needs, wants, or dispositions in common. These
individuals do not comprise a "society" and they are not compelled
by "social forces" or "independent variables." They need not be obsessed with each other's doings, nor constantly frustrated by "relative deprivation," nor are they engaged ineluctably in a perpetual
siege of their resources in order to indulge in an endless transformation of "wants" into "needs," or an incessant redistribution of their
possessions according to some principle of comparability which the
terms of their association cannot supply.

Such people understand that they are subscribing to, not obeying, a body of laws, which laws are the result of the deliberations of
rulers or officeholders in authority. Authority here is not understood as "informal" or "tacit" power or influence, but as the specific engagement to rule, associated with an office of rule, exercised
under agreed-upon terms, producing rules to which citizens may
subscribe.

In this view,

> Power is not identifiable with authority and it is not even
> among the considerations in terms of which an office of
> government is recognized to have authority. The difference is
> categorical. The contingent features of its apparatus of power
> are neither formally nor substantively related to the constitu-
> tional shape of the office or rule.[31]

The elucidation of the ideal character, in short, makes explicit
the implicit aim of civil association to establish and maintain
authoritative rule. To put it differently, one might say that it is the

30. Oakeshott, *On Human Conduct*, 23–24.
31. Michael Oakeshott, "The Vocabulary of the Modern European State,"
Political Studies 23 (1975): 212–13.

already existing commitment in the thinking of individuals on the road to being *cives* in a *civitas*, and it prompts their respective imaginations toward the creation of institutional relations that are separable from mere relationships of power, interest, or hope for an imagined end-state.

The clarity of this conceptual distinction will not be equaled in actuality. The achievement is in continual need of protection and renewal. Those who have sought to do this have had to assume certain attitudes about what sort of beings they and their fellows are and, in turn, what sorts of relationships they could enjoy. The fact that such beings do not perfectly exhibit the conduct that their self-understanding logically requires has nothing to do with the elucidation of that self-understanding. We are reminded of the difference between an "ideal character" and the world of historic actuality the ideal character illuminates. To conceive "power" and "authority" as separable and, as a consequence, to exercise whatever ingenuity is available to concretize that distinction in practices among individuals is a tribute to the capacity of human beings to govern themselves by the ideas they hold of the direction they ought to take.

The achievement is undermined when authority is defined as the building of consensus, the proclamation of unifying goals, or the gaining of influence by advancing interests. Authority is appropriate precisely to an association of human beings whose view of their association has already ruled out common goals and consensus, and who share no fixed principles to determine social importance. They will subscribe to rules not because they have been cajoled or paid off, not because it is in their interest, and not because they have been blackmailed or threatened, but because the rules proceed from those holding offices constituted to make rules. Consider the credibility gap of modern, democratic politics: To make building consensus, the prerequisite to exercising authority insures that no authority will be exercised since it is the lack of consensus (and the awareness of the arbitrariness of "consensus") that makes authority indispensable.

It is true that in actual political life what seems authoritative to some will seem to others to be the mere exercise of power. Perhaps there is no relation among individuals in society that can exempt itself from this ambiguous condition. Authority is an abatement of but not a permanent release from the ambiguities surrounding this engagement.

Oakeshott challenges the instrumentalism of modern thought, posing its antithesis in order to reopen the inquiry into the nature of civic association, the relationship between authority, the rule of law, and the status of the individual:

> Laws are unavoidably indeterminate prescriptions of general adverbial obligations. They subsist in advance and in necessary ignorance of the future contingent situations to which they may be found to relate. . . . Therefore, the second necessary condition of association in terms of the rule of law is an office endowed with authority and charged with the duty to ascertain (according to some conditional rules of evidence) what has been said or done on a particular occasion brought to its notice because it is alleged not to have subscribed adequately to an obligation imposed by law. . . . A court of law is concerned with a particular contingent action or utterance in respect of its conformity with the conditions of existing obligations. . . . Deliberation, here, is an exercise in retrospective casuistry. . . . Nor may it regard itself as the custodian of a public policy or interest in favour of which . . . to resolve the disputed obligation. . . . In a court of law "justice" must exhibit itself as the conclusion of an argument designed to show as best it may that *this* is the meaning of the law in respect of this occurrence.[32]

And

> Here, then, is a mode of human relationship . . . abstract: a relation not of persons but of *personae*. Association, not in terms of doing and the enjoyment of the fruits of doing, but of procedural conditions imposed upon doing: laws. Relationship, not in terms of efficacious arrangements for promoting or procuring wished-for substantive satisfactions (individual or communal), but obligations to subscribe to

32. Michael Oakeshott, "The Rule of Law," in *On History and Other Essays* (1983), 144–46.

non-instrumental rules: a moral relationship. Rule, not in terms of the alleged worth, "rationality" or "justice" of the conditions these rules prescribe, but in respect of the recognition of their authenticity.[33]

III. Taking Natural Law Seriously

Dworkin and Oakeshott defend conflicting strains within the complex tradition of liberalism. Each portrays an ideal whose presuppositions exclude those of the alternative. In one, taking rights seriously is the defining end of the rule of law, appealing to a possible, substantive relationship among competing political claims. In the other, extrinsic standards for assessing the *ius* of *lex* undermine the rule of law, transforming the civil association from a "moral" association, wherein agents obligate themselves to abide by rules adherence to which specifies no particular satisfaction of individual or group wants or claims, into a struggle for power even if pursued through the judicial system.

A third voice presents itself in John Finnis' reformulation of classical natural law. He seeks to pass between the normative speculations of neo-positivist or utilitarian theorists, and the stark proceduralism of the pure rule of law. He recognizes that a legal order has a symbolic meaning for political life. What the legal order forbids, promotes, or permits, among the ways human beings seek to flourish, contributes to the articulation of the self-identification of a polity. If the law inevitably intimates something above and beyond its own procedures, if law has an existential meaning, then it behooves the theorist to inquire whether he must remain caught between the uncontrolled insertion of normative preferences into law which leads to imposing the view of a part on the whole; and the converse aim radically to individualize questions of meaning, rendering them essentially private, resisting or denying the need of natural sociality to express itself in a common, but supra-ideological, form that enjoys voluntary recognition.

---

33. Oakeshott, "The Rule of Law," 148.

Finnis thus engages to show that there are universal, human goods implicitly or explicitly sought by all human beings out of natural inclination. At this level, one speaks of natural desires, not of moral choices, to do this as opposed to that in actual, contingent circumstances. If human flourishing is in seeking specific ways to fulfill the natural desires in individual human lives, law is necessary to securing conditions that support such seeking. It is necessary, therefore, to relate the natural desires to the contingent conditions in which their satisfaction is sought, and law is one medium through which this may be deliberatively, reflectively done.

In reviewing the effort of modern legal theorists to analyze and comprehend law "on the basis of non-evaluative characteristics only," Finnis finds incorrigible differences of opinion about "what is *important* and *significant* in the field of data and experience with which they are all equally and thoroughly familiar."[34] At best modern legal philosophy, despite its suspicion of the possibility of knowledge of objective good, manages to retain a sense of moral evil. But this opens the way to uncontrolled moral speculation, and the connection between law and moral good must become "uncertain and floating."[35]

Continuing scrutiny of the prevailing state of affairs is undeniably important, but if disciplined knowledge is to illuminate our self-understanding and direction it must do so as an aid to converting the prejudices of the theorist, and of the theorist's culture, "into truly reasonable judgments about what is good."[36]

Remarkably, Finnis accepts that this cannot be accomplished "by some inference from the facts of the human situation."[37] A judgment, synthesizing insight into the natural desires or natural goods with a wide acquaintance with the actual conditions of society, must be made. There is a dichotomy between what we value and the "facts," but if the natural basis of value is acknowledged, then there is

---

34. John Finnis, *Natural Law and Natural Rights*, 2d ed. (Oxford: Oxford University Press, 2011), 9.
35. Finnis, *Natural Law and Natural Rights*, 14.
36. Finnis, *Natural Law and Natural Rights*, 17.
37. Finnis, *Natural Law and Natural Rights*, 17.

a substructure of evaluation which persists through altering contingent conditions. Judgment is to be distinguished from non-rational expressions of preference for one cultural possibility against another. A natural law theory "undertakes a critique of practical viewpoints . . . to distinguish the practically unreasonable from the practically reasonable . . . to identify conditions and principles of practical right-mindedness, of good and proper order."[38] The scientific study of law must look beyond itself for the final meaning of the search that motivated scientific investigation in the first place.

The movement from the prelegal to the legal is not the experientially final step. As a movement in self-consciousness, it opens the way to self-critical examination to discover the foundation of good which motivated the movement at the outset.

With the articulation of order appears the question of its rightness or goodness. Yet we cannot fully visualize goodness from the conspectus of wants and satisfactions through which initial response to the felt need of goodness is made. Implicit is a quest for additional insight to illuminate the deeper need that is revealed as opposed to a mere repetition in technical terms of the incomplete understanding that the order already possesses.

Efforts to mediate between need and its illumination cannot be avoided, only disguised. We are moved by the good which moves us to seek it. Our acceptance of the seeking is a choosing, but that we choose diminishes in importance as the seeking of which we are agents finally encompasses us. Self-determination is transformed into the ordering of the self in compliance with the object of its search.

Seeking well-being will not eliminate chronic disagreement about the various paths chosen to pursue well-being. Finnis presents natural law theorizing as compatible with a disjunction between "facts" and "norms" which cannot be eliminated by elucidating principles of well-being or flourishing. Man is his own agent in establishing the connection between his sensed incompletion and flourishing, and he must will to harmonize them. As Finnis puts it, one experiences "one's nature . . . from the inside, in the form of one's inclinations"

38. Finnis, *Natural Law and Natural Rights*, 18.

recognizing "that the object of the inclination which one experiences is an instance of a general form of good."[39] Thereafter, one is further prompted to be reasonable in the pursuit of goods prompted by the inclinations. But to attempt to be reasonable demands that we theorize reasonableness. Natural law becomes apparent in experience but is completed by intellectual illumination constituted in reason.

Knowing of goods and understanding the requirements of reasonableness in pursuit of them can be a unity only when we make them so in action. The basic goods must be sought in all actions that can qualify as moral but they do not themselves specify actions. We act in deciding how to pursue the goods which we have identified, and we express our understanding of what we have identified in chosen actions. Reason absorbs the implications of particular experience, organizing them according to the requirements of goodness. Reasonableness, then, includes both comprehensive awareness of conditions and a self-critical awareness of the response necessary to those conditions in order to keep goodness in sight.

Finnis finds the whole of humanity bound together in search of a fulfillment that is common to all, albeit manifested in a diversity with unspecified boundaries. Inclination to good is not antithetical to diversity; it is the source of diversity.

While such natural diversity intimates the importance of "liberty" or "authenticity" as conditions of seeking good, they do not exhaust the desirabilities to be identified as good. Exclusive devotion to liberty or authenticity limits the understanding of good and distorts it. Finnis lists seven basic goods which he takes to be self-evident: life, knowledge, play, aesthetic experience, sociability/friendship, practical reasonableness, and religion.[40] They enjoy equal, non-hierarchical status. The effort to organize our experience coherently while trying to satisfy all the basic goods, now emphasizing some, now others, according to circumstances, constitutes moral existence.

---

39. Finnis, *Natural Law and Natural Rights*, 34.
40. John Finnis, *Fundamentals of Ethics* (Washington, D.C.: Georgetown University Press, 1983), 50–51.

The organizing judgment we make constitutes our self-interpretation implicating both the conditions under which we live and the goods we seek in the context of those conditions. Our responses show what the circumstances mean to us in light of our understanding of the goods. Such judgments are more or less adroit, but the standard will always be the responsiveness to the goods given the conditions.

Finnis thus explicitly rejects a "thin theory" of human goods which identifies "as the basic human goods those goods which *any* human being would need *whatever his objectives* . . . the goods identified by a thin theory will be what it is rational for any human being to want whatever else his or her preferences."[41] The defense of thin theories is based on a practical judgment of "fear that anything other than a thin theory of the good will entail an authoritarian politics."[42] This fear leads many to an arbitrary insistence on the insuperable subjectivity of all stipulations of good.

To Finnis, however, mere choosing among goods does not define human flourishing. The choice of goods to pursue, even though issuing from a subject, is open to assessment both by the subject who has chosen, and by others, independently of the fact that the manifestation of choice is associated with any particular individual. What is chosen must dignify the choosing. That is, what is chosen completes the meaning of the choosing, and any defense of the essential contribution of choosing to human flourishing will fail if the choices themselves are exempted from, or fail to be eligible for, defense. Man does not live to choose but chooses in the hope of living well (in a manner that can enjoy confirmation both by himself and others). Liberty and authenticity must

> find their proper place in any accurate (i.e., "full", non-emaciated . . .) theory of the human good. Indeed, only such a theory can make secure for them the dignity of being recognized as objective goods, truly worthwhile (rather than

---

41. Finnis, *Natural Law and Natural Rights*, 48–49.
42. Finnis, *Fundamentals of Ethics*, 50.

merely the matrix for the pursuit of "subjective" desires and satisfactions).[43]

We are moved toward fulfillment in the full, not the thin, sense "prior to any intelligent consideration of what is worth pursuing" but what we need to know is "discernible only to one who . . . intelligently directs, focuses, and controls his urges, inclinations, and impulses."[44] Diversity flows from the variability with which human beings undertake this practical task and that diversity conceals within itself a universal aspiration which does not permit diversity to be an end in itself. On the other hand, the fact that diversity is not an end in itself does not mean either that diversity is not real or that we should try to bring diversity to an end. Not only is it not possible to suppress diversity, it is undesirable to reject diversity. Diversity brings forth far more concrete experience of the possibilities of human well-being than could otherwise be possible or imaginable in the reflections of any human minds, or articulable in any actual regime.

In the midst of this diversity, the theorist must become transparent to himself. In our circumstances that will mean creating a dialogue between liberal rights theorists and exponents of the non-emaciated theory of good. Finnis believes this is possible because "the modern grammar of rights provides a way of expressing virtually all the requirements of practical reasonableness."[45] For Finnis, taking rights seriously establishes that an order can be known to be just only when participants can choose to assent. That choice carries with it duties of respect for the order which is to be secured through agreement. Finnis seeks to bring respect for rights into a recast Aristotelian perspective that is not restricted to a defense of individual or group liberty or authenticity:

> reference to rights . . . is simply a pointed expression of what is implicit in the term "*common* good," namely that *each* and everyone's well-being, in each of its basic aspects, must be

43. Finnis, *Fundamentals of Ethics*, 50; see also Finnis, *Natural Law and Natural Rights*, 221–23.
44. Finnis, *Natural Law and Natural Rights*, 103.
45. Finnis, *Natural Law and Natural Rights*, 198.

considered and favoured at *all* times by those responsible for co-ordinating the common life.[46]

And,

> On the one hand, we should not say that human rights, or their exercise, are subject to the common good. . . . On the other hand, we can appropriately say that most human rights are subject to or limited by each other and by other *aspects* of the common good, aspects which could probably be subsumed under a very broad conception of human rights but which are fittingly indicated (one could hardly say, *described*) by expressions such as "public morality," "public health," "public order."[47]

But then the problem of making this reciprocity specific in a particular order must be faced. Specificity is perpetually an uncertainty seeking certainty. Generally held notions of rights and duties in particular orders will potentially and actually vary in meaning in some measure from one person to the next. Orderliness cannot consist only in consensus. There must be a strong commitment to the continual resolution of conflicts as they arise. What is to guide conflict resolution? Finnis argues,

> There is, I think, no alternative but to hold in one's mind's eye some pattern, or range of patterns, of human character, conduct, and interaction in community, and then to choose such specifications of rights as tend to favour that pattern, or range of patterns. In other words, one needs some conception of human good, of individual flourishing in a form (or range of forms) of communal life that fosters rather than hinders such flourishing.[48]

There remains the possibility of conflict between the regard for every human being as a locus of flourishing and the necessities of policy which dictate that some goods and some individuals be

---

46. Finnis, *Natural Law and Natural Rights*, 114.
47. Finnis, *Natural Law and Natural Rights*, 218.
48. Finnis, *Natural Law and Natural Rights*, 219–20.

preferred. Practical reasonableness requires only that we never intend to serve exclusively any one good or set of goods, or the good of any one or set of individuals to the exclusion of the others. Yet even if policymakers or statesmen accept all this, in the necessities of their position they may associate practical reasonableness with any ranking of the basic goods that fit their aims.

Finnis certainly wishes to take rights seriously. This means to him that every human being is entitled to consideration and respect, and that no one is permitted to pursue a policy in which someone or group may be destroyed as an end in itself. Nor, says Finnis, may anyone or group be destroyed as the means to some other possibly worthy end. One thinks of nuclear deterrence and the polarity between pacifism and the requirement of practical reasonableness to defend all the basic goods, not just life.

The aim of these dialectical arguments is clearly to moralize the use of power. It is easier to imagine this in the domestic society than in the international. It is easier to suppose that in the former some consensus on the range of patterns of permissible conduct might emerge effectively. It is also in the domestic realm that casuistry is less likely to be reduced to a cold logic of proportionality and intentionality, that rulers and ruled alike may be better able to act as if the basic values are not mere abstractions but "are aspects of the real well-being of flesh-and-blood individuals" and thus that judgments will be arrived at "by a steady determination to respect human good in one's own existence and the equivalent humanity or human rights of others."[49]

Nevertheless, the purpose of Finnis' arguments is to evoke a vision of the final reconciliation of rights and duties on a universal scale, without falling into mere apocalyptic moralizing. He intends to show the implicit universal striving of humanity and what, in principle, such striving would have to achieve in order to find final satisfaction. This is what he meant in saying that "the modern grammar of rights provides a way of expressing virtually all the requirements of practical reasonableness." The grammar is set out in the legal tradition which resists the separation of rights from duties. To

49. Finnis, *Natural Law and Natural Rights*, 225–26.

understand the tradition of the rule of law is to understand the systematic effort to establish the technical requirements of human flourishing. To leave it at this, however, would be to obscure the motivating ends which this technical effort presupposes whether they are openly acknowledged or not.

The modern grammar of rights may provide a way for expressing the fact that all human beings are loci of flourishing, for recognizing a universal humanity. But it is also necessary to show that the comprehensive understanding of the basic goods is inherent in the experience of actual human beings prior to its philosophical expression. In seeing that the basic goods are not imposed upon, but are derived from, experience, the redemption of rights becomes possible.

The reconciliation between an ancient vision and a modern vocabulary is further constituted for Finnis in an outlook informed by reflection on the meaning of providence. The idea of absolute rights is an idiomatic formulation of an ancient philosophical and theological challenge to all forms of utilitarianism or consequentialism which Finnis chooses to refer to collectively as "proportionalism." The challenge is summed up in the principle: "There are some acts which cannot be justified by any end," or, as in the Pauline Epistles, "Evil may not be done for the sake of good."[50] In affirming these principles, the Judeo-Christian tradition affirms God's providence:

> We can see that the collision between proportionalism and Christianity has its origins in the proportionalist's implicit proposal to undertake the very responsibility that Christianity, like Judaism, ascribes to God Himself . . . the proportionalist's imaginary perspective, as a God-like figure surveying possible worlds and choosing the world that embodies greater good or lesser evil, as in perspective that is simply not open to human practical reason.[51]

There are no "pre-moral choices" which then can be moralized or not according to later consequences. Implicated in the choices

50. Finnis, *Fundamentals of Ethics*, 109–10.
51. Finnis, *Fundamentals of Ethics*, 111.

from the outset is a manifestation of the chooser's degree of illumination with respect to what the good requires.

Exemplary for Finnis is the Socratic principle that it is better to suffer wrong than to do it. To be able to say this is to understand that no matter what calculations of future outcomes may be entertained, the action is also a self-enactment, not a disembodied choice. The Socratic pattern would be one of those Finnis would include as part of the range of patterns of human flourishing.

Socrates' pronouncement that he spent his life trying to be good rather than seeming to be good means here that no states of affairs can be known to be coming to be which absolve him from the question of the rightness of his life.[52] The human world is a compendium of interactions the ramifications of which are so complex that it is impossible fully to evaluate the actual state of affairs. Politics is inevitably the pursuit of intimations, and all calculations are intimations too. Finnis denies that there can be a proportionalist ethic. In this respect, Finnis has surely departed from many features of contemporary thinking while yet seeking to come to terms with it.

On the other hand, political life is real and resists such arguments no matter how philosophically powerful. Thus, in identifying the *nature* of law, the experiential foundation from which all *concepts* of law arise, Finnis finds the reference point for testing the adequacy of concepts of law, and the basis for a potential reconciliation of natural or human rights with natural law. He evokes the ancient tension between politics and philosophy. His practical strategy is to challenge calculating qualifications to the acknowledgment of rights while holding back from postulating that their unqualified acknowledgment would be the prelude to an inevitable, final moral self-transformation in the human condition.

Such a transformation would require us to define an "aggregate collective good" that, as a concept, is incoherent since the common good of a community cannot be measured as an aggregate.[53] Individuals and societies may imagine that they can solve their problems by presupposing objectives which are taken to be sufficiently

52. Plato, *Gorgias*, 527.
53. Finnis, *Natural Law and Natural Rights*, 253.

comprehensive of the common good as to produce the aggregate collective good when they are attained. But this will never be possible because there are no objectives of this character actually available to human beings. On the contrary, all objectives put forward to serve this purpose depend for their apparent unifying significance on suppressing other objectives of equal or greater significance in realizing human well-being. In the final analysis, the claims of certain knowledge that such efforts would have to sustain are a "cosmic impertinence."[54]

"Facts" and "norms" are only to be brought together in continuing acts of judgment. We must seek their reconciliation in the sense that it is always sought, believing that the seeking is the finding and thus akin to an end in itself. By the latter is meant that in seeking one is in conformity to what is good even if one is neither identical with goodness nor goodness fully incarnated.

54. Finnis, *Natural Law and Natural Rights*, 111–18.

What Can We Learn from Michael Oakeshott's Effort to Understand Our World?

I

M Y INTENTION ON THIS OCCASION IS, first, to say something about what sort of activity Oakeshott understood political philosophy to be; and, second, what he thought the philosophical study of politics might reveal about the world in our time and place.

Although Oakeshott never spent much time talking about influences on his thinking, he did mention a few influences that show us something about his approach. He admired Montaigne's *Essays* and often described himself as a writer of essays. For example, he described his masterpiece, *On Human Conduct*, as a set of three essays whereas most readers would take it to be a systematic whole. An essay is a tentative expression of how one understands oneself and

Printed with permission from Timothy Fuller. This lecture was presented in 2020 to the Laboratory of Research on "Politics, Behavior, and Media" at Pontifical Catholic University of São Paulo in Brazil, with the following introductory remarks: "I want to thank Professor Luiz Bueno and the members of the Laboratory for inviting me to discuss the significance of the work of Michael Oakeshott, the leading British political philosopher of the twentieth century. I also remember fondly the time when Daniel Marchiori and later Felipe Cardoso worked on Oakeshott's thought with me in Colorado Springs. I am most happy to be with you all even if, for the time being, only remotely."

how one understands what is going on in the world. For Oakeshott, the essay is an act of self-disclosure about how one sees things. It is also an invitation to others to say how they see things and thus to keep alive the conversation of mankind regarding the most important matters. In such acts of self-disclosure and response human beings are at their most human.

Oakeshott also acknowledged Hegel for understanding our world as the continuous experience of oppositions to be mediated, reconciled only to disclose further oppositions to be mediated in the continuous flow of experience which constitutes the historical character of the human condition. Oakeshott did not adopt the progressive theory of history with which Hegel is often credited, but he did adopt Hegel's method of explaining what is going on in the world in terms of fundamental oppositions in search of reconciliation. I will provide illustrations of this from many places in his writings.

Oakeshott described himself as a skeptic who would do better if only he knew how to do better. In this he invoked the skepticism of Montaigne along with the dictum of Hegel that the main lesson we learn from history is that we do not learn from history if by learning from history we imagine that the oppositions we must deal with are identical to those of the past and are susceptible to the same responses. The owl of Minerva takes flight at dusk; our wisdom is largely gained in the retrospective contemplation of what is past. This insight might moderate our tendency to rush headlong into the future, lacking as we do answers in advance.

Here also is the influence of David Hume on Oakeshott's thinking, especially Hume's essay on the skeptic. There Hume remarks that "philosophic devotion . . . like the enthusiasm of a poet, is the transitory effect of high spirits, great leisure, a fine genius, and a habit of study and contemplation."[1] However, Hume says, such a state cannot sustain itself. It must reattach to the actualities of common, historical existence. Hume thus recommends a virtuous temper to counteract alienation from the world. To lose connection to the dailiness of life is to lose sight of the weakness of philosophy's

---

1. David Hume, *Essays: Moral, Political, and Literary*, ed. Eugene F. Miller, rev. ed. (Indianapolis: Liberty Fund, Inc., 1994), 167.

claim to authority. When Hume wrote this he was recalling the "Allegory of the Cave" in Plato's *Republic*.

Reflection at its best "insensibly refines the temper" against the illusions of passion and quiets the mind without inducing that indifference which would diminish the pleasures of life. If there is no philosophical cure for the human condition, there may be a philosophical cure for the philosophical ill: The philosopher has encountered problems he cannot solve. Thus the skeptic philosophizes also about philosophizing, warning against the pretension that philosophy should rule. Hume had already recognized that the age of ideology was dawning, that the lust for abstract theorizing was growing, that the classical defense of moderation was in decline, that philosophers were tempted to become politicians.

II

Oakeshott, acknowledging Montaigne and Hume, and deriving his method of analysis from Hegel, thus describes himself as a skeptic who would "do better if only he knew how."[2] In this Oakeshott was formulating his own response to the possibilities and perils of the modern situation. For him, the philosophic examination of politics seeks to describe the character of political activity quite apart from defending or attacking particular policies. The philosophic examination of politics is not an effort to participate in current arguments but rather to understand why the arguments take the form they do.

Politics is a self-contained manner of human activity; it does not require an independent theory to get it going, to maintain its momentum, or to carry out its self-chosen activities. The philosopher, Oakeshott says, speaks in the indicative or descriptive mood, expressing in other words what has already been expressed in the words and actions of daily life. The practitioner of politics does not require this exposition from the philosopher, often choosing to ignore the philosophic description altogether.

Speaking indicatively, Oakeshott said that politics is the "activity of attending to the general arrangements of a set of people whom

2. Michael Oakeshott, *Rationalism in Politics* (1962), 111.

chance or choice have brought together."[3] More specifically, this usually means "the hereditary co-operative groups" called "states." The modern state began to come into being long before us and may persist long after us. We never possess a blank slate on which we may write what we want. To think we can start from scratch is to suffer an illusion. This illusion is nonetheless evident in our world and must be noticed as a feature of the rhetoric of politics.

For Oakeshott, "politics springs neither from instant desires, nor from general principles, but from the existing traditions of behaviour themselves."[4] "Arrangements," in short, are neither merely desires nor merely principles. They are a manner of living, a way of life, composed over time by the myriad choices of individuals in the society of each other, establishing practices through which they render their association concrete and humanly possible.

Such arrangements, of course, have consequences. They are the product of intelligence responding to its surrounding circumstance according to its understanding of those circumstances. In responding, human beings discover "intimations" to pursue, possibilities which are not necessary implications but present themselves as significant. There are always more such intimations than can be followed up at any moment. Choices among the possible avenues of exploration must be made. Political debate makes its appearance here: "relevant political reasoning will be the convincing exposure of a sympathy, present but not yet followed up, and the convincing demonstration that now is the appropriate moment for recognizing it."[5]

There is no logically implied direction to be discovered, no self-evidently right intimation among all the intimations that come in for consideration. Human beings find their purposes in life in constructing purposes as they respond to their circumstances. All such responses, no matter how far removed from our own sympathies, are exhibitions of intelligence at work with intermittent success. We cannot specify our final goal or *the* final goal. We may be able to

---

3. Oakeshott, *Rationalism in Politics*, 112.
4. Oakeshott, *Rationalism in Politics*, 123.
5. Oakeshott, *Rationalism in Politics*, 124.

minimize the chance of disaster "if we escape the illusion that politics is ever anything more than the pursuit of intimations; a conversation, not an argument."[6] On this point, we might respond to Oakeshott that such conversation nevertheless regularly becomes stridently argumentative.

For some the philosopher may have a depressing effect when the philosopher is obliged to say that in politics, "men sail a boundless and bottomless sea; there is neither harbor for shelter nor floor for anchorage, neither starting-place nor appointed destination. The enterprise is to keep afloat on an even keel; the sea is both friend and enemy; and the seamanship consists in using the resources of a traditional manner of behaviour in order to make a friend of every hostile occasion."[7] (One will note that the postulate of this view is expressed in Montaigne's advice about making a friend of death.)

Perhaps with regret the philosopher puts aside the possibility of superhuman wisdom, but also perhaps with relief points to the traditions without which we would fall into a morass of random choices. The emphasis is on the capacity of human intelligence to continue to use the resources of its history. There is confidence that intelligence is not likely to be exhausted. In our moment, the responsibility is ours. It is not likely to be the final moment, and, in any case, we cannot act as if it were. We do not and cannot know that. Nor can we unmake the inheritance we have. History cannot be taken back. Thus we must go on.

Tradition, says Oakeshott, "is not susceptible of the distinction between essence and accident, knowledge of it is unavoidably knowledge of its detail: to know only the gist is to know nothing."[8] Intimacy with tradition may yield stability without rest. Politics is best conducted in the attitude of energetic sobriety. This attitude results from having grown up hearing the already ongoing voices of one's world, and having learned to speak with them. The study of history, properly conducted, will introduce us to the detailed, concrete nature of our way of life, and will illustrate on a broader scale what is

6. Oakeshott, *Rationalism in Politics*, 125.
7. Oakeshott, *Rationalism in Politics*, 127.
8. Oakeshott, *Rationalism in Politics*, 128–29.

true of our own experience. The lesson will be that a manner of living indicates how we may conduct ourselves but not what we are required to do, nor where we are required to go. We may gain inspiration, Oakeshott thought, from "thinkers and statesmen who knew which way to turn their feet without knowing anything about a final destination."[9]

Political philosophy—philosophic reflection on the character of politics—may help us to think straighter about the concepts we employ. Here and there it may reduce the incoherency of our thinking. But it has no capacity to guarantee success in political activity. All of the foregoing reflections may be seen as the effort of a political philosopher to escape from his own occupational illusions by looking directly at the object of his investigation, namely, politics itself.

There we see what political actors actually succeed in doing: they pursue the intimations of the traditions of which they are a part. They may deny this and seek to do something else. Ideologies promise that we can escape the world we have inherited. Proponents of ideologies can sometimes persuade others that they have escaped this limitation. They can rename the Tower of Babel and vary its architectural nuances. They can attempt to pursue perfection as the crow flies. They can also become cynical graspers after power for its own sake. What, finally, they cannot do is to fend off the reassertion of the human condition as it has always been.

Fortunately, the death of false ideas is not identical to the death of the human spirit. It arises from its own ashes. Nevertheless, it would be to the good to avoid recipes for the production of ash heaps where possible. Sensible politicians will do so. Philosophers cannot produce sensible politicians, but they can be irritating reminders of the limits of politics. Philosophers might notice sensible politicians and speak their praises simply by describing them. In so doing, they perform a not altogether useless task. Their task is to understand why the world is the way it is, not to postulate a program to liberate us into a world beyond change or to reach the end of history.

Political philosophers in a special sense are thus of a conservative disposition. This is not to be confused with what is currently

9. Oakeshott, *Rationalism in Politics*, 131.

discussed as "conservatism" whether paleo- or neo-. Oakeshott's reference is specifically to a disposition from which no obvious generalizations about views on specific policy questions may be drawn. The political philosopher is not in the business of determining of which ideas it may be said that their time has come, or gone. This conservative disposition reveals the nature of the skeptical way. Plans to eliminate contingency, or to "give the government back to the people," or to achieve "peace in our time," or to "make poverty history," claim a potential for control the historical record does not support.

If one were to ask Oakeshott, "Why ought governments to accept the current diversity of opinion and activity in preference to imposing upon their subjects a dream of their own?" His reply is "Why not? Their dreams are no different from those of anyone else; and if it is boring to have to listen to the dreams of others being recounted, it is insufferable to be forced to re-enact them. We tolerate monomaniacs, it is our habit to do so; but why should we be *ruled* by them? . . . Government . . . does not begin with a vision of another, different and better world, but with the observation of the self-government practised even by men of passion in the conduct of their enterprises. . . . The intimations of government are to be found in ritual, not in religion or philosophy; in the enjoyment of orderly and peaceable behaviour, not in the search for truth or perfection."[10] Here is Oakeshott's critique of the enlightenment project, and of rationalism in politics, in the wake of the horrendous events of the twentieth century. What then is the proper role of governing? For Oakeshott, it begins with the rule of law.

Governing involves the making and enforcing of rules of conduct. Rules of conduct are not prescriptions for how we ought to live. They are adverbial conditions, specifying that, whatever we choose to do, we must do it under certain conditions. Such conditions may help or hinder us in the pursuit of our aims. The function of the rules of conduct, however, is neither to help nor to hinder, neither to pronounce in favor of nor against particular self-chosen pursuits of individuals, but to encourage the capacity for self-regulation.

10. Oakeshott, *Rationalism in Politics*, 187–88.

Governing provides a structure of laws. When successful, it will reduce the number of unfortunate collisions among interests. It will insure compensation for injuries. It will punish those who refuse to abide by rules of conduct. But government is "not the management of an enterprise, but the rule of those engaged in a great diversity of self-chosen enterprises . . . not concerned with concrete persons, but with activities . . . not concerned with moral right and wrong . . . not designed to make men good or even better."[11] Such a government seeks only "necessary loyalty" because it is indifferent to truth and error alike. Such a government may expect "respect and some suspicion, not love or devotion or affection."[12] Oakeshott is describing procedural governance as the means to allow for the widest range of human self-regulation through voluntary transactions.

Rules of conduct will have to change over time, of course. Such modification as is necessary "should always reflect and never impose, a change in the activities and beliefs of those who are subject to them, and should never on any occasion be so great as to destroy the *ensemble*."[13] Even armed with this disposition it will not necessarily be an easy or simple task to act in accord with it: "To rein-in one's own beliefs and desires, to acknowledge the current shape of things, to feel the balance of things in one's hand, to tolerate what is abominable, to distinguish between crime and sin, to respect formality even when it appears to be leading to error, these are difficult achievements."[14]

Reflection of this sort fosters being at home in the world. As with Montaigne, we discern a pattern of movement from natural harmony at birth to the disharmony of youthful exuberance, to the reflective return to the world which we must inhabit and which differs from the one of our poetic images and political fancies. There is no rule enforcing this upon us. We may experience this with greater or lesser grace, but it is the capacity to find the days of age equal to the days of youth which qualifies us for undertaking political activity.

11. Oakeshott, *Rationalism in Politics*, 189.
12. Oakeshott, *Rationalism in Politics*, 192.
13. Oakeshott, *Rationalism in Politics*, 190.
14. Oakeshott, *Rationalism in Politics*, 195.

There is a parallel between the wisdom of the philosopher and the practical insight of the mature politician. But they do not need each other to come to them. Oakeshott thought we should be thankful if they can live safely together in the same polity.

III

Throughout his writings, Oakeshott explored a number of oppositions in search of mediation which characterize the modern situation. Among them are these:

Empirical politics—Ideological politics
Politics of Skepticism—Politics of Faith
Nomocracy—Teleocracy
Morality of habit and affection—Morality of reflective thought
Civil Association—Enterprise Association

I will say something about each of these oppositions and offer a tentative conclusion about what we can learn from them about our world, divided as it is between impatience and disillusionment.

The distinction between the empirical style of politics and the ideological style of politics was a central feature of "Political Education," Oakeshott's inaugural lecture as Professor of Political Science, presented at the London School of Economics and Politics in 1951. The "empirical" style suggests a kind of ad hoc response to the kaleidoscopic array of issues one confronts every day, a kind of not well-organized pragmatism often generating contradictory responses. Opposing this style is the ideological style which, impatient with the disorderly character of the prevailing order, seeks an independently designed plan for the society—a model of how one imagines the society ought to look—coupled with the demand for the power to impose that design in order to bring to an end the sloppiness of the existing situation. The opposition between the empirical and the ideological style is mediated by recognizing the possibility of an orderly but revisable set of judgments as to what it is possible to achieve, involving something like the practical judgment described by Aristotle in the *Nicomachean Ethics* and the *Politics*.

At about the same time as his 1951 lecture, Oakeshott was writing a book which he never published, the typescript of which only came to light after his death in 1990. The book subsequently published with the title *The Politics of Faith and the Politics of Scepticism*. The "politics of faith" describes the utopian or millennialist aspirations to direct our existence toward a final stage of harmony and relief from the ordeal of history. Marx's belief in the final withering away of the state in favor of a post-political tranquility is one classic image. The "politics of scepticism" arises as a warning against concentrated centralized power, exemplified in the modern constitutional state. Oakeshott thought that both of these were modern responses to the emergence of the modern state beginning about 500 years ago, setting up a polarized field of argument in which each side energizes its opposite even as it seeks to dominate. Each responded to the centralization of power in the modern state beyond anything found in the premodern period, particularly as the technology of control expanded in unprecedented ways—an issue we currently clearly worry about, for example, in the era of the surveillance state. For Oakeshott, modern history is characterized by the unresolved opposition between the politics of faith and the politics of skepticism which he thought was observable in all modern states. The current debate over the "constitutional state" versus the "post-constitutional state" instantiates this conflict.

In his lectures on the history of political thought at LSE, Oakeshott developed a theory of law based in the opposition between "nomocracy" and "teleocracy." The first, nomocracy, refers to the rule of law strictly speaking as a set of procedural norms to provide the background conditions which reinforce the capacity of individuals to interact with each other through self-regulation, reinforced by the law, promoting mutual recognition and accommodation. The alternative, teleocracy, implies that there is a specific arrangement of human beings to be achieved, defined as an end or goal to be reached through government regulation adjusting and directing self-regulation. This is often described nowadays as the rule of experts. In its moderate form it advocates the use of governmental power to nudge people in the right direction through limited coercion. Current debates about the "administrative state" or the "deep state" reflect the underlying unresolved opposition of our time. One recent legal theorist has described this opposition as the difference between the rule *of* law, and rule *through* law.

In his 1948 essay, "The Tower of Babel,"[15] Oakeshott distinguished between the morality of "habit and affection" and the morality of "reflective thought." He thought that in our time we have increasingly resorted to the morality of reflective thought. This means increasing suspicion of inherited moral habits, even suspicion of all tradition altogether. In a way this means continually second guessing ourselves, continually questioning our motives, feeling that we cannot expect others to observe the same rules of conduct that we may continue to respect. Oakeshott thought that this must lead to constant anxiety and unease. It is not that traditional notions of conduct disappear but that we allow ourselves to be embarrassed by them.

Finally, in *On Human Conduct* Oakeshott presented the opposition between "civil association" and "enterprise association." He thought that this was the most comprehensive description of the oppositional character of modern history which he had been attempting to describe throughout his study of modern politics. One can see the connection of this description of the oppositionality to the other attempts that go back to his efforts beginning with *Experience and Its Modes* in 1933, and expressed also in his 1939 book, *Social and Political Doctrines of Contemporary Europe*, and in his Harvard lectures of 1958, *The Morality and Politics of Modern Europe*. In *On Human Conduct* (1975), Oakeshott elaborates at great length the distinction between a society of largely self-governing, self-regulating individuals supported by the rule of law or nomocracy, and the idea of the modern state as a managerial enterprise involving the pursuit of a single goal in which governors manage us through laws and regulations, treating us as individuals who play our roles in a vast division of labor pointing to a unified outcome or end, at which point the conversation of mankind will become a song in unison.

If we consider all these attempts, these essays to understand ourselves and the world we inhabit, we might say that the fundamental

15. Michael Oakeshott, "The Tower of Babel," in *Rationalism in Politics*, 59–79.

opposition in the twenty-first century is between impatience with the failure of the end of history to materialize and disillusionment with the proclamation of its coming. We have become suspicious of the enlightenment project but we find it difficult to give it up. Like Icarus we have flown too close to the sun; unlike Icarus we have survived our fall and must make sense of what has happened to us.

Thus Oakeshott: "The predicament of Western morals, as I read it, is first that our moral life has come to be dominated by the pursuit of ideals, a dominance ruinous to a settled habit of behaviour; and, secondly, that we have come to think of this dominance as a benefit for which we should be grateful or an achievement of which we should be proud. And the only purpose to be served by this investigation of our predicament is to disclose the corrupt consciousness, the self-deception which reconciles us to our misfortune."[16]

This conclusion is one aspect of Oakeshott's self-disclosure; it suggests stoic resignation regarding the human condition since the world must be as it is and as it will come to be. Beyond that, however, there was cheerfulness and enthusiasm for life discernible to anyone who knew him. This is evident in his 1929 essay, "Religion and the World,"[17] where he criticizes "worldliness," the disposition haunted by guilt about what has passed and intense anxiety about what is to come. The result is to depreciate present possibilities, seeking perhaps desperately to live elsewhere than in the moment one has been given which nevertheless remains inescapable. To overcome this was, I believe, the point of view informing Oakeshott's life work. Echoing Montaigne, Oakeshott sought to overcome the anxieties of self-consciousness through openness to the intimations of immortality, where immortality is understood not as a future state of affairs but as the poetic experience transcending the dailiness of life.

16. Oakeshott, "Tower of Babel," 79.
17. Michael Oakeshott, "Religion and the World," in *Religion, Politics, and the Moral Life*, 27–38.

Selected Works by Michael Oakeshott

"The Concept of a Philosophical Jurisprudence." *Politica* 3, 1938.
Reprinted in *Michael Oakeshott: The Concept of a Philosophical
Jurisprudence: Essays and Reviews 1926–51*. Edited by Luke
O'Sullivan. Charlottesville, VA: Imprint Academic, 2007.

Experience and Its Modes. Cambridge: Cambridge University Press,
1933. Reprint, Cambridge: Cambridge University Press, 1966. Both
editions contain the same pagination.

Hobbes on Civil Association. Berkeley: University of California Press,
1975. Reprinted, with a foreword by Paul Franco. Indianapolis:
Liberty Fund, Inc., 2000.

Introduction to *Leviathan* by Thomas Hobbes, vii–lxvi. Edited by
Michael Oakeshott. Blackwell's Political Texts. Oxford: Blackwell,
1946.

Lectures in the History of Political Thought. Edited by Terry Nardin and
Luke O'Sullivan. Exeter: Imprint Academic, 2006.

Morality and Politics in Modern Europe: The Harvard Lectures, 1958.
Edited by Shirley Letwin, with an introduction by Kenneth Minogue. New Haven: Yale University Press, 1993.

On History and Other Essays. New York: Barnes and Noble, 1983.
Reprinted, with a foreword by Timothy Fuller. Indianapolis: Liberty
Fund, Inc., 1999.

On Human Conduct. Oxford: Clarendon, 1975.

"A Place of Learning." *Colorado College Studies* 12 (January 1975):
6–29.

The Politics of Faith and the Politics of Scepticism. Edited and with an introduction by Timothy Fuller. New Haven: Yale University Press, 1996.

Rationalism in Politics and Other Essays. London and New York: Methuen, Basic Books, 1962. New and expanded edition, with a foreword by Timothy Fuller. Indianapolis: Liberty Fund, Inc., 1991.

Religion, Politics, and the Moral Life. Edited by Timothy Fuller. London and New Haven: Yale University Press, 1993.

Religion and the Moral Life. Cambridge: The "D" Society Pamphlets, no. 2, 1927.

The Social and Political Doctrines of Contemporary Europe. Cambridge: Cambridge University Press, 1939.

The Voice of Liberal Learning: Michael Oakeshott on Education. Edited by Timothy Fuller. New Haven and London: Yale University Press, 1989. Reprinted, with a foreword and introduction by Timothy Fuller. Indianapolis: Liberty Fund, Inc., 2001.

The Voice of Poetry in the Conversation of Mankind. London: Bowes & Bowes, 1959.

What Is History? And Other Essays. Edited, with an introduction by L. D. O'Sullivan. Exeter: Imprint Academic, 2004.

Index

absolute rights, 250, 269

achievement: of authority, 69, 74; of
civil association, 33, 57, 259; of
coherence, 162, 193; of democratic
politics, 75; of human spirit, 74;
immortality through, 135, 136;
modes of experience and, 4, 125,
168; moral, 226; of perfection, 142,
180; of perpetual peace, 207; of
political morality, 113; practicality
and, 17, 141, 159, 188; in pursuit of
perfection, xviii; in rule of law, 53,
120; of self-knowledge, 15; of social
justice, 112

Adams, Andy: *The Log of a Cowboy*, 77

administrative state, 281–82

affection: desirability of, 21; in
friendship, 40; morality of, 282;
mortal, xx, 12*n*18, 102, 201; in
personal relationships, 87; skepticism and, 45, 46; Stoic views of, 42.
See also love

Aquinas, Thomas, 230

Arendt, Hannah, 91–93

Aristotle: on civil association, 55; on
human conduct, 87; *Nicomachean
Ethics*, 160, 192, 280; on polis-life,
230–31; *Politics*, 280; on wisdom, 70

Augustine (saint): *The City of God*,
139*n*34; on human spirit's quest
for fulfillment, 86; on political
transformation, 117; on politics
as necessary evil, 118; religious
imagination of, 83; on temporality,
132; two-cities doctrine, 103, 139,
139*n*34, 220

authoritarianism, 58, 170, 265

authority, 54–75; achievement of, 69,
74; ambivalence toward, 55; civil
association and, 32–33, 54–57,
68, 75, 106–7, 174–76, 258; civil
disobedience to, 65–67; consensus
building as prerequisite to, 33,
259; democratization of, 65–66;
duplication of, 61; functions of, 55,
70–73; intimations of, 61; inverse
relationship with perfection, 70;
judicial, 40, 251–52; *Leviathan* on,
58; limitations of, 71, 74; literature
review, 58; in modern states, 112,
122, 175; moral, 150; power vs.,
32–33, 57, 58, 258–59; pure theory

Fackenheim, Emil: *Metaphysics and Historicity*, 228
faith: cultivation of, 112; politics of, 118–19, 122, 171, 176, 210–11, 226–27, 281; reason as substitute for, 115; in salvation, 220; theoretical understanding of, 140. *See also* religion and spirituality
Finnis, John, 261–70
Flathman, Richard: on civil disobedience, 65–67; on democratization of authority, 65–66; on political liberalism, 67; *The Practice of Political Authority*, 58; on resolute irresolution, 55, 68; on submission to authority, 59–65
Foster, Michael: *Mystery and Philosophy*, 84
Franco, Paul, 85–88, 90
freedom: abstractions of, 17; coherence in tension with, 188–89; in democracy, 113; initial vs. terminal, 73, 74; as intelligent response, 173; intersection with human spirit, 86; in legal interpretations, 40; from material interest, 134; objective vs. subjective, 249; in political philosophy, 156, 162–64, 184; in practical world, 194, 195; premeditation of, 37; progress of, 69; radical temporality and, 200–201; of thought, 219, 225; universal, 116–17. *See also* autonomy
Friedman, Richard, 86, 88–90
friendship, xvii, 21, 38–40, 98, 264
Fuller, Lon, 89

Gadamer, Hans-Georg, 238–41, 243–46; *Truth and Method*, 238–40
Glorious Revolution, 147–48
government: authoritarian, 58, 170, 265; civil association and, 33, 34; depersonalized relations of, 205; foundations of, 148; intimations of, 52, 278; power of, 104–5, 119, 154, 172, 176, 180, 182, 227, 281; self-government, 51–52, 113, 278–79, 282; skepticism and, 25. *See also* democracy; political authority
Griffith, Guy: *A Guide to the Classics or How to Pick a Derby Winner*, x

happiness, 40, 42, 44, 158, 187, 208, 218. *See also* pleasure; satisfaction
Hart, H. L. A., 89
Hegel, G. W. F.: on consequences of ideas, 88; on human experience, 103; on human spirit's quest for fulfillment, 86; incarnational theology of, 115; on learning from history, 131; *Phenomenology of Spirit*, 123, 167; *Philosophy of History*, 229; philosophy of religion, 84; on progressive theory of history, 273; "rational will" tradition and, 230; on undoing of past successes, 200; on universal freedom, 116
Heidegger, Martin, 81, 246
hermeneutics, defined, 245
Himmelfarb, Gertrude, 214
history and historicism, 228–46; Collingwood on, 234–37, 239–43; critiques of, 238–39, 241, 243, 244; Gadamer on, 238–41, 243–46; knowledge of, 229, 234, 241; learning from, 131, 273; as mode of experience, 8–9n9, 125–27, 131, 168, 189–90, 232–34; Oakeshott on nature and limits of, 232–34; philosophy of, 110, 192, 215, 219–21, 234; political philosophy and, 229–34, 237–46; politics of, 141, 168–69; predictive, 207, 210; progressive theory of, 273;

impatience: in modern states, 280,
283; in pursuit of perfection, 21;
revolutionary forms of, 224;
youthfulness and, xvi, xvii, 26,
108. *See also* patience
incoherence: detection of, 161, 192;
incipient, 4, 162, 193; intimations
of, 13; in politics, 167; of practical
world, 16, 217; of thought, 50, 277.
See also coherence
individualism: burden of obligations
in, 22; in civil association, 54–57,
174, 176, 256–57; defense by appeal
to rule of law, 90; learning and, 38;
morality of, 15; of Oakeshott, xv,
69, 92, 105, 173; self-disclosure and,
31; self-enactment and, 31, 73;
universal freedom and, 116; in
world of ideas, 11. *See also*
autonomy
intimations: of authority, 61; of
coherence, 9; discovery of, 275; of
good, 71–72; of government, 52, 278;
of human experience, 133, 143,
199; of immortality, xx, 12*n*18,
102, 140, 283; of incoherence,
13; poetic, 19, 27, 103; in political
philosophy, 153–55, 158–60, 188;
politics as pursuit of, 49–51, 91,
153–55, 158–60, 168, 181–83,
186–89, 214–16, 276; of satisfaction, 10, 181; of tradition, 277

judicial authority, 40, 251–52

Kant, Immanuel: cosmopolitan point
of view, 117; liberalism of, 111, 115;
on moralized politics, 113, 208;
"An Old Question Raised Again:
Is the Human Race Constantly
Progressing?," 207–9; on perpetual
peace, 207; on predictive history,
207, 210

Kedourie, Elie, xiii, 166
knowledge: contingent character of,
100; criteria for defining, 128;
historical, 229, 234, 241; integration of, 132; mind as offspring of,
14; of natural law, 114; political,
149; rationalism and, 103; in
republican order, 91; of rule of law,
114; scientific, 131; Socrates on
claims to, 146; traditional, 50, 91;
world of, 7, 131. *See also* self-
understanding; wisdom

Laski, Harold, 95
Laslett, Peter, x, 166
law. *See* natural law; rule of law
learning: appropriation and, 101;
degeneration of, xviii; from history,
131, 273; human conduct and, 3,
14–15, 31; individualism and, 38;
liberal, xi, xii, xiv, xviii, 76. *See also*
education; universities
legal philosophy, 86–89, 247, 262.
See also rule of law
Letwin, Bill, xii, xiii
Letwin, Shirley, x, xii–xiii, xvi–xvii
Leviathan (Hobbes): on authority, 58;
Hobbes's introduction to, 205–6;
on mortality, 99; Oakeshott's
characterization of, 15, 84, 99, 232;
Oakeshott's introduction to, ix, 76,
80, 166, 166*n*1, 197, 229–30
Leyden, Wolfgang von, xiii, 166
liberalism: authority and, 58, 67;
criticisms of, 115; in democracy,
113; education and, 173; of Kant,
111, 115; of Mill, 111, 115, 214; of
Oakeshott, 105; perfectionist ideal
and, 118; power dispersal in, 86,
105; progressivism and, 85, 111;
resolute irresolution and, 55, 68
liberal learning, xi, xii, xiv, xviii, 76
liberty. *See* freedom

This book was typeset in Warnock, a typeface
created by Robert Slimbach in honor of Adobe cofounder
John Warnock. Its classic yet contemporary appearance
performs a wide variety of tasks with elegance.

Printed on paper that is acid-free and meets
the requirements of the American National Standard for
Permanence of Paper for Printed Library Materials,
Z39.48-1992. ∞

Book design by Chris Crochetière, BW&A Books, Inc.,
Oxford, North Carolina
Typography by Westchester Publishing Services,
Danbury, Connecticut
Index by Indexing Partners, Rehoboth Beach, Delaware
Printed and bound by Sheridan Books, Inc., Chelsea, Michigan